Did the Reformers Misread Paul?

A Historical-Theological Critique of the New Perspective

T0385280

STUDIES IN CHRISTIAN HISTORY AND THOUGHT

Did the Reformers Misread Paul?

A Historical-Theological Critique of the New Perspective

Aaron T. O'Kelley

Foreword by Gregg R. Allison

Paternoster is an imprint of Authentic Media
52 Presley Way, Crownhill, Milton Keynes, Bucks, MK8 0ES

www.authenticmedia.co.uk
Authentic Media is a division of Koorong UK, a company limited by guarantee
(registered charity no. 270162)

09 08 07 06 05 04 03   8 7 6 5 4 3 2 1

British Library Cataloguing in Publication Data A catalogue record for this
book is available from the British Library

ISBN 978–1–84227–794–2

Typeset by the author
Printed and bound in Great Britain
for Paternoster

Series Preface

This series complements the specialist series of Studies in Evangelical History and Thought and Studies in Baptist History and Thought for which Paternoster is becoming increasingly well known by offering works that cover the wider field of Christian history and thought. It encompasses accounts of Christian witness at various periods, studies of individual Christians and movements, and works which concern the relations of church and society through history, and the history of Christian thought.

The series includes monographs, revised dissertations and theses, and collections of papers by individuals and groups. As well as 'free standing' volumes, works on particular running themes are being commissioned; authors will be engaged for these from around the world and from a variety of Christian traditions.

A high academic standard combined with lively writing will commend the volumes in this series both to scholars and to a wider readership.

For Joni
"An excellent wife is the crown of her husband"—Proverbs 12:4

Contents

FOREWORD

The 'new perspective on Paul' has riveted the attention of theologians and biblical scholars over the course of the last several decades. For the most part, its proponents and opponents wage battle over the proper understanding of Second Temple Judaism and the right interpretation of the apostle Paul's affirmations about justification, grace, law, faith, works, legalism, and the like. One crucial area of consideration, however, has been largely overlooked in this discussion: a historical study of the nature of the clash over the doctrine of justification between Roman Catholicism and Protestantism in the sixteenth century Reformation. The proponents of the new perspective assume that late medieval Catholicism was a graceless religion; thus, they conclude that the Reformation debate about justification and grace has negatively influenced our reading of Paul, who was not facing a graceless Second Temple Judaism and thus must have addressed some other matter than the divine initiative in saving fallen human beings by faith. Even many opponents of the new perspective assume that grace had no role to play in the Catholic notion of salvation that was so roundly criticized by the Reformers. This assumption significantly colors the new perspective's perspective—that of both its proponents and opponents.

Thankfully, this assumption is addressed by the book you are about to read. Aaron O'Kelley, noting the dearth of historical study on the sixteenth century Catholic-Protestant divide—or, at the minimum, the lack of applying the fruit of that study to the new perspective debate—wrote his fine Ph.D. dissertation—now, this book—to rectify that situation. As you read it, you will better understand several prevailing themes: the Protestant embrace of the divine insistence on perfect obedience rather than the partial compliance permitted in Catholic theology; the Protestant emphasis on an alien righteousness (that of Jesus Christ) over against the personal righteousness championed by the Catholic sacramental system offering grace for the meriting of eternal life; the Protestant highlighting of the imputation of righteousness versus the prominence of an infused righteousness within Catholic soteriology; and the Protestant concentration on the dichotomy between the law and the gospel in place of the law-gospel synergy promoted by Catholicism. At the same time, you will also appreciate the Catholic grounding of salvation in the grace of God, which means that Protestantism did not face off against Pelagianism but some form of modified semi-Pelagianism. Additionally, you will clearly see how the parallelism between Second Temple Judaism and the apostle Paul, on the one hand, and medieval Catholic soteriology and the Protestant material principle of justification by grace through faith alone, on the other hand, is actually far stronger than the new perspective sees. The conclusions to which this book will lead you are that 'the traditional, Reformation view of Paul's polemic and his corresponding doctrine of justification' is upheld and that the new perspective needs serious reconsideration.

Aaron O'Kelley is one of a growing cadre of young, promising theologians who, even as recent Ph.D. graduates, are making notable contributions to both evangelical and non-evangelical scholarship. His fine historical research, applied masterfully to a contemporary subject, is a model of how evangelical theologians can and must join their voices to important discussions. Addressing a difficult topic that has caused a seismic shift in the doctrine of justification, he writes lucidly, develops his points logically and thoroughly, treats the positions of others fairly, and champions the historical Protestant position winsomely.

May this book receive a wide reading so that it can make the impact it deserves to and must make!

Gregg R. Allison
Professor of Christian Theology
The Southern Baptist Theological Seminary, Louisville, KY

Acknowledgements

Written works such as this one are never produced solely by the efforts of one person. I gladly acknowledge my debt of gratitude to many others who have made the completion of this work possible. I am a man who has been blessed with life and opportunity to devote a great deal of energy for a significant amount of time to the study of the glorious doctrine of justification. I thank the God who counts me righteous in his sight, not because I have my own merits to plead, but because of the atoning work of his Son. I thank him for that truth in and of itself and also for the privilege of searching out its depths in study and writing. I pray that my weaknesses may not obscure the glory of the truth and that God would bless this work as he sees fit, by his grace and for his glory.

One of the primary means that my gracious God has used to guide this work to completion has been the insight and support of other people. I deeply appreciate the work of my editor, Michael Parsons, for taking an interest in the manuscript and guiding me through the process of preparing it for publication. When this project originally took shape as a doctoral dissertation at the Southern Baptist Theological Seminary, Gregg Allison provided invaluable direction along the way, and I am grateful for his willingness to write the foreword. Several others read earlier versions of the manuscript and offered helpful feedback, including David Puckett, Tom Schreiner, and Carl Trueman. I am also grateful to Albert Mohler for his willingness to read a prepublication version of the manuscript. I enjoyed helpful email correspondences with Mark Seifrid regarding Luther's doctrine of justification and with George Hunsinger regarding Calvin's doctrine. Kevin McFadden's encouraging words were instrumental in prompting me to bring this work to the press. The contribution of each person has made it better than it would have otherwise been, and thus to each one I am thankful, though of course I must take sole responsibility for all deficiencies that remain.

I appreciate the work of the helpful staff members at three different libraries where I conducted most of my research: Boyce Library on the campus of the Southern Baptist Theological Seminary, White Library on the campus of Louisville Presbyterian Theological Seminary, and Summar Library on the campus of Union University. With their help, I was able to track down many old resources that would have otherwise been virtually impossible to obtain.

In the span of years that I have worked to produce this book, I have had the privilege to serve as a pastor to two different churches. To the members of Corn Creek Baptist Church in Milton, Kentucky, your prayers and support of me during my seminary days were invaluable. To the members of Cornerstone Community Church in Jackson, Tennessee, it is my joy to labor among you. To my fellow pastors at Cornerstone—Tom Fox, Lee Tankersley, and Nathan Young—I thank God for each one of you and am grateful for your pastoral oversight.

I must also acknowledge the help of my family, without which this project never could have been pursued at all. My parents and in-laws helped ease some of the challenges of our seminary years with their prayers and support. While my two precious sons, Benjamin and Ethan, at present have little understanding of what I have been doing typing away on this computer for so many hours, I am thankful for the joy they have brought into my life every step of the way. I pray that in years to come they will understand and rejoice in the wonderful reality of the justification of the ungodly by grace alone, through faith alone, in Christ alone. This work is dedicated with great affection and gratitude to Joni, my wife, who endured many, many hours apart as I researched, wrote, edited, and revised. With patience and support she has met every demand placed upon her as a result of my commitment to this book, and so she, more than any other person, has helped make its completion possible.

Aaron O'Kelley
Jackson, Tennessee
January 2013

Abbreviations

BJRL	*Bulletin of the John Rylands University Library of Manchester*
BOO	*Doctoris Seraphici S. Bonaventurae S. R. E. Episcopi Cardinalis Opera Omnia* (Quaracchi: Ex Typographia Collegii S. Bonaventurae, 1882-1902)
CR	Corpus Reformatorum (Halle: C. A. Schwetschke, 1834-1900; reprint, New York: Johnston Reprint Corp., 1964)
CTQ	*Concordia Theological Quarterly*
JETS	*Journal of the Evangelical Theological Society*
JTS	*Journal of Theological Studies*
LCC	Library of Christian Classics
LW	*Luther's Works*, American ed., ed. J. Pelikan (St. Louis: Concordia, 1955-1986)
NTS	*New Testament Studies*
OPT	*Guillelmi de Ockham Opera Philosophica et Theologica ad Fidem Codicum Manuscriptorum Edita* (New York: Franciscan Institute, 1967-)
OS	*Ioannis Calvini Opera Selecta*, ed. P. Barth and G. Niesel (Munich: Chr. Kaiser, 1926-62)
TynBul	*Tyndale Bulletin*
WA	*D. Martin Luther's Werke, kritische Gesamtausgabe* (Weimar: H. Böhlaus Nachfolger, 1883-)
WTJ	*Westminster Theological Journal*

CHAPTER 1

Introduction

Since 1977, the field of Pauline studies has been influenced dramatically by the rise of the so-called 'new perspective on Paul'. While the new perspective is a diverse movement with a diversity of claims, arguments, and viewpoints, it is held together by a common reaction to the Lutheran paradigm of reading Paul. The movement's proponents argue that a new perspective on Paul is necessary because Protestantism has long accepted a false view of Paul's Jewish context, leading to a faulty understanding of Paul's polemic against Judaism. The result has been a misreading of Paul, particularly with regard to his doctrine of justification. More than any other work, E.P. Sanders' *Paul and Palestinian Judaism* has provided the historical foundation upon which new perspective proponents have built their case.[1] By arguing that Second Temple Judaism exhibited a grace-based pattern of religion, as opposed to the legalistic caricature portrayed by New Testament scholars in the Lutheran tradition, Sanders laid the groundwork for a paradigm shift in Pauline studies. A number of scholars have concluded, largely as a result of Sanders' work, that historic Protestantism has misread Paul in significant ways because of a tendency to impose foreign categories onto him, namely, the categories of grace and merit that defined the debates of the Reformation.[2] As they argue, Sanders' insights into Second Temple Judaism indicate the unlikelihood that Paul's doctrine of justification stands opposed to a doctrine of works-righteousness, for, steeped in grace as it was, Judaism did not uphold such a doctrine. Thus, Sanders' work has generated a hermeneutical presupposition that has led to a reinterpretation of Paul's polemic and, consequently, a reinterpretation of his doctrine of justification.

The new perspective has elicited responses from a number of scholars who

---

[1] E.P. Sanders, *Paul and Palestinian Judaism: A Comparison of Patterns of Religion* (Minneapolis: Fortress, 1977).

[2] For an excellent survey of the work of a number of scholars associated with the new perspective on Paul, see Stephen Westerholm, 'The New Perspective at Twenty-Five', in D.A. Carson, Peter T. O'Brien, and Mark A. Seifrid (eds), *Justification and Variegated Nomism*, vol. 2, *The Paradoxes of Paul* (Grand Rapids: Baker Academic, 2005), pp. 1-17.

hold to more traditional views.[3] These responses have focused primarily on the nature of Second Temple Judaism and/or the exegesis of relevant Pauline passages. At least one aspect of the debate, however, has yet to be explored adequately, and that is whether the new perspective's claims concerning Second Temple Judaism, when read in light of the debates of the Reformation era and beyond, actually warrant the significant modifications that its proponents offer for the interpretation of Paul.[4] If, for the sake of argument, one grants that Sanders has accurately described Second Temple Judaism as a grace-based religion, does this observation necessarily overthrow the Reformation reading of Paul?

Thesis

This study will argue that the new perspective's hermeneutical presupposition generated by Sanders' view of Second Temple Judaism is a *non sequitur*; as such, it does not overturn the Reformation paradigm for interpreting Paul's doctrine of justification. The hermeneutical presupposition does not follow specifically because Sanders' argument has no bearing on the categories that defined the concepts of grace, merit, and justification in the Reformation debates. Although some exegetical observations will be noted in the conclusion, this study is not primarily exegetical in nature. It is, rather, an argument that addresses the presupposition that new perspective proponents bring to the Pauline epistles. If that presupposition, which is the driving force behind the perceived need for a 'new perspective' on Paul, can be shown to be unwarranted, then the traditional, Reformation view of Paul's polemic and his corresponding doctrine of justification will stand vindicated no matter how one evaluates Sanders' portrayal of Second Temple Judaism. It must not be denied

---

[3] Friedrich Avemarie, *Tora und Leben: Untersuchungen zur Heilsbedeutung der Tora in der frühen rabbinischen Literatur* (Tübingen: Mohr Siebeck, 1996); D.A. Carson, Peter T. O'Brien, and Mark A. Seifrid, (eds), *Justification and Variegated Nomism* (2 vols; Grand Rapids: Baker Academic, 2001-2004); R. Scott Clark (ed), *Covenant, Justification, and Pastoral Ministry: Essays by the Faculty of Westminster Seminary California* (Phillipsburg, NJ: P & R, 2007); A. Andrew Das, *Paul, the Law, and the Covenant* (Peabody, MA: Hendrickson, 2001); Simon J. Gathercole, *Where Is Boasting? Early Jewish Soteriology and Paul's Response in Romans 1-5* (Grand Rapids: Eerdmans, 2002); Seyoon Kim, *Paul and the New Perspective: Second Thoughts on the Origin of Paul's Gospel* (Grand Rapids: Eerdmans, 2002); John Piper, *The Future of Justification: A Response to N. T. Wright* (Wheaton, IL: Crossway, 2007); Guy Prentiss Waters, *Justification and the New Perspectives on Paul: A Review and Response* (Phillipsburg, NJ: P & R, 2004); Stephen Westerholm, *Perspectives Old and New on Paul: The 'Lutheran' Paul and His Critics* (Grand Rapids: Eerdmans, 2004).

[4] This question has been addressed by Bart Anders Eriksson, 'Luther, Paul and the New Perspective' (Th.M. thesis, University of Toronto, 2004), but this investigation is limited only to Luther.

that the new perspective has brought much-needed attention to Paul's own historical context, an emphasis that has yielded much exegetical and theological fruit. Nevertheless, what this study will suggest is that, because of the failure of Sanders' thesis to warrant the kind of hermeneutical presupposition that drives the new perspective's approach to Paul, what is needed is not a new perspective on Paul but a further refining of the old one in light of recent scholarly discussion. The relationship between Jews and Gentiles need not be an unwelcome guest at the table of the Reformation doctrine of *sola fide*.[5]

The New Perspective and Justification

The significance of this study lies in its focus on the doctrine of justification, which Calvin regarded as 'the main hinge on which religion turns'.[6] For centuries this doctrine has been the primary soteriological divide between Roman Catholics and Protestants. *Sola fide* has provided the distinguishing contours of the Reformation tradition.[7] It is, therefore, a matter of great importance when a movement in Pauline studies asserts that Paul's own understanding of justification was very different.

The doctrine of justification that arose from the Reformation and has persisted in both the Lutheran and Reformed traditions since that time has been enshrined in the Lutheran *Formula of Concord*:

> We believe, teach, and confess [t]hat our righteousness before God is this: God forgives our sins out of pure grace, without any work, merit, or worthiness of ours preceding, present, or following. He presents and credits to us the righteousness of Christ's obedience [Romans 5:17-19]. Because of this righteousness, we are received into grace by God and regarded as righteous.

---

[5] Some scholars who have incorporated insights from the new perspective as a way of refining rather than overturning the old one include Tim Chester, 'Justification, Ecclesiology, and the New Perspective', *The Northern Training Institute Papers* 12 (March 2008), pp. 1-14; Bruce W. Longenecker, *The Triumph of Abraham's God: The Transformation of Identity in Galatians* (Nashville: Abingdon, 1998); Francis Watson, *Paul, Judaism, and the Gentiles: Beyond the New Perspective* (Grand Rapids: Eerdmans, 2007); Michael Bird, *The Saving Righteousness of God: Studies on Paul, Justification, and the New Perspective* (Eugene, OR: Wipf and Stock, 2007). Some of these works give too much ground to the new perspective, but it is refreshing to see a more chastened approach, one that incorporates new insights without promoting a sweeping paradigm shift.
[6] John Calvin, *Institutes of the Christian Religion* 3.11.1 (ed. John T. McNeill, trans. Ford Lewis Battles, LCC vols. 20-21; Philadelphia: Westminster, 1960), 1, p. 726
[7] A good historical survey of *sola fide* is provided by Samuel E. Waldron, 'Faith, Obedience, and Justification: Current Evangelical Departures from *Sola Fide*' (Ph.D. diss., The Southern Baptist Theological Seminary, 2005), pp. 1-131.

We believe, teach, and confess that faith alone is the means and instrument through which we lay hold of Christ. So in Christ we lay hold of righteousness that benefits us before God [Romans 1:17], for whose sake this faith is credited to us for righteousness (Romans 4:5).[8]

With even greater theological precision, this doctrine of justification has been proclaimed for centuries by the preeminent Reformed confession, *The Westminster Confession of Faith*:

Those whom God effectually calleth, he also freely justifieth: not by infusing righteousness into them, but by pardoning their sins, and by accounting and accepting their persons as righteous; not for anything wrought in them, or done by them, but for Christ's sake alone; not by imputing faith itself, the act of believing, or any other evangelical obedience to them, as their righteousness; but by imputing the obedience and satisfaction of Christ unto them, they receiving and resting on him and his righteousness by faith; which they have not of themselves, it is the gift of God.[9]

As a new perspective on Paul has emerged in the wake of E.P. Sanders' work on Judaism, this doctrine, at least insofar as its major contours have been attributed to Paul, has been called into question. Arguing that the grace/works antithesis of the Reformation is anachronistic when read into Paul, some scholars have concluded that Paul's polemic must be aimed, not at legalism, but nationalism, and that his primary concern in unfolding his doctrine of justification is not the standing of individual sinners before God but the relationship between Jews and Gentiles in God's covenant purpose. Thus, the phrase 'works of the law' that appears at crucial junctures in Paul's letters as a foil to faith (Rom. 3:20, 28; Gal. 2:16; 3:2, 5, 10) must be taken to connote primarily the badges of Jewish identity, most notably circumcision, food laws, and Sabbath, not good works in general.[10] According to the new perspective, Paul's concerns are less anthropological than they are sociological and

---

[8] *The Formula of Concord* 3.2-3 [3.4-5], in *Concordia: The Lutheran Confessions*, 2nd ed. (ed. Paul Timothy McCain; St. Louis: Concordia, 2006), p. 480.

[9] *The Westminster Confession of Faith* 11.1, in *Creeds and Confessions of the Christian Tradition* (ed. Jaroslav Pelikan and Valerie Hotchkiss; New Haven, CT: Yale University Press, 2003), 2, p. 620.

[10] James D.G. Dunn, 'The New Perspective on Paul', in *The New Perspective on Paul: Collected Essays* (Tübingen: Mohr Siebeck, 2005), pp. 98-101; idem, 'Works of the Law and the Curse of the Law (Galatians 3.10-14),' in *New Perspective*, pp. 115-16; N.T. Wright, *The Letter to the Romans: Introduction, Commentary, and Reflections*, in *The New Interpreter's Bible*, vol. 10 (ed. Leander E. Keck; Nashville: Abingdon, 2002), pp. 460-61. Dunn has softened his claims on this point in more recent publications. See James D.G. Dunn, 'New Perspective View', in James K. Beilby and Paul Rhodes Eddy (eds), *Justification: Five Views* (Downers Grove, IL: IVP Academic, 2011), p. 193.

redemptive-historical.

N.T. Wright's view on this question has been most prominent.[11] According to Wright, justification is an eschatological declaration of covenant membership. God justifies, that is, declares to be in the covenant, those who belong to him. At the final judgment this declaration will be based on works, though in a redefined sense. Final justification, then, is not a justification by faith, at least not in the traditional Reformation sense of *sola fide*.[12] What, then, is justification by faith? For Wright it is the present anticipation of that eschatological verdict. It is the doctrine that gives assurance to believers that they have been reckoned covenant members in the present in anticipation of their final justification by works. In other words, justification by faith assures believers now that God's work, once begun, will not fail to be completed (Phil. 1:6). For Wright, faith does not appropriate the righteousness of Christ for the sinner; the imputation of righteousness is no part of Paul's doctrine of justification.[13] Rather, faith (which is exhibited by both Jews and Gentiles) is the badge of covenant identity that stands opposed to the boundary markers, or 'works of the law', that nationalistic Jews upheld proudly as evidence of their covenant identity to the exclusion of outsiders. Significantly, for Wright justification is not initiatory; it does not change one's legal standing, nor is it associated with conversion. It is, rather, a divine recognition of what is already the case.[14] Those who are in the covenant are justified by faith, that is, declared

---

[11] N.T. Wright, 'New Perspectives on Paul', in *Justification in Perspective: Historical Developments and Contemporary Challenges* (ed. Bruce L. McCormack; Grand Rapids: Baker Academic, 2006), pp. 243-64; idem, *What Saint Paul Really Said: Was Paul of Tarsus the Real Founder of Christianity?* (Grand Rapids: Eerdmans, 1997), pp. 113-33; idem, *Paul: In Fresh Perspective* (Minneapolis: Fortress, 2005), pp. 120-22; see also Piper, *The Future of Justification* and Wright's rejoinder in *Justification: God's Plan and Paul's Vision* (Downers Grove, IL: IVP Academic, 2009).

[12] 'We now discover that this declaration, this vindication, occurs twice. It occurs in the future, as we have seen, on the basis of the entire life a person has led in the power of the Spirit—that is, it occurs on the basis of "works" in Paul's redefined sense.' Wright, 'New Perspectives on Paul', p. 260.

[13] 'Righteousness is not an object, a substance or a gas which can be passed across the courtroom.' Wright, *What Saint Paul Really Said*, p. 98.

[14] 'What, then, is this vindication, this *dikaiōsis*? It is God's declaration that a person is in the right—that is, (a) that the person's sins have been forgiven and (b) that he or she is part of the single covenant family promised to Abraham. Notice the opening phrase: God's *declaration that*. Not "God's bringing it about that" but God's authoritative declaration of what is in fact the case.' Wright, 'New Perspectives on Paul', p. 260. However, in a more recent work, Wright appears to contradict himself: 'When the judge in the lawcourt justifies someone, he does not give that person his own particular "righteousness." He *creates* the status the vindicated defendant now possesses, by an act of declaration, a "speech-act" in our contemporary jargon' (Wright, *Justification*, p. 69, emphasis original). If this and similar statements in Wright's more recent publication (pp. 91, 135) indicate that he has changed his mind and now regards the verdict of

to be what they already are because they exhibit the badge of covenant membership.

Besides Wright, James D.G. Dunn has been the other most prominent proponent of the new perspective on Paul, and he has likewise sought to modify the traditional Protestant formulation of justification.[15] In his Pauline theology, Dunn begins his discussion of justification by addressing the key phrase 'the righteousness of God', arguing that 'righteousness' is a relational term that refers to the fulfillment of one's obligations to another in the context of a relationship.[16] God's righteousness, then, is 'God's fulfilment of the obligations he took upon himself in creating humankind and particularly in the calling of Abraham and the choosing of Israel to be his people.'[17] Within the context of this discussion of God's righteousness as the fulfillment of his salvific obligations, Dunn describes justification by faith in a manner very similar to Wright. He argues that it involves God's reckoning of covenant membership, particularly with reference to the Gentiles, in fulfillment of his salvific purpose.[18] That it is by faith as opposed to 'works of the law' is a statement of universality, an argument against Jewish nationalism, not Jewish legalism.[19]

In the early days of the new perspective, Dunn argued (as Wright would subsequently) that justification is not a term indicating transfer but status recognition:

> God's justification is not his act in first *making his* covenant with Israel, or in initially accepting someone into the covenant people. God's justification is rather God's acknowledgment that someone is in the covenan[t]—whether that is an *initial* acknowledgment, or a *repeated* action of God (God's saving acts), or his *final* vindication of his people.[20]

---

justification as a synthetic, rather than an analytic, statement, then it is a most welcome development. Nowhere, however, does Wright say that he has changed his mind, and thus the apparent contradiction remains in his work.

[15] James D.G. Dunn, 'The New Perspective on Paul'; idem, 'The Justice of God: A Renewed Perspective on Justification by Faith', in *New Perspective*, pp. 187-205; James D.G. Dunn and Alan M. Suggate, *The Justice of God: A Fresh Look at the Old Doctrine of Justification by Faith* (Grand Rapids: Eerdmans, 1993); James D.G. Dunn, *The Theology of Paul the Apostle* (Grand Rapids: Eerdmans, 1998), pp. 334-89.

[16] Dunn, *The Theology of Paul*, pp. 340-46. As Dunn indicates, credit for this 'Hebraic' understanding of righteousness goes to H. Cremer, *Die paulinische Rechtfertigungslehre im Zusammenhange ihrer geschichtlichen Voraussetzungen* (Gütersloh: Bertelsmann, 1900). Wright likewise adheres to this understanding of righteousness. See Wright, *What Saint Paul Really Said*, pp. 95-111.

[17] Dunn, *The Theology of Paul*, p. 342.

[18] Dunn, *The Theology of Paul*, p. 344; idem, *The Justice of God*, p. 25.

[19] Dunn, *The Theology of Paul*, pp. 354-79.

[20] Dunn, 'The New Perspective on Paul', p. 97, emphasis original.

However, in subsequent publications Dunn's language has changed somewhat on this issue. Justification by faith appears in a chapter entitled 'The Beginning of Salvation' in his Pauline theology, and he tends to speak more freely of justification as transfer terminology than does Wright.[21]

One final example to be noted here of the new perspective's impact on the doctrine of justification is to be found in Richard B. Hays, whose article on justification in *The Anchor Bible Dictionary* clearly defines the doctrine in terms of covenant membership:

> Insofar as 'righteousness' may be ascribed to the human beneficiaries of God's grace (cf. such passages as Phil. 3:9; Rom. 9:30-10:4), this righteousness should be interpreted primarily in terms of the covenant relationship to God and membership within the covenant community. . . . 'Righteousness' refers to God's covenant-faithfulness which declares persons full participants in the community of God's people. This declaration has a quasi-legal dimension, but there is no question here of a legal fiction whereby God juggles his heavenly account books and pretends not to notice human sin. The legal language points rather to the formal inclusion of those who once were 'not my people' in a concrete historical community of the 'sons of the living God' (Rom. 9:25-26). (Justification is only one of the metaphors that Paul can use to describe this act of inclusion by grace; elsewhere he can speak, for example, of 'adoption', as in Gal. 4:5 and Rom. 8:15.)[22]

Hays' rejection of the Lutheran paradigm is clear, as is his identification of justification as a declaration that marks off God's covenant people. What is not clear from the article, however, is whether Hays agrees with Wright that justification is non-initiatory. The quote above seems to imply that Hays considers justification an event that changes one's status from 'out' to 'in', but ultimately he does not address this question directly.

The new perspective on Paul represents the harvest of seeds sown by Krister Stendahl a half-century ago in an article that suggested that Paul, even from the time of Augustine, has been forced to address questions that had little

---

[21] This is the case not only in his acknowledgement that justification involves 'the initial acceptance by God into restored relationship', but also in the ongoing aspect of justification, whereby 'the human partner will ever be dependent on God justifying the ungodly'. Dunn, *The Theology of Paul*, p. 386. These statements represent some remaining Lutheran themes in Dunn. See also James D.G. Dunn, 'The New Perspective: Whence, What, and Wither?' in *New Perspective on Paul: Collected Essays*, pp. 1-88, where Dunn acknowledges several aspects of the Lutheran tradition of reading Paul that he finds legitimate.

[22] Richard B. Hays, 'Justification', in *The Anchor Bible Dictionary* (ed. David Noel Freedman; New York: Doubleday, 1992), 3, pp. 1131-32. See also Richard B. Hays, *The Letter to the Galatians: Introduction, Commentary, and Reflections*, in *The New Interpreter's Bible* (ed. Leander E. Keck; Nashville: Abingdon, 2000), 11, pp. 236-38.

significance in his own first-century context, questions about how individual sinners might find a gracious God.[23] Out of these concerns the Reformation doctrine of justification emerged. As the new perspective has argued, however, Paul's primary concern was not about individual sinners facing God as judge but about God's global purpose of redemption that encompasses both Jews and Gentiles, uniting them into one covenant community. Understood in this manner, justification need no longer constitute a rigid barrier between Protestants and Catholics. Both sides have missed the mark to some degree, and some measure of theological rapprochement might be possible if both sides recognize justification for the great ecumenical doctrine that it is.[24] In light of the fact that *sola fide* has been the defining soteriological distinctive of the Reformation tradition, this claim on the part of new perspective proponents merits careful scrutiny. Of significance for this study is the fact that these modifications to the doctrine of justification stem from one important work published in 1977, to which attention must now be given.

E.P. Sanders' *Paul and Palestinian Judaism*

Two of Sanders' stated purposes in his 1977 work were 'to destroy the view of Rabbinic Judaism which [was at the time] still prevalent in much, perhaps most, New Testament scholarship' and then 'to establish a different view of Rabbinic Judaism'.[25] Sanders traced the prevalent view in need of destruction from Ferdinand Weber through three prominent scholars (among others) who appropriated Weber's view and made it dominant in New Testament scholarship: Wilhelm Bousset, Paul Billerbeck, and Rudolf Bultmann.[26] Scholars in this school of thought characterized Judaism as a religion in which works earn salvation by a careful weighing of merits against demerits at the final judgment, entailing as a significant corollary the denial or downplaying of God's grace in Israel's election.[27] Sanders argued that this view of Judaism,

---

[23] Krister Stendahl, 'The Apostle Paul and the Introspective Conscience of the West', *Harvard Theological Review* 56 (1963), pp. 199-215; subsequently published in Krister Stendahl, *Paul Among Jews and Gentiles* (Philadelphia: Fortress, 1976), pp. 78-96.

[24] Wright (*What Saint Paul Really Said*, pp. 158-59) has sounded this note strongly. Dunn has also to a lesser extent in *The Theology of Paul*, p. 344.

[25] Sanders, *Paul and Palestinian Judaism*, p. xii.

[26] Sanders, *Paul and Palestinian Judaism*, pp. 33-59.

[27] Sanders, *Paul and Palestinian Judaism*, p. 54. Interestingly, Sanders argued that those who followed Weber continued to promote a legalistic view of Judaism even while they ignored Weber's view of the Rabbinic narrative of Israel's history, namely, that Israel forfeited the grace of God in the golden calf incident and, subsequently, had to pursue salvation based on a system of weighing merits against demerits. According to Sanders, this narrative was foundational to Weber's portrayal of Judaism, for it provided a coherent, even if incorrect, means of harmonizing the grace of election with the

though lacking warrant from the evidence, did serve a theological purpose, especially for the Lutheran tradition:

> The supposed legalistic Judaism of scholars from Weber to Thyen (and doubtless later) serves a very obvious function: It acts as the foil against which superior forms of religion are described. It permits, as Neusner has said, the writing of theology as if it were history. One must note in particular the projection on to Judaism of the view which Protestants find most objectionable in Roman Catholicism: the existence of a treasury of merits established by works of supererogation. We have here the retrojection of the Protestant-Catholic debate into ancient history, with Judaism taking the role of Catholicism and Christianity the role of Lutheranism.[28]

Arguing that the prevailing view of Judaism among New Testament scholars was a caricature created by the theology of the Lutheran tradition, Sanders sought to expose it as a falsehood.

Sanders' methodology involved surveying the Tannaitic literature, the Dead Sea Scrolls, and the Apocrypha and Psuedepigrapha in an effort to determine a common 'pattern of religion', which he defined as 'the description of how a religion is perceived by its adherents to *function*. "Perceived to function" has the sense not of what an adherent does on a day-to-day basis, but of *how getting in and staying in are understood*: the way in which a religion is understood to admit and retain members is considered to be the way it "functions".'[29] According to Sanders, the relevant sources reveal a pattern of religion that may be defined as 'covenantal nomism'.[30] This phrase ties together both the gracious and legal aspects of Second Temple Judaism. The covenant, as an expression of God's electing grace, has priority. Once in the covenant by grace, Israelites maintain their covenant status by keeping the law as a proper response to the grace of God. Perfect obedience to the law is neither demanded nor necessary, for the law itself contains provision for atonement. With eight propositions, Sanders defined covenantal nomism as follows:

> (1) God has chosen Israel and (2) given the law. The law implies both (3) God's promise to maintain the election and (4) the requirement to obey. (5) God rewards obedience and punishes transgression. (6) The law provides for means of atonement, and atonement results in (7) maintenance or re-establishment of the

---

legalistic system of earning salvation. That Weber's followers simply dropped this narrative from consideration is, therefore, surprising.

[28] Sanders, *Paul and Palestinian Judaism*, p. 57. Here Sanders refers to Jacob Neusner, *The Rabbinic Traditions about the Pharisees Before 70* (Leiden: Brill, 1971), 3, pp. 359-63.

[29] Sanders, *Paul and Palestinian Judaism*, p. 17, emphasis original.

[30] Sanders, *Paul and Palestinian Judaism*, p. 75.

covenantal relationship. (8) All those who are maintained in the covenant by obedience, atonement and God's mercy belong to the group which will be saved. An important interpretation of the first and last points is that election and ultimately salvation are considered to be by God's mercy rather than human achievement.[31]

By unfolding covenantal nomism as the pattern of religion of Palestinian Jews in the Second Temple period, Sanders sought to dismiss the caricature prevalent in New Testament scholarship prior to 1977 and replace it with a portrayal of Judaism free from Protestant distortions.

The final section of *Paul and Palestinian Judaism* addresses Paul. Sanders' most significant argument about the apostle, in light of the thesis of the book, is that Paul's polemic against the law and Judaism did not stem from anthropological considerations, either to the effect that fallen humanity could not keep the law or that even an attempt to keep the law would constitute sin.[32] Rather, Paul's polemic stemmed from his Christology, and his thinking moved from solution to plight. Having found Christ to be the savior of all people, Paul then worked backwards to the conclusion that all people needed saving. More specifically, if all people needed saving, then the law must have been incapable of saving. And thus Paul opposed Judaism, with its devotion to the law, not because he found it inadequate on its own terms but because he saw that Christ's exclusivity and universality entailed the end of the law for believers.[33] Sanders' conclusion about Paul's polemic fits his prior conclusion that works-righteousness does not constitute the essence of Second Temple Judaism.

Comparing, then, one pattern of religion with another, Sanders ultimately concluded that Paul represents a different pattern than covenantal nomism, a pattern that finds its center in participatory rather than covenantal categories.[34] However, these two patterns do overlap at one significant point: grace and works. According to Sanders, 'Paul is in agreement with Palestinian Judaism. …There are two aspects of the relationship between grace and works: *salvation is by grace but judgment is according to works; works are the condition of remaining "in", but they do not earn salvation.*'[35] If Paul agreed with the prevailing view among his kinsmen on these matters, then the traditional Protestant view of Paul would seemingly require some revision.[36]

---

[31] Sanders, *Paul and Palestinian Judaism*, p. 422.

[32] The latter point was argued by Rudolf Bultmann, *Theology of the New Testament* (ed. and trans. Kendrick Grobel; New York: Charles Scribner's Sons, 1951), 1, p. 264.

[33] Sanders, *Paul and Palestinian Judaism*, pp. 474-511.

[34] Sanders, *Paul and Palestinian Judaism*, pp. 511-15; 543-52.

[35] Sanders, *Paul and Palestinian Judaism*, p. 543, emphasis original.

[36] Sanders further developed his analysis of Paul in *Paul, the Law, and the Jewish People* (Philadelphia: Fortress, 1983) and, at a more popular level, in *Paul* (New York: Oxford University Press, 1991).

Sanders' Judaism and the New Perspective

Sanders' work on Paul has not had near the influence in Pauline studies as has his work on Second Temple Judaism. Convinced that Sanders has proven that the 'Lutheran' Paul is an anachronism, proponents of the new perspective have diverged in multiple directions as they have unfolded different visions of Paul. Thus, there is no single 'new perspective' on Paul. What unites these various perspectives is their common rejection of the Protestant grace/works antithesis as the key to Paul's doctrine of justification, a rejection that has grown out of the perception that the whole of the Reformation tradition has misread Paul by forcing him to address sixteenth-century questions about soteriology foreign to his own context.

In the decades following Sanders' groundbreaking work, the new perspective on Paul has emerged largely as a result of a perceived historical link between a legalistic medieval Catholicism and a misrepresented legalistic first-century Judaism. A refrain that describes the shortcomings of the traditional Protestant reading of Paul has been repeated over the years by prominent proponents of the new perspective. Their argument may be summarized as follows:

1. Sixteenth-century Roman Catholicism was legalistic.[37]
2. The Reformers opposed this legalism with their doctrine of justification.
3. This doctrine of justification emerged from, but also helped to shape, a certain way of reading Paul that depended on having a legalistic foil in his own context, a role attributed to Judaism.
4. In fact, Jews of Paul's day were not legalists; they believed strongly in the grace of God.
5. Thus, the Roman Catholic legalism of the sixteenth century has caused Protestants to misrepresent Judaism and misread Paul.

In *Paul and Palestinian Judaism*, Sanders did not go quite so far in his argumentation. To be sure, he criticized New Testament scholars of the nineteenth and twentieth centuries for allowing their (Lutheran) theology to impact the way they understood Second Temple Judaism, but he did not specifically argue that the whole of the Reformation tradition was at fault in this regard. His primary concern was to correct a faulty view of Judaism that stemmed from Weber, not to evaluate the prevailing Protestant view of Paul. References to the Reformers or to major theologians who gave shape to the Protestant doctrine of justification are scant throughout his work. In this regard, some who have followed Sanders' work have taken his premise further than he did in an attempt to argue, not only that the Weber/Bousset/Billberbeck/ Bultmann school of interpretation has been skewed by a misrepresentation of Judaism, but that historic Protestantism itself shares in this unfortunate mistake.

---

[37] Here 'legalism' refers to the attempt to earn salvation by human effort.

Wright initially leveled this charge in 1978, when he first identified with the new perspective (before that phrase had been coined) in an article, previously delivered as a lecture, entitled 'The Paul of History and the Apostle of Faith'.[38] Here Wright took aim directly at 'one particular misunderstanding of Paul which has dogged the footsteps of Pauline studies, particularly (though by no means exclusively) in the Lutheran tradition'. That misunderstanding, he claimed, rests on a false view of Second Temple Judaism: 'My case here is simply stated: the tradition of Pauline interpretation has manufactured a false Paul by manufacturing a false Judaism for him to oppose.'[39] Alluding to the work of Sanders, Wright argued that 'the real Judaism was not a religion of legalistic works-righteousness'. This misrepresentation, he concluded, has resulted from the imposition of Protestant-Catholic debates onto the first century.[40]

The same charge has been leveled in many of Wright's subsequent publications. The following examples are taken from his 1986 commentary on Colossians:

> Paul's critique of Judaism does not aim, as in the old caricature, at 'legalism', the supposed attempt to earn righteousness through good works.[41]

> What Jewish scholars rejected as *Paul's* misunderstanding of Judaism is *itself* a misunderstanding of Paul, based on the standard Protestant (mis)reading of Paul through Reformation spectacles.[42]

Wright's 1997 monograph on Paul includes the following statements:

> Since the publication in 1977 of Ed Sanders' *Paul and Palestinian Judaism*, the fat has been in the fire. Everything we know about Paul, or thought we knew, has had to be re-examined. Sanders argued, basically, that the normal Christian, and especially Protestant, readings of Paul were seriously flawed because they attributed to first-century Judaism theological views which belonged rather to medieval Catholicism.[43]

> There [in 4QMMT], 'justification by works' has nothing to do with individual

---

[38] N.T. Wright, 'The Paul of History and the Apostle of Faith', *TynBul* 29 (1978), pp. 61-88.
[39] Wright, 'The Paul of History', p. 78.
[40] Wright, 'The Paul of History', pp. 79-80.
[41] N.T. Wright, *The Epistles of Paul to the Colossians and to Philemon: An Introduction and Commentary*, Tyndale New Testament Commentaries (Grand Rapids: Eerdmans, 1986), p. 30.
[42] Wright, *Colossians*, p. 108, emphasis original.
[43] Wright, *What Saint Paul Really Said*, p. 114.

Jews attempting a kind of proto-Pelagian pulling themselves up by their moral bootstraps and everything to do with the definition of the true Israel in advance of the final eschatological showdown.[44]

Paul has no thought in this passage [Rom. 3:21-31] of warding off a proto-Pelagianism, of which in any case his opponents were not guilty.[45]

Wright's 2002 commentary on Romans repeats the same idea:

One of the great gains of the last quarter of a century in Pauline scholarship has been to recognize that Paul's contemporaries—and Paul himself prior to his conversion—were not 'legalists', if by that we mean that they were attempting to earn favor with God, to earn grace as it were, by the performance of law-prescribed works. Paul's fellow Jews were not proto-Pelagians, attempting to pull themselves up by their moral shoelaces. They were, rather, responding out of gratitude to the God who had chosen and called Israel to be the covenant people and who had given Israel the law both as a sign of that covenant membership and as the means of making it real.[46]

In his 2009 rejoinder to John Piper, Wright makes the same claim:

It was the relentless insistence on the wickedness of Judaism, the folly of arrogant self-righteous lawkeeping on the one hand and the gloom of depressing lawkeeping on the other, the sense of Judaism as 'the wrong kind of religion', and so on—all of which slurs, though frequent in many would-be Christian traditions, were always far more endemic in Lutheranism than in Calvinism—that represented the problem to which Sanders, following Moore, Davies, Schoeps, Stendahl and others, was offering a fresh solution. God gave Israel the Torah as a way of life for the people with whom he had already entered into covenant, and whom he had now rescued from slavery. The Torah was itself the covenant charter, setting Israel apart from all the other nations: which other country, Israel was to ask itself, has laws like these? All the 'obedience' that the law then required would fall under the rubric of 'response to God's saving grace', even when this was not explicitly mentioned.[47]

---

[44] Wright, *What Saint Paul Really Said*, p. 119.

[45] Wright, *What Saint Paul Really Said*, p. 129.

[46] Wright, *Romans*, pp. 460-61.

[47] Wright, *Justification*, pp. 72-73. Wright's larger discussion in this section of the book (pp. 71-77) draws on the differences between Lutheranism and Calvinism with respect to the law as part of an argument that the 'old perspective', because of its greater emphasis on discontinuity between the law and the gospel, is the unique heir of the Lutheran tradition. While there is some truth in this analysis, Wright's sweeping caricature of the Lutheran view of the law and his failure to understand the nuances of

Wright's indebtedness to Sanders is evident, as is his concern that Protestantism has long misread Paul in part because of a faulty view of Second Temple Judaism.

Dunn has repeatedly made the same charge. In 1983 he coined the phrase 'The New Perspective on Paul' by publishing an article by that title.[48] Dunn opened his argument with a discussion of Sanders before moving on to his own understanding of Paul. Along the way he sought to expose the problem with historic Protestant exegesis of Paul's letters:

> Looked at from another angle, the problem is the way in which Paul has been understood as the great exponent of the central Reformation doctrine of *justification by faith*. As Krister Stendahl warned twenty years ago, it is deceptively easy to read Paul in the light of Luther's agonized search for relief from a troubled conscience. Since Paul's teaching on justification by faith seems to speak so directly to Luther's subjective wrestlings, it was a natural corollary to see Paul's opponents in terms of the unreformed Catholicism which opposed Luther, with first century Judaism read through the 'grid' of the early 16th century Catholic system of merit. To a remarkable and indeed alarming degree, throughout this century the standard depiction of the Judaism which Paul rejected has been the reflex of Lutheran hermeneutic.[49]

This charge has been leveled repeatedly in subsequent publications, as a few examples will indicate. In an article originally published in 1985, Dunn argued the following:

> What I have been pleading for in effect is a shift in perspective—from one dominated by the categories of the Reformation debates, to one properly set within the horizons of the social world of first century Judaism. When such a shift is carried through it releases a flood of fresh light on the issues confronting Paul and on his response to them. A key example is the phrase *ta erga tou nomou*, 'the works of the law'. The fact that Paul uses it only in the context of his argument with other Jewish Christians (or Jews) is usually recognized by commentators. But sooner or later (usually sooner) the perspective slips and the assumption begins to dominate the exegesis that by 'works of the law' Paul means the attempt

---

the Reformed tradition's view of the law (on which see chapters 3 and 4 below) significantly weakens the force of his argument here.

[48] James D.G. Dunn, 'The New Perspective on Paul', *BJRL* 65 (1983), pp. 95-122; subsequently published in *New Perspective* pp. 89-110. Subsequent references are to the latter publication.

[49] Dunn, 'The New Perspective on Paul', pp. 91-92, emphasis original.

to win God's favour by human achievement, or some such paraphrase.[50]

In 1992 the argument appeared again:

> Luther had striven to please God by his acts of penitence and good works. The Church of his day taught that salvation could be gained by merit, the merit of the saints, that the time spent in purgatory could be diminished by the purchase of indulgences. That was what the discovery of justification by faith had freed him from. It was all too easy to read Paul's experience through the same grid. What Luther had been delivered from was also what Paul had been delivered from. As the medieval church taught salvation by merit and good works, so must the Judaism of Paul's day. It was a degenerate religion precisely because it was legalistic, dependent on human effort, and self-satisfied with the results. And the Pharisees were the worst of all—narrow minded, legalistic bigots.
>
> In vain might Jewish scholars protest: this was not the Judaism they knew. Possibly another form of early Judaism of which no trace now remains—in the diaspora, from where Paul came, perhaps. But not traditional Judaism, with its emphasis precisely on repentance (a category strikingly absent from Paul) and atonement—that is, on God's provision for sin.[51]

Again, the refrain appears in Dunn's 1998 magnum opus, *The Theology of Paul the Apostle*:

> The negative side of this emphasis [on justification by faith since the time of the Reformation] was an unfortunate strain of anti-Judaism. Paul's teaching on justification was seen as a reaction against and in opposition to Judaism. As Luther had rejected a medieval church which offered salvation by merit and good works, the same, it was assumed, was true of Paul in relation to the Judaism of his day.[52]

A final example comes from Dunn's contribution representing the new perspective in a 2011 book on justification:

> Within this tradition of Christian anti-Jewishness, it is hardly surprising that Paul was regarded, by Jews as well as Christians, as the archetype of this anti-Jewishness, as hostile to the Judaism he once espoused. Nor is it very surprising that the assumption became more or less given, that Paul opposed Judaism because of its negative and anti-Christian (so un-Christian) character. This became the default perspective of Protestantism, principally because Martin

---

[50] Dunn, 'Works of the Law and the Curse of the Law', pp. 115-16 (originally published in *NTS* 31 [1985], pp. 523-42).

[51] Dunn, 'The Justice of God', p. 192 (originally published in *JTS* 43 [1992], pp. 1-22).

[52] Dunn, *The Theology of Paul*, pp. 336-37.

Luther understood Paul's reaction against Judaism in the light of his own reaction against medieval Catholicism. The degeneracy of a Catholicism that offered forgiveness of sins by the buying of indulgences mirrored for Luther the degeneracy of a Judaism that taught justification by works. In Lutheranism, Paul's distinction between gospel and law became an antithesis between Christianity and Judiasm. If 'gospel' was the expression of grace, then 'law' was the antonym to 'grace'. In Jewish (mis)understanding, 'law' was 'a summons to achievement'. And 'works of the law' were but 'man's self-powered striving to undergird his own existence in forgetfulness of his creaturely existence'.[53]

Like Wright, Dunn has used Sanders' thesis to expose what he perceives to be the weakness of the traditional Protestant reading of Paul.

Although less prominent as a proponent of the new perspective, Hays has made the same charge:

> Martin Luther found in Paul's dichotomy between 'faith' and 'works of the law' a hermeneutical principle that provided the theological impetus for the Reformation. Luther interpreted 'works of the law' as a metaphor for all human striving for God's approval. Thus, he saw in Gal. 2:16 a contrast between earning salvation through meritorious performance of good deeds and receiving salvation through faith alone (*sola fide*). This doctrine provided him with a powerful polemical weapon against the practices and teachings of the sixteenth-century Roman Catholic Church. Luther's reading of Paul exercised widespread influence on subsequent Christian interpreters, who associated the attempt to earn salvation through good works with Pharisaic Judaism and, therefore, saw Paul as announcing a radical break with the Jewish understanding of God and salvation.
>
> The difficulty with this account of the matter is that it rests upon a caricature of Judaism, as E.P. Sanders has demonstrated in his watershed study *Paul and Palestinian Judaism*. Judaism has never taught that individuals must earn God's favor by performing meritorious works; members of the covenant people are already embraced by God's gracious election and mercy. Obedience to the Law is not a condition of getting in; rather, it is a means of staying in the covenant community. Sanders describes this Jewish pattern of religion as 'covenantal nomism'. Nearly all scholars who study early Judaism and Christianity now acknowledge that Sanders's description of Palestinian Judaism is basically correct.[54]

---

[53] Dunn, 'New Perspective View', pp. 179-80. Significantly, Dunn's quotations in the last two sentences quoted here come, not from any Reformer or theologian of the post-Reformation period, but rather from Käsemann and Bultmann, respectively. It is all too easy for new perspective proponents to slide from criticism of Luther to criticism of twentieth-century Lutherans.

[54] Hays, *Galatians*, p. 239.

It is difficult to imagine a clearer account of the new perspective's understanding of its own origin.

Other new perspective proponents have traced a paradigm shift in Pauline studies to Sanders' thesis, which they generally regard as firmly established.[55] While Stendahl may have anticipated Sanders by raising questions about the traditional approach to Paul's writings, there can be no doubt that Sanders has given the new perspective its primary historical foundation. What has become clear throughout this discussion is that the new perspective on Paul depends for its existence on a foil, namely, the traditional Protestant approach to reading Paul.[56] The new perspective holds to a particular thesis about this foil, namely, that it arose from the imposition of sixteenth-century categories derived from debates over grace and merit onto the Pauline writings, in the process tearing Paul away from his own context and misrepresenting the Judaism of his day. The primary offenders in this regard are New Testament scholars in the Weber/Bousset/Billerbeck/Bultmann stream. While it may be apparent that the chastisement these scholars have received from Sanders and company is well-deserved, it must be noted here that such chastisement cannot be legitimately applied to the whole of the Reformation tradition without further argument. That Lutheran New Testament scholars four-hundred years after Luther might have misrepresented Judaism in light of their own theology seems to be entirely probable. That these misrepresentations can be blamed for the rise of the whole of the Lutheran tradition, or of historic Protestantism itself, is a claim with an enormous logical gap. Richard Gaffin has, in passing, drawn attention to this subtle move made by new perspective proponents:

> I leave to the side here the general tendency, as it seems to me, of the 'new perspective' too readily to lump together the Reformation with modern Protestantism prior to Sanders as the target of its criticisms; such similarities as there may be between Luther and Bultmann, for instance, are upon more careful reflection little more than merely formal.[57]

By arguing that the discovery of a grace-based Judaism overturns the way Paul has been read among Protestants since the sixteenth-century, new perspective

---

[55] Francis Watson, *Paul, Judaism and the Gentiles* (New York: Cambridge University Press, 1986), pp. 1-22; Neil Elliot, *The Rhetoric of Romans: Argumentative Constraint and Strategy in Paul's Dialogue with Judaism* (Sheffield, UK: Sheffield Academic, 1990), pp. 146, 212; Daniel Boyarin, *A Radical Jew: Paul and the Politics of Identity* (Berkeley: University of California Press, 1994), pp. 11, 41-56; Terence L. Donaldson, *Paul and the Gentiles: Remapping the Apostle's Convictional World* (Minneapolis: Fortress, 1997), pp. 3-27. Stephen Westerholm provides an excellent survey of the paradigm shift in Pauline studies in *Perspectives Old and New on Paul*, pp. 3-258.

[56] This is most often called the 'Lutheran' approach, but it would also include historic Protestantism more broadly, including the Reformed tradition.

[57] Richard B. Gaffin, 'Review Essay: Paul the Theologian', *WTJ* 62 (2000), p. 132.

proponents not only make a historical claim about Judaism; they make a historical claim about the Reformation itself. This study will, in part, investigate the validity of that claim.

The Hermeneutical Presupposition of the New Perspective

Sanders' *Paul and Palestinian Judaism* has generated a hermeneutical presupposition among new perspective proponents, one that could be stated simply as follows: *covenantal nomism could not have served as Paul's foil in the promotion of a doctrine of justification that resembles that of the Reformation.* Expanded into a more complete explanation, the presupposition could be given in four propositions:

1. The antithesis of grace/faith and works in Paul seems to suggest categories of grace and human merit that formed the contours of the debate over justification during the Reformation.

2. However, as E.P. Sanders has demonstrated, Second Temple Judaism upheld a pattern of religion that was based on grace, not works.

3. Therefore, Paul could not have opposed a doctrine of merit, for there was no such doctrine in his historical context.

4. Therefore, the antithesis of grace/faith and works in Paul must be defined in categories other than those that framed the Reformation debate over justification.

This presupposition has been identified before by none other than Francis Watson, who, although formerly identified with the new perspective, now seeks to move beyond it, as the subtitle of a more recent edition of his *Paul, Judaism, and the Gentiles* indicates.[58] In 2001 Watson wrote the following:

> In interpreting the relevant Pauline texts, the new perspective repeatedly performs a characteristic exegetical manoeuvre in three steps. Here's how it works. *Step one*: we observe that a Pauline text appears to be contrasting the logic of the gospel with the logic of a Jewish or Jewish Christian understanding of the law. Paul speaks of grace over against law, faith over against works; he seems to set believing the gospel of divine saving action over against practising the law. *Step two*: we know, however, that the point of these Pauline antitheses *cannot* be to contrast the gospel's emphasis on divine agency with a Jewish emphasis on human agency. If we think that we see this antithesis between divine and human agency in Paul, we're still held captive by the ideology of the Reformation,

---

[58] Francis Watson, *Paul, Judaism, and the Gentiles: Beyond the New Perspective* (Grand Rapids: Eerdmans, 2007).

resulting as it must do in a hostile caricature of Judaism. But how do we know that an antithesis between divine and human agency *cannot* be present in Paul's texts? Because Sanders has taught us that Judaism was and is a religion of grace; and, on this matter, Sanders speaks not only the truth but also the whole truth and nothing but the truth. *Step three*: we must therefore read the Pauline antithesis differently, as an 'ecclesiological' statement about the nature of the people of God. For Paul, 'faith' represents an *inclusive* understanding of God as including non-law-observant Gentiles; 'works' represents an *exclusive* understanding of the people of God according to which full conversion to the practice of Judaism is a necessary precondition of salvation. What Paul is propounding is, in effect an inclusive, universal, liberal form of Jewish covenant theology.[59]

This hermeneutical presupposition seems to be driven by the prior assumption that only a strict merit theology could serve as a foil to the Reformation doctrine of *sola fide*. Only Weber's Judaism could have served as a foil to Luther's Paul. In fact, an investigation of the way the doctrine of justification was framed during the Reformation and beyond will demonstrate that such is manifestly not the case. The Reformers and their successors never faced pure Pelagianism, just as (if one grants Sanders' point for the sake of argument) Paul never faced pure legalism. Yet pure Pelagianism was not necessary for *sola fide* to arise. The true foil to *sola fide* was the medieval Catholic synthesis of law and gospel, the mixture of grace and human effort that is not unlike the monocovenantal pattern of Sanders' Judaism.[60] In fact, the distinguishing mark

---

[59] Francis Watson, 'Not the New Perspective' (paper presented at the British New Testament Conference, September 2001), p. 14, as cited in S.M. Baugh, 'The New Perspective, Mediation, and Justification', R. Scott Clark (ed), *Covenant, Justification, and Pastoral Ministry: Essays by the Faculty of Westminster Seminary California* (Phillipsburg, NJ: P & R, 2007), p. 140, emphasis original.

[60] The term 'monocovenantal' refers to a soteriological synthesis between demand and promise or, in Christian terminology, between law and gospel. The term 'bicovenantal' refers to a soteriological distinction between law and gospel, such that the pursuit of one for justification mutually excludes the other. Although covenant theology is clearly bicovenantal (referring to the two covenants of works and grace), I will use the term 'bicovenantal' more broadly to include any theological position that distinguishes law from gospel as two different ways of relating to God, whether within the framework of a covenant of works/covenant of grace or not. The use of these terms is dependent on Michael S. Horton, *Covenant and Salvation: Union with Christ* (Louisville: Westminster John Knox, 2007), pp. 80-101; idem, 'Which Covenant Theology?' in R. Scott Clark (ed), *Covenant, Justification, and Pastoral Ministry: Essays by the Faculty of Westminster Seminary California*, (Phillipsburg, NJ: P & R, 2007), pp. 197-227. Horton has noted again the similarities between Sanders' Judaism and medieval Catholicism in his 'Traditional Reformed Response [to the New Perspective View]', in James K. Beilby and Paul Rhodes Eddy (eds), *Justification: Five Views* (Downers Grove, IL: IVP Academic, 2011), pp. 201-07.

of the Reformation doctrine of *sola fide* is not that it rests on grace as opposed to works. Rather, what distinguishes *sola fide* from the Roman Catholic doctrine of justification is that the former declares that justification occurs on the basis of an alien righteousness. The need for this alien righteousness arises from a divine demand for perfect obedience, which then gives rise to a clear law-gospel distinction (bicovenantalism), wherein justification may be pursued by faith or by works, but never both at the same time. It is in these categories, and not in a simplistic contrast between grace and works, that the Reformation doctrine of justification was forged. For this reason, Sanders' thesis about Second Temple Judaism has no bearing on the categories that defined justification during the Reformation. Therefore, the hermeneutical presupposition that has resulted from his work simply does not follow.

Methodology

The foregoing claim will be demonstrated by an investigation of the development of the doctrine of justification in the Reformation and post-Reformation periods. It will be shown that the doctrine of *sola fide* arose because of the Protestant conviction that God demands perfect obedience for salvation, and this demand leaves open two distinct paths to right standing before him: the path of works and the path of faith. These two paths do not intersect. One must obey the law of God perfectly or receive by faith the imputed righteousness of Jesus Christ in order to be justified before God. Law and gospel must not be mixed together. Because of the universality of sin, the law's demands cannot be met, and thus the only hope for humanity is the way of faith.

Chapter 2 will set the historical-theological background for this argument by surveying the themes of grace and merit in several prominent representatives of the late medieval Catholic tradition, culminating in the definitive declaration of the Council of Trent. Chapter 3 will demonstrate that the key element that distinguishes the Reformation doctrine of justification in Luther, Melanchthon, and Calvin in opposition to Rome is not that the former proclaimed justification by grace through faith, but rather that they proclaimed justification by grace alone through faith alone, on the basis of an alien righteousness. Chapter 4 will then trace further developments of the doctrine of justification in the post-Reformation period, developments that indicate that the necessity of perfect obedience, the distinction between law and gospel, and the doctrine of alien righteousness continued to define the Protestant view of justification, thereby bringing to maturity the 'old perspective' on Paul. The concluding chapter will then apply the observations of chapters 2, 3, and 4 to the question at hand, the hermeneutical presupposition of the new perspective, revealing it to be unwarranted and expendable.

The thesis of this study having been demonstrated, the final chapter will also take the argument one step further by sketching in some exegetical observations that indicate that Paul's polemic moves in the same orbit as that of the Reformers and their heirs. Is there any evidence in Paul that would indicate a bicovenantal theology dependent on a divine demand for perfect obedience and issuing forth in a doctrine of alien righteousness? If so, could this argument have been formulated against a Jewish or Jewish-Christian theology that was essentially gracious in character and yet upheld Torah observance as at least a partial basis of final justification? How might these observations square with Paul's doctrine of judgment according to works and James' doctrine of justification by works? Because this study is not primarily exegetical in nature, these questions can only be answered in a preliminary way, pointing out areas for more fruitful work to be done by others.

CHAPTER 2

Grace and Merit in Late Medieval Theology

If the case for a grace-based Judaism overturns the Reformation reading of Paul by undermining the legalistic foil imported from medieval Catholicism, the implication would seem to be that medieval Catholicism was not a grace-based religion. If, however, the medieval Catholic Church did hold to an essentially gracious framework for its soteriology, and yet the Reformation doctrine of justification still emerged in response to it, then it would appear that the new perspective on Paul that has arisen in Sanders' wake has offered a claim about the significance of a grace-based Judaism that does not follow. This chapter will demonstrate that such is indeed the case. Medieval Catholicism was not legalistic in the sense that it eliminated grace from the soteriological equation. It was not characterized by an undiluted Pelagianism, nor did it promote a doctrine by which self-attained merits are weighed against demerits at the final judgment. The medieval Catholic doctrine of justification, in its diversity of formulations, adheres to a pattern that places primacy on divine grace and then incorporates human merit as part of the legal basis of final salvation. It was this doctrine, in whatever way it may have been formulated, that the Reformers rejected. This claim will be demonstrated by an investigation of some prominent works of the pre-Reformation scholastic tradition—beginning with Peter Lombard's *Sentences*—and moving on to the definitive decree of the Council of Trent on justification in 1547.[1]

As this survey will demonstrate, the Catholic Church of the Middle Ages did not consider perfect obedience to be a requirement for right standing with God. Although conceived in different ways, medieval theologians viewed salvation,

---

[1] The purpose of this chapter is to set a theological context for the next chapter addressing justification among the Reformers. The approach followed here is to bookend the Reformation by tracing a theological pattern that reveals continuity between pre-Reformation scholasticism and the Council of Trent. In Sanders' terminology, this chapter will reveal a common 'pattern of religion' among the pre-Reformation scholastics and Tridentine theology. Although Trent is not technically 'medieval' in chronology, it will be treated here because of its location at a time of historical transition out of the medieval period and because of its conceptual ties to the medieval theology that preceded it. Some of the Roman Catholic 'sparring partners' of the Reformers, omitted from discussion here, will be noted in the next chapter in connection with specific polemical works that they provoked.

including its legal dimension, as a result of the grace of God working in conjunction with an imperfect human obedience. This theological issue, and not legalism *per se*, became the central dividing line between Rome and the Reformers. Because of their commitment to the necessity of a perfect righteousness as the legal basis of justification, the Reformers and their heirs upheld a clear distinction between divine demand and divine gift (law and gospel), entailing a doctrine of alien righteousness as a necessity for the salvation of sinners. Roman Catholic soteriology developed very differently because it did not include a requirement for perfect obedience, leading to a synthesis of law and gospel and an outright rejection of alien righteousness in its polemic against the Reformation. These categories define the debates over justification of the sixteenth century and beyond, and they are categories basically left untouched by Sanders' thesis on Second Temple Judaism. Whether a religion is grace-based or not is essentially irrelevant to the discussion at hand. Any religion that fails to distinguish between law and gospel, or between the principle of doing and that of receiving by faith, comes under the attack of the Reformation doctrine of justification, as the grace-based Catholicism of the late Middle Ages certainly did.

The Pre-Reformation Scholastic Tradition

Catholic theologians of the late medieval period use the terminology of grace primarily in connection with the infusion of charity. For the purpose of this study, however, any kind of unmerited divine favor shown to human beings will be included in the discussion of their theology of grace, whether the specific term *gratia* is used or not, for it is unmerited divine favor that is the primary connotation of grace in Sanders's portrayal of covenantal nomism. In the centuries that preceded the Reformation, grace was not a peripheral theme in soteriology. It was, without question, the dominant theme. No theologian from this period would have denied that salvation is by grace. However, this fact alone does not tell the whole story, for no distinctive Reformation soteriology could have arisen if there were not more nuance to the discussion. Therefore, it is necessary to look more closely at the contours of late medieval Catholic soteriology in order to see precisely how the Reformation doctrine of justification emerged in response to it, beginning in the twelfth century.

PETER LOMBARD'S *SENTENCES*

In his monumental work *Iustitia Dei*, Alister McGrath argues that the medieval scholastic doctrine of justification is essentially an outworking and clarification of Augustine's teaching, namely, that to justify is to make someone just; justification is a moral transformation that occurs by the grace of God, which thereby sets the sinner right in relation to God.[2] Peter Lombard (c. 1095/1100-1161) contributed to this development by producing the most enduring theological textbook of the late medieval period, the *Four Books of Sentences* (*Libri IV Sententiarum*). This work, which consists largely of quotations from Augustine, will be the starting point for this survey.[3]

The Lombard's soteriology is rooted in divine grace, and the doctrine of grace as set forth in the *Sentences* is broadly Augustinian. It begins with a principle of discrimination, a doctrine of predestination by which God has determined from eternity that certain people will, by his grace, 'be good and blessed', receiving eternal life.[4] God's mercy, and thus his eternal decree of predestination, cannot be merited, lest grace be emptied of its character as grace.[5] There is an asymmetry between predestination and reprobation. The Lombard explains the latter as a subset of foreknowledge, which, in distinction from predestination, is not causative.[6] Furthermore, while reprobation is not strictly merited, divine hardening (the enactment of the decree of reprobation in time) is a divine judgment that is given in response to sin, and thus mercy and hardening do not exist as arbitrary parallel concepts. The Lombard seeks to honor God for the good end attained by the elect and place blame for damnation squarely on sinners. However, while the Lombard's doctrine of predestination is Augustinian in character, noticeably lacking in his discussion is any notion of irresistible grace.[7]

The Lombard's soteriology begins with the sovereign grace of God, but

---

[2] Alister E. McGrath, *Iustitia Dei: A History of the Christian Doctrine of Justification*, 3rd ed. (New York: Cambridge University Press, 2005), p. 56.

[3] On Peter Lombard's theology of grace, see Marcia L. Colish, *Peter Lombard* (New York: Brill, 1994), 2, pp. 488-507; Philipp W. Rosemann, *Peter Lombard* (New York: Oxford University Press, 2004), pp. 135-43; Karlfried Froehlich, 'Justification Language in the Middle Ages', in H. George Anderson, T. Austin Murphy, and Joseph A. Burgess (eds), *Justification by Faith: Lutherans and Catholics in Dialogue VII*, (Minneapolis: Augsburg, 1985), pp. 143-61; Aage Rydstrøm-Poulsen, *The Gracious God: Gratia in Augustine and the Twelfth Century* (Copenhagen: Akademisk Forlag, 2002), pp. 343-91.

[4] 'Therefore, he has predestined from eternity some future good and blessed people, that is, he has chosen that they might be good and blessed, and he has predestined good things for them.' Peter Lombard, *Libri IV Sententiarum* 1.35.4 (Quaracchi: Ex Typographia Collegii S. Bonaventurae, 1916), 1, p. 221. All English translations from this work are my own.

[5] 'However, if we seek merit for hardening and for mercy, we find merit for hardening, but in fact we find no merit for mercy, since there is no merit for mercy, lest grace be emptied, if it is not given freely, but is given in exchange for merits.' Peter Lombard, *Sententiarum* 1.41.1 (Collegii S. Bonaventura, 1, p. 253).

[6] He writes of predestination 'by which God chose [*elegit*] from eternity whom he willed', in contrast to reprobation, 'by which he foreknew [*praescivit*] from eternity certain future people to be wicked and damned'. Peter Lombard, *Sententiarum* 1.41.1 (Collegii S. Bonaventurae, 1, p. 254).

[7] Colish, *Peter Lombard*, 1, p. 289.

human free will also plays a prominent role in the acquisition of merit that leads to eternal life, as Colish notes: 'There can be no merit without free will. And, when God rewards the meritorious, He rewards not Himself but the virtues that moral agents have made their own ingrained character traits.'[8] Grace and merit are not mutually exclusive concepts. The end that God ordains by grace (eternal life) is itself attained by merit, but this merit in turn arises from grace: 'For the principal cause of good acts of merit is grace itself, by which free will is kindled and healed, and also the human will is helped, so that it might be good.'[9] In the *Sentences* this process occurs by a synergistic interplay between the grace of God and the human will. God's grace enables the acquisition of merit by providing its necessary condition.[10] By operative grace (*gratia operans*) God brings a sinner from the state of sin into the state of justification through faith, thereby providing the necessary precondition for free will to merit eternal life. The sinner who is justified by operative grace is not, in the Reformation sense, declared righteous; he or she is, in the Augustinian sense, made righteous. By cooperative grace (*gratia cooperans*) God assists the will that has been healed and directed toward good, making its good aims effective for merit. Operative grace precedes a good will, and cooperative grace follows it.[11] Grace begins and completes the process of salvation, but there is a division of labor that occurs throughout the process, leaving room for free will to attain merit before God.

Faith may be said to merit justification and eternal life, but only as an acceptable figure of speech:

> For if faith itself, the prevenient virtue, were said to be an act of the mind, which is a merit, then it would have its origin from free will; but because it is not, it is said to be a merit *in this way*: that its act is a merit, but only if charity is present, without which neither believing nor hoping is meritorious of life.[12]

In other words, faith does not originate from free will; it is a gift of God's

---

[8] Marcia L. Colish, 'Peter Lombard', in G.R. Evans (ed), *The Medieval Theologians: An Introduction to Theology in the Medieval Period* (Malden, MA: Blackwell, 2001), p. 175.
[9] Peter Lombard, *Sententiarum* 2.27.7 (Collegii St. Bonaventurae, 1, p. 448).
[10] Colish, *Peter Lombard*, 1, p. 289.
[11] Having quoted from Augustine's *De Gratia et Libero Arbitrio*, the Lombard writes, 'Behold, it is sufficiently opened by these words, what operative grace and cooperative grace are: for it is operative [grace] that precedes a good will, for by it the will of a man is freed and prepared to be good, and to will the good effectively; cooperative grace, in fact, follows by helping a good will.' Peter Lombard, *Sententiarum* 2.26.1 (Collegii St. Bonaventurae, 1, pp. 436-437); see also sections 2.27.1—2.28.2; Colish, *Peter Lombard*, 2, pp. 488-89.
[12] Peter Lombard, *Sententiarum* 2.27.9 (Collegii St. Bonaventurae, 1, p. 449).

operative grace.[13] The *sine qua non* of all merit is charity, which the Lombard identifies as the Holy Spirit himself.[14] When faith is joined to charity, it is capable of producing acts that are meritorious of eternal life, and in this way faith can be said to be meritorious. Merit only applies to acts that proceed from free will,[15] and this means that faith itself cannot qualify; nevertheless, meritorious acts do proceed from faith.

Justification is particularly connected to the two sacraments of baptism and penance, for it is by means of baptism that justification is first received, and it is by means of penance that it is restored after being lost through mortal sin. The Lombard defines a sacrament as 'so great a sign of the grace of God and a form of invisible grace, that it might bear the image of it and be the cause of it. Therefore, the sacraments were instituted not only for the grace of signifying, but also for that of sanctifying'.[16] The sacraments are indeed signs of grace, but not mere signs; they are themselves the instrumental causes of grace, which comes to the believer by virtue of the atonement of Christ. Because baptism is the initial sacrament, it is the one connected to the reception of justifying grace, for justification is nothing other than a definitive transition from a state of sin to a state of grace. Concerning baptism, the Lombard writes, 'Therefore, the thing [i.e., substance or content] of this sacrament is justification.'[17] Penance restores justifying grace to those who, subsequent to baptism, have lost it. Here the Lombard's influence has been particularly significant for the subsequent development of Roman Catholic theology, for in his day there was no widespread agreement that penance even constituted a sacrament. The popularity of the *Sentences* in subsequent generations helped set the trajectory for the teaching solidified at the Council of Trent, a sacramental theology that endures to this day.[18] In particular, the Lombard's omission of a physical element from the definition of a sacrament made possible the inclusion of penance among the sacraments and thereby linked much subsequent theological

---

[13] 'For faith, by which you are justified, is given to you freely.' Peter Lombard, *Sententiarum* 2.26.3 (Collegii St. Bonaventurae, 1, p. 439).

[14] Peter Lombard, *Sententiarum* 2.27.9 (Collegii St. Bonaventurae, 1, p. 449).

[15] '[T]here is no merit in man, which is not through free will.' Peter Lombard, *Sententiarum* 2.27.7 (Collegii St. Bonaventurae, 1, p. 448).

[16] Peter Lombard, *Sententiarum* 4.1.4 (Collegii St. Bonaventurae, 2, p. 746).

[17] Peter Lombard, *Sententiarum*, 4.3.9 (Collegii St. Bonaventurae, 2 p. 761). In the previous paragraph the Lombard had written, 'and this is the thing [i.e., substance] of this sacrament, namely, interior cleansing'. The parallel nature of these statements indicates that for Peter Lombard, justification is nothing other than interior cleansing.

[18] Rosemann, *Peter Lombard*, pp. 159-68, places the Lombard's doctrine of penance in its historical-theological context. On Trent's doctrine of penance, see Council of Trent 7, 14 in *Decrees of the Ecumenical Councils*, vol. 2, *Trent-Vatican II* (ed. Norman P. Tanner; Washington, DC: Georgetown University Press, 1990), pp. 684, 703-09.

discussion of justification to the sacramental system.[19]

The Lombard affirms Jerome's metaphor that penance is a second plank after shipwreck.[20] While both baptism and penance are instrumental causes of justification, baptism is a sacrament only, while penance, which has both an exterior and an interior aspect, is both a sacrament and a virtue of the soul.[21] Rosemann argues that 'inner penance is a virtue of the mind because, like all other virtues, it is an indissociable effect of charity, which, in turn, has its source in Christ, and in our adherence to Him in faith'.[22] And since charity is none other than the Holy Spirit, the interior aspect of penance must be linked to the internal working of the Holy Spirit, a work that is manifested outwardly in acts of confession and satisfaction. And so, while the sacrament, taken as a whole, is both a sign and an instrumental cause of grace, it is itself the result of grace through the gift of the Holy Spirit. Whether referring to first justification (at baptism) or subsequent justification (through penance), the Lombard's doctrine is one of justification by grace, with the sacramental system functioning as a gracious provision for the weakness of humanity.

In summary, for Peter Lombard, salvation begins in God's sovereign, discriminating decree of predestination from eternity. In time, however, eternal life is merited by those who are, first, justified by operative grace through baptism, thereby being enabled to perform meritorious works, and, second, assisted in their works by cooperative grace. Those who fall from grace have recourse to the sacrament of penance, which is a sign, instrument, and even an effect of divine grace. A divine demand for perfect obedience is not a factor in this equation. The Lombard acknowledges that perfect fulfillment of the commandment to love God with all of one's heart is impossible to fulfill in this life.[23] Yet he still upholds a doctrine whereby eternal life is merited by works of charity that flow from faith. Furthermore, he envisions at the final judgment two groups who receive salvation: the elect who 'wipe away the stains of life with tears and hide them with the covering of alms' and the elect who 'even

---

[19] McGrath, *Iustitia Dei*, pp. 120-22. To be sure, penance includes an outward act, but there is no physical element like water, bread, or wine as part of the sacrament.

[20] Peter Lombard *Sententiarum* 4.14.1 (Collegii St. Bonaventurae, 2, p. 819).

[21] 'Baptism is only a sacrament, but penance is said to be both a sacrament and a virtue of the soul. For there is interior penance and exterior penance: the exterior is the sacrament, and the interior is the virtue of the soul; and both are the cause of salvation and justification.' Peter Lombard, *Sententiarum* 4.14.1 (Collegii St. Bonaventurae, 2, p. 849).

[22] Rosemann, *Peter Lombard*, p. 166.

[23] 'Nevertheless, that precept ["Love God with your whole heart"] is not fulfilled inwardly by man in this mortal life, except in part, not from the whole, since we love in part, just as *we know in part* [1 Cor. 13:9]; in the future, however, it will be fulfilled from the whole.' Peter Lombard, *Sententiarum* 3.27.6 (Collegii St. Bonaventurae, 2, p. 676).

surpass the precepts of the law by the virtue of perfection'.[24] The latter group will not even face judgment but will instead participate in administering it. The bare fact that the Lombard envisions that some, who are sinners incapable of perfect love for God in this life, will obtain surplus merit in the end indicates that the standard for eternal life is not perfection. Because of God's grace given through Christ and the sacraments, even sinners are capable of going beyond what God requires of them to attain eternal life. While the dominant note in the Lombard's soteriological scheme is grace, it is worked out in such a way that incorporates an imperfect human obedience as the instrumental, yet meritorious, cause of final salvation. Furthermore, it presupposes a doctrine of divine grace whereby God lowers his standard to accommodate the weakness of fallen humanity, enabling those who are incapable of loving God wholeheartedly to merit eternal life.

THOMAS AQUINAS' *SUMMA THEOLOGICA*

Thomas Aquinas (1225-1274) represents the pinnacle of the Catholic scholastic tradition. As such, his views on grace, merit, and justification deserve attention as a prominent pattern in the mosaic of late medieval theology. This survey will focus on his most mature and enduring work, the *Summa Theologica*.[25]

Thomas treats the subject of grace at length in the First Part of the Second Part (*Prima Secundae*) of the *Summa Theologica*, particularly Questions 109-112, followed by a treatment of justification (Question 113) and merit

---

[24] Peter Lombard, *Sententiarum* 4.47.3 (Collegii St. Bonaventurae, 2, pp. 1019-20). Here the Lombard quotes Gregory. The word 'perfection' does not refer to perfect obedience to God's law here, for the Lombard admits that there is no possibility of that.

[25] The literature on Thomas's view of grace includes Albrecht Ritschl, *A Critical History of the Christian Doctrine of Justification and Reconciliation* (trans. John S. Black; Edinburgh: Edmonston and Douglas, 1872), pp. 74-81; Reginald Garrigou-Lagrange, *Grace: Commentary on the* Summa Theologica *of St Thomas, Ia IIae, q. 109-14* (trans. The Dominican Nuns; St. Louis: Herder, 1952); Bernard Lonergan, *Grace and Freedom: Operative Grace in the Thought of St. Thomas Aquinas* (ed. J. Patout Burns; Toronto: University of Toronto Press, 2000); Bruce McCormack, 'What's at Stake in Current Debates over Justification? The Crisis of Protestantism in the West', in Mark Husbands and Daniel J. Treier (eds), *Justification: What's at Stake in the Current Debates* (Downers Grove, IL: IVP, 2004), pp. 85-90; Bernard McGinn, 'The Development of the Thought of Thomas Aquinas on the Reconciliation of Divine Providence and Contingent Action', *The Thomist* 39 (1975), pp. 741-52; Joseph Wawrykow, *God's Grace and Human Action: 'Merit' in the Theology of Thomas Aquinas* (Notre Dame, IN: University of Notre Dame Press, 1995); idem, 'Grace', in Rik Van Niewenhove and Joseph Wawrykow (eds), *The Theology of Thomas Aquinas* (Notre Dame, IN: University of Notre Dame Press, 2005), pp. 192-221. Wawrykow ('Grace', pp. 206-09) notes significant development in Thomas' doctrine of grace from the earlier *Scriptum Super Libros Sententiarum* to the later *Summa Theologica*. Because the latter represents Thomas' mature thought, and because its influence is by far more enduring, this study will focus on the latter.

(Question 114). However, his discussion of these topics presupposes and completes the discussion of predestination addressed in the First Part (*Prima Pars*), Question 23, and must, therefore, be read in light of it.[26] Thomas' doctrine of predestination is the foundation of his doctrine of grace, rooting the salvation of sinful human beings completely in the sovereign will of God. He affirms that the love of God differs from human love in that human love is roused by what it perceives to be good, whereas divine love is the cause of good in that which is loved.[27] For this reason, predestination has no respect to foreknown merit in those predestined to life, for all merit in them is the result of God's prior love for them.[28] Thomas specifically rejects what he terms the view of 'the Pelagians', although what he actually describes as such resembles a semi-Pelagian doctrine whereby God gives grace in response to those who prepare themselves for it by their own power. Thus, for Thomas, predestination is unconditional,[29] although there is an asymmetrical relationship between predestination to life and reprobation to eternal condemnation. The former occurs by God's active will and the latter by his permission.[30]

Significantly, Thomas' discussion of predestination intersects with his doctrine of merit prior to the more comprehensive discussion of the latter in Question 114. He argues that 'predestination as an effect can be considered in two ways, as to its parts and in its entirety'. Considered in its parts, one aspect of predestination may be considered the cause of another, and in this manner it is legitimate to say that glory is given by God on the basis of merit, so long as it is understood that human merit is itself the result of God's predestination.[31]

---

[26] Wawrykow, 'Grace', p. 199.

[27] 'Election and love, however, are differently constituted in God, and in ourselves; because in us the will in loving does not cause good; but we are incited to love by the good which already exists; and so election in us precedes love. In God, however, it is just the reverse. For His Will, which, in loving, He wishes good to someone, is the cause of good possessed by some in preference to others.' Thomas Aquinas, *The 'Summa Theologica' of St. Thomas Aquinas* 1.23.4 (trans. Fathers of the English Dominican Province; London: R & T Washbourne, 1911), pp. 321-22. The Latin text for this section is available in Thomas Aquinas, *Summa Theologiae* (ed. Thomas Gilby; New York: McGraw-Hill, 1967), vol. 5.

[28] Thomas Aquinas, *Summa Theologica*, 1.23.5 (trans. Fathers of the English Dominican Province), pp. 322-27.

[29] 'Why He chooses some for glory, and reprobates others, has no reason; except the Divine Will.' Thomas Aquinas, *Summa Theologica* 1.23.5 (trans. Fathers of the English Dominican Province), p 327. In this context Thomas explains that God's design in predestination and reprobation is to display his goodness by mercifully sparing the elect and by justly punishing the reprobate.

[30] 'Therefore, as Predestination includes the will to confer grace and glory; so also Reprobation includes the will to permit a person to fall into sin, and to impose the punishment of damnation on account of that sin.' Thomas Aquinas, *Summa Theologica* 1.23.3 (trans. Fathers of the English Dominican Province), p. 320.

[31] Thomas Aquinas, *Summa Theologiae* 1.23.5 (ed. Gilby), 5, pp. 124-27.

Thus, Thomas argues that, when considered as to its parts, predestination to life includes the predestination of merits that will gain life. God ordains the end of eternal life for his elect, and he also ordains the means by which they will attain that end, namely, at least some degree of merit. Salvation is all of grace, and yet it is still earned in some sense. A grace-based soteriology does not preclude a form of works-righteousness. Thomas' doctrine of grace begins with a strong doctrine of unconditional divine predestination to life.

In the First Part of the Second Part (*Prima Secundae*), Thomas begins his discussion of grace by addressing the need for grace (Question 109). Article 2 of this question asks whether man can will and do good apart from grace.[32] Here Thomas introduces an important anthropological distinction: the difference between human nature as originally created and human nature as corrupted by the fall. In the state of integrity, man is capable of performing the good that is proportionate to his nature, but he cannot perform the transcendent good (*bonum superexcedens*) that is meritorious. In the state of corruption, man is not even capable, apart from grace, of performing that which is proportionate to his created nature; thus, for fallen man, grace is necessary, first to provide healing to his nature and then to empower him to perform the transcendent good necessary for merit.[33] In a subsequent discussion (Article 4) Thomas denies the 'Pelagian heresy' that man can fulfill the precepts of the law apart from grace. While this would be possible for man in his unfallen state, it is impossible for fallen man; Thomas clearly affirms a doctrine of original sin that has left humanity helpless apart from divine assistance.[34] It comes as no surprise, then, that in the following article (Article 5) he denies the possibility of meriting eternal life apart from grace.[35] In the midst of this discussion, Thomas reiterates a point previously made in the question regarding predestination. Answering an objection to his position, he argues that man does indeed perform works that merit eternal life, but these works are themselves the

---

[32] The generic term 'man' will be used here because of its ability to represent the human race as a whole and also to denote a generic individual at the same time. The term 'human being' cannot denote the former, and 'humanity' cannot denote the latter. The term 'man' best captures the sense of the Latin *homo* as used by Thomas in this context.

[33] 'And thus in the state of perfect nature man needs a gratuitous strength superadded to natural strength for one reason, viz., in order to do and wish supernatural good; but for two reasons, in the state of corrupt nature, viz, in order to be healed, and furthermore in order to carry out works of supernatural virtue, which are meritorious.' Thomas Aquinas, *Summa Theologica* 1-2.109.2 (trans. Fathers of the English Dominican Province), pp. 326-28. The Latin text for this section may be found in Thomas Aquinas, *Summa Theologiae* (ed. Cornelius Ernst; New York: McGraw-Hill, 1972), vol. 30.

[34] Thomas Aquinas, *Summa Theologiae*. 1-2.109.4 (ed. Ernst), 30, pp. 80-85; cf. Thomas Aquinas, *Summa Contra Gentiles* 4.50-52 (ed. and trans. Charles J. O'Neil; Notre Dame, IN: University of Notre Dame Press, 1957), 4, pp. 212-23.

[35] Thomas Aquinas. *Summa Theologiae* 1-2.109.5 (ed. Ernst), 30, pp. 84-87.

result of grace.[36] For Thomas there is no possibility of eternal life, especially for man in his corrupt nature, apart from grace.

He takes the concept of grace still farther. In the sixth article of Question 109 he asks whether a man can prepare himself for grace on his own apart from grace. What he has in mind here pertains to the distinction between habitual grace and *auxilium divinum*, that is, divine assistance. Habitual grace is the infusion of virtue into the soul, and justification occurs when, by reception of habitual grace, one is transferred from a state of sin into a state of grace. But before habitual grace can be received, the soul must be formed, that is, prepared to receive it. Thomas affirms that grace is necessary even for the preparation to receive grace; more specifically, *auxilium divinum*—divine assistance that occurs on a specific occasion, which enables man to do something that is pleasing to God—must precede habitual grace in justification in order to prepare the soul to receive it. Man is incapable on his own of even preparing himself for grace.[37] It follows, then, as Thomas argues in the next article (Article 7), that man cannot rise up from sin to a state of justice apart from grace. Here he offers a definition of justification: returning from the state of guilt to the state of justice, a moral transformation that can only occur by grace.[38] In article 10 Thomas goes still one step further on the necessity of grace, arguing that one who is established in grace cannot persevere in it apart from grace.[39] From preparation to receive grace, to its reception in justification, to perseverance in grace, to works meritorious of eternal life, Thomas views the whole process of salvation as one that depends on the grace of God, rooted in his electing love and predestination.[40]

Question 110 addresses the nature of grace, a discussion not directly related to this study. It only needs to be observed here that, for Thomas, grace is more than a divine disposition toward the creature; it is a quality that is actually infused into the soul.[41] Question 111 then addresses the divisions of grace. For the purpose of this study, the most important division of note is that seen

---

[36] 'Man, by his will, does works meritorious of everlasting life; but as Augustine says, in the same book, for this it is necessary that the will of man should be prepared with the grace of God.' Thomas Aquinas, *Summa Theologica* 1-2.109.5 (trans. Fathers of the English Dominican Province), p. 333.

[37] Thomas Aquinas, *Summa Theologiae* 1-2.109.6 (ed. Ernst), 30, pp. 86-91.

[38] 'Therefore by himself he cannot be justified, i.e., he cannot return from a state of sin to a state of justice.' Thomas Aquinas, *Summa Theologica* 1-2.109.7 (trans. Fathers of the English Dominican Province), 337.

[39] Thomas Aquinas, *Summa Theologiae* 1-2.109.10 (ed. Ernst), 30, pp. 104-07.

[40] It is worthwhile to note here the five effects of grace that Thomas sets forth in Question 111, article 3: 'the first is, to heal the soul; the second, to desire good; the third, to carry into effect the good proposed; the fourth, to persevere in good; the fifth, to reach glory'. Thomas Aquinas, *Summa Theologica* 1-2.111.3 (trans. Fathers of the English Dominican Province), pp. 361-62.

[41] Thomas Aquinas, *Summa Theologiae* 1-2.110.1-4 (ed. Ernst), 30, pp.108-23.

previously in Peter Lombard: the distinction between operative and cooperative grace. Thomas' discussion here is much more nuanced than that of the Lombard. Whether referring to habitual grace or to the *auxilium*, grace may be divided into the two categories of operative and cooperative. Habitual grace has a twofold effect, related first to being and then to activity. Just as heat works internally on its object and then radiates outward from it, so does habitual grace work both inwardly and outwardly. As it pertains to being, habitual grace that heals or justifies the soul is termed 'operative' (*operans*), for God alone is the agent involved in its working. But as habitual grace becomes the principle of meritorious works, by which one performs actions that are pleasing to God that proceed from free will, it is termed 'cooperative' (*cooperans*), for it involves the human will in an active capacity. The same distinction pertains to grace as *auxilium*: in specific instances in which divine assistance comes to a person, the interior act of the will, by which it is moved to the good by God, occurs by operative grace. The external act of the will, by which it carries out a specific act that is good and pleasing to God, occurs by cooperative grace.[42]

The foregoing distinction is important because it forms the outline by which Thomas goes on to discuss the effects of grace in Questions 113 and 114. The first effect of grace he discusses is justification (Question 113), which is the effect of operative grace. The second effect he discusses is merit (Question 114), which is the effect of cooperative grace. For Thomas, justification is a process that consists of four logically successive elements: (1) the infusion of grace; (2) the movement of free will toward God by faith; (3) the movement of free will away from sin; (4) forgiveness of sins.[43] These elements arise from Aristotelian physics. Because justification is a movement of the soul from a state of sin to a state of justice, it must begin with the act of the mover, proceed to the movement of the object, and culminate in the object's arrival at its end. God moves the soul by the infusion of grace, resulting in a twofold movement of free will, both toward God and away from sin, culminating in the divine blessing of the forgiveness of sins. Because any act may be defined by its end, Thomas does at times define justification as the forgiveness of sins.[44] This

[42] Thomas Aquinas, *Summa Theologiae* 1-2.111.2 (ed. Ernst), 30, pp. 128-33. Wawkyrow, 'Grace', pp. 196-99, provides a helpful discussion of the distinction between operative and cooperative grace. Lonergan, p. 38, summarizes aptly: 'For grace operates inasmuch as the soul is purely passive; it cooperates inasmuch as the soul is both passive and active.'

[43] Thomas Aquinas *Summa Theologiae* 1-2.113.6 (ed. Ernst), 30, p. 180). McGrath, *Iustitia Dei*, pp. 63-67, places this fourfold pattern within its historical-theological context.

[44] 'And because movement is named after its term *whereto* rather than from its term *whence*, the transmutation whereby anyone is changed by the remission of sins from the state of ungodliness to the state of justice, borrows its name from the term *whereto*, and is called *justification of the ungodly*.' Thomas Aquinas, *Summa Theologica* 1-2.113.1 (trans. Fathers of the English Dominican Province), p. 381.

definition cannot be considered exhaustive, as though Thomas views justification in primarily forensic terms. For Thomas, the forgiveness of sins is the culmination of a movement of the soul that begins with the infusion of grace, and justification, properly considered, is nothing less than the process by which the soul is moved from a state of sin to a state of justice. Although justification is a process with logically successive elements, it nevertheless happens in an instant.[45]

The second effect of grace, which is merit, occurs by cooperative grace. After affirming that man can merit something from God,[46] Thomas argues that it is impossible for man to merit eternal life apart from grace.[47] Even in the original state that would not have been possible, for man would still have needed grace to reach beyond his natural capacities and gain eternal life.[48] Much more, then, is grace necessary for man in his fallen state, for before he can receive the grace that enables him to surpass his created nature, he must first receive grace in order to be reconciled to God and have his sins forgiven.[49] In essence, justification must precede the possibility of meriting eternal life; that is, operative grace must precede cooperative grace. Man in a state of grace can merit eternal life by condign merit, that is, the merit of strict equivalence, if the meritorious work is considered as proceeding from the grace of the Holy Spirit.[50] However, insofar as meritorious work proceeds from free choice, it is impossible for man to merit anything from God by condign merit but only by the merit of congruence, that is, in a way that is proportionate to man's capacity but is not strictly equivalent to the value of his works before God.[51] By condign merit, then, God crowns his own works in man. By congruous merit, God graciously accommodates himself to man's limited capacity.

Grace works primarily through the virtue of charity in order to obtain the merit of eternal life.[52] Man can merit growth in charity, for growth in charity is a means to the end of eternal life, which is also merited.[53] Thus both the end (eternal life) and one of the means to that end (growth in charity) are merited. However, man cannot merit the first grace for himself,[54] nor can he merit

---

[45] Thomas Aquinas, *Summa Theologiae* 1-2.113.7 (ed. Ernst), 30, pp. 182-89.

[46] Thomas Aquinas, *Summa Theologiae* 1-2.114.1 (ed. Ernst), 30, pp. 200-03.

[47] Thomas Aquinas, *Summa Theologiae* 1-2.114.2 (ed. Ernst), 30, pp. 204-07.

[48] Thomas Aquinas, *Summa Theologiae* 1-2.114.2 (ed. Ernst), 30, p. 204.

[49] Thomas Aquinas, *Summa Theologiae* 1-2.114.2 (ed. Ernst), 30, pp. 204-07.

[50] Thomas Aquinas, *Summa Theologiae* 1-2.114.3 (ed. Ernst), 30, pp. 206-08.

[51] 'If it [man's meritorious work] is considered as regards the substance of the work, and inasmuch as it springs from free-will, there can be no condignity because of the very great inequality. But there is congruity on account of an equality of proportion.' Thomas Aquinas, *Summa Theologica* 1-2.114.3 (trans. Fathers of the English Dominican Province), p. 408.

[52] Thomas Aquinas, *Summa Theologiae* 1-2.114.4 (ed. Ernst), 30, pp. 210-13.

[53] Thomas Aquinas, *Summa Theologiae* 1-2.114.8 (ed. Ernst), 30, pp. 222-24.

[54] Thomas Aquinas, *Summa Theologiae* 1-2.114.5 (ed. Ernst), 30, pp. 212-15.

restoration to grace after he has fallen from it due to sin.[55] Given Thomas' anthropology, this is not a surprising conclusion. Whether one has never been justified or has fallen from the state of grace, one is in a corrupt state that requires healing prior to the possibility of attaining merit. Therefore, the grace that justifies and the grace that restores cannot be merited. Nor is man in the state of grace able to merit perseverance in grace on the way to glory. However, once he reaches the final state, his irreversible perseverance in grace is secured by an act of free will, and thus perseverance in the state of glory is the result of merit.[56]

Thomas affirms that God is the principal cause of grace, and the sacraments are the instrumental cause, '[f]or it is manifest that through the sacraments of the New Law man is incorporated into Christ'.[57] Baptism wipes away all sin and remits all eternal punishment due to sin because it incorporates a person into the passion of Christ.[58] Given the fact that Thomas earlier defined justification as the forgiveness of sins, it is evident that baptism effects justification.[59] Baptism is also the means by which virtue is infused, which is likewise a component of the process of justification outlined earlier.[60] The sacrament of penance restores justification that has been lost by wiping away all mortal sin.[61] Grace is not a private transaction between God and the individual; it takes place in the context of the Catholic Church, by means of the sacramental system.

The foregoing discussion will suffice to draw out a soteriological pattern. For Thomas Aquinas, salvation is by grace from beginning to end. The elect are chosen and predestined by the will of God alone, without reference to foreknown merits in them. God's love for them precedes and creates their worthiness, not vice versa. In order to be saved in the end, man in his fallen state must first, by divine operative grace, be prepared to receive the infusion of habitual grace. This infusion is an act of God alone, which leads to a twofold movement of the will and results in justification, or the transfer from a state of

---

[55] Thomas Aquinas, *Summa Theologiae* 1-2.114.7 (ed. Ernst), 30, pp. 218-21.

[56] Thomas Aquinas, *Summa Theologiae* 1-2.114.9 (ed. Ernst), 30, pp. 224-29.

[57] Thomas Aquinas, *Summa Theologiae* 3.62.1 (ed. and trans. David Bourke; New York: McGraw-Hill, 1974), 56, p. 53.

[58] Thomas Aquinas, *Summa Theologiae* 3.69.1-3 (ed. James J. Cunningham; New York: McGraw-Hill, 1974), 57, pp. 122-32. Thomas affirms that baptism does not, however, remit temporal punishments for sin.

[59] Thomas indicates in passing that baptism effects justification when he addresses the problem of an insincere reception of the sacrament: 'Consequently in order that a man be justified by Baptism, his will must needs embrace both Baptism and the baptismal effect.' Thomas Aquinas, *Summa Theologica* 3.69.9 (trans. Fathers of the English Dominican Province), p. 182.

[60] Ibid. 3.69.4 (ed. Cunningham, 57:132-35).

[61] Thomas Aquinas *Summa Theologiae* 3.86.1 (ed. Reginald Masterson and T. C. O'Brien; New York: McGraw-Hill, 1965), 60, pp. 72-77.

sin to a state of justice. Justification does not guarantee eternal life. It only restores man's fallen nature and places him in a state of grace before God, a state in which he may potentially merit eternal life or lose grace because of mortal sin. There is no dichotomy between grace and merit; merit is itself the result of grace, not only the divine electing grace by which God predestines the elect to salvation, but also the cooperative grace by which man through charity merits eternal life. In a state of grace, man can merit growth in charity, but he cannot merit perseverance until the final state. Grace is by far the dominant note in this soteriological pattern. However, this grace does not preclude a doctrine of human merit and a form works-righteousness.

Given the fact that eternal life can be merited by restored sinners whose obedience in this life is never perfect, it is clear that Thomas does not regard perfect obedience as a requirement for final salvation.[62] With his doctrine of purgatory Thomas does leave room for a satisfaction of God's justice for venial sins that remain within the redeemed at the time of death, and this doctrine indicates a view of divine justice as thorough and unmitigated, though one that is certainly not divorced from abundant divine mercy.[63] Nevertheless, this doctrine does not have quite the same effect as the Reformers' understanding of a divine demand for perfect obedience, for purgatory exists for Thomas precisely so that those who have merited eternal life by charity, though they have fallen far short of perfect obedience, may not be hindered from the beatific vision because of their venial sins. In other words, the mere existence of the category 'venial sin', a category of sin that can co-exist with the merit of eternal life, demonstrates that perfect obedience is not necessary for salvation, for if perfection is the divine standard, no sin can be venial. For Thomas, the principles of doing and receiving are mixed together, and even though God is

---

[62] Thomas affirms that it is possible to attain a kind of perfection of charity in this life, but it is not the perfection that the saints will know in heaven, nor does it prohibit the commission of venial sins. Furthermore, not all who possess charity (and thus will be saved if they die in this state of grace) attain to this kind of earthly perfection, thereby proving that perfect obedience is not a requirement for final salvation. See Thomas Aquinas, *Summa Theologiae* 2-2.24.8 (ed. R. J. Batten; New York: McGraw-Hill, 1974), 34, pp. 56-61.

[63] 'For it sometimes happens that during their lives people have not done full penance for the sins they have committed, but for which they have been sorry in the end. Since the order of divine justice demands that punishment be undergone for sins, we must hold that souls pay after this life the penalty they have not paid while on earth. This does not mean that they are banished to the ultimate misery of the damned, since by their repentance they have been brought back to the state of charity, whereby they cleave to God as their last end, so that they have merited eternal life. Hence we conclude that there are certain purgatorial punishments after this life, by which the debt of penalty not previously paid is discharged.' Thomas Aquinas, *Compendium of Theology* 181 (trans. Cyril Vollert; St. Louis: Herder, 1947), 197; cf. idem, *Summa Contra Gentiles* 4.91.6 (trans. O'Neil) 4, p. 336.

entirely responsible for salvation, the soteriological pattern is one that does not clearly distinguish between demand and gift, between law and gospel.

BONAVENTURE'S *BREVILOQUIUM*

Bonaventure (1217-1274) ranks as the thirteenth-century Franciscan counterpart to the Dominican Thomas Aquinas. His two works, *Journey of the Mind to God* and *Breviloquium*, are generally regarded as his masterpieces. The latter, a condensed, yet substantive treatment of the spectrum of theological topics, is an ideal source from which to glean his doctrines of grace and merit.[64] He addresses the grace of the Holy Spirit in chapter 5, followed by a treatment of the sacraments in chapter 6. These two chapters constitute an area of interest for this study.

Bonaventure argues that eternal blessedness consists of possessing God, the supreme Good. However, this Good is beyond anything that humanity in its creaturely limitations could merit. Therefore, grace is necessary to elevate humanity and so bring it to God.[65] The primary action in salvation is a divine condescension, not a self-wrought human elevation. As it condescends to humanity's creaturely limitations, divine grace operates by a process of inward transformation that makes a person worthy of eternal blessedness:

> If, then, the rational soul is to become worthy of eternal beatitude, it must partake of the God-honoring flow. Because this inpouring, rendering the soul deiform, comes from God, conforms to God, and leads to God as an end, it restores our spirit as the image of the most blessed Trinity, affecting it not only as part of the order of creation, but also in terms of the righteousness of the will and of the repose of beatitude.[66]

In order to be acceptable to God, the soul must exhibit the vigor of virtue, the splendor of truth, and the fervor of love, and these qualities, out of reach of the natural capacity of humanity, are the effects of grace.[67]

---

[64] On Bonaventure's theology of grace, see Gordon R. Payne, 'Augustinianism in Calvin and Bonaventure', *WTJ* 44/1 (1982), pp. 1-31; Christopher M. Cullen, *Bonaventure* (New York: Oxford University Press, 2006), pp. 153-64; Etienne Gilson, *The Philosophy of St. Bonaventure* (trans. Dom Illtyd Trethowan and Frank J. Sheed; Paterson, NJ: St. Anthony Guild, 1965), pp. 391-425.

[65] '[N]o one is worthy to arrive completely at that highest good, since it is completely above all limits of nature, unless, when God condescends to him, he himself is elevated above himself.' Bonaventure, *Breviloquium* 5.1.3 (Collegii St. Bonaventurae, *BOO*) 5, p. 252. Unless otherwise indicated, all English translations from this work are my own.

[66] Bonaventure, *Breviloquium* 5.1.3, in *The Works of Bonaventure* (ed. and trans. José de Vinck; Paterson, NJ: St. Anthony Guild, 1963), 2, p. 182.

[67] 'Finally, since our mind is not made similar to the blessed Trinity according to the rectitude of choice except through the *vigor of virtue*, the *splendor of truth*, and the *fervor of love*; and the *vigor of virtue purges* the soul, *establishes* and *elevates* it; the

The grace of the Holy Spirit functions in two primary ways: as a help toward the attainment of merit and as a remedy for sin.[68] With regard to merit, Bonaventure distinguishes between grace in a general sense, in a special sense, and in its proper sense. In a general sense, grace is simply concurrence, the power of God that sustains everything in existence and enables the successful performance of every creaturely act.[69] In a special sense, grace is that which prepares the soul for the reception of the Holy Spirit. This actual grace is known as 'grace freely given' (*gratia gratis data*), and it corresponds to the *auxilium divinum* as set forth by Thomas.[70] In its proper sense, grace is the divine assistance that enables the acquisition of merit. This is known as 'grace that makes pleasing' (*gratia gratum facientis*, often translated 'sanctifying grace'), otherwise known as 'habitual grace', that which is possessed in the soul of the justified. This grace precedes all merit.[71] Because merit is that which renders a person pleasing to God,[72] and yet because merit is itself the result of grace, Bonaventure's soteriology fits the pattern seen thus far in which salvation occurs by grace through the means of works. As free will cooperates

---

splendor of truth illuminates the soul, *reforms* it and *assimilates* it to God; the *fervor of love perfects* the soul, *revives* it and *joins* it to God, and by all these things man becomes *pleasing and acceptable* to God.' Bonaventure, *Breviloquium* 5.1.6 (Collegii St. Bonaventurae), 5, p. 253, emphasis original.

[68] This distinction is introduced in Bonaventure, *Breviloquium* 5.2.1 (Collegii St. Bonaventurae), 5, p. 253. The first aspect is treated in chapter 2 and the second in chapter 3.

[69] '[G]*enerally*, it is said to be a divine help freely and graciously extended to the creature . . . without this kind of assisting grace we are able neither to perform anything nor to remain in *being*.' Bonaventure, *Breviloquium* 5.2.2 (Collegii St. Bonaventurae), 5, p. 253, emphasis original.

[70] '*In particular*, grace is said to be a help divinely given, so that whoever prepares himself to receive the gift of the Holy Spirit, by him he might arrive at a state of merit; and such a kind of grace is said to be *freely given*, and without this no one sufficiently does what is in him [*facit quod in se est*], in order to prepare himself for salvation.' Bonaventure, *Breviloquium* 5.2.2 (Collegii St. Bonaventurae), 5, p. 253, emphasis original. Bonaventure does not use the phrase *facere quod in se est* here in the same sense in which it would later be used by the *via moderna* (see below). For Bonaventure, preparatory grace must precede human effort, whereas the *via moderna* views grace as a divine response to the one who does what is in him.

[71] '*Properly*, grace is truly said to be a help divinely given for the sake of meriting, which indeed is said to be the gift of *grace that makes pleasing*, without which nothing is able to be merited, either to make progress in good or to arrive at eternal salvation. For grace itself, like a root of meriting, precedes all merits.' Bonaventure, *Breviloquium* 5.2.2 (Collegii St. Bonaventurae), 5, p. 253, emphasis original. De Vinck's translation uses the phrase 'sanctifying grace'.

[72] 'And on that account every root of meriting is founded on sanctifying grace, which makes man worthy to God'. Bonaventure, *Brevoloquium* 5.2.3 (Collegii St. Bonaventurae), 5, p. 254.

with sanctifying grace, grace merits its own increase, leading to an inward transformation by which free will makes its own what belongs to grace.[73]

Bonaventure's discussion of grace as a remedy for sin (Chapter 3 of Part 5) is essentially a discussion of the doctrine of justification, which he envisions as a synergistic process in which actual grace (*gratia gratis data*) prepares the soul for sanctifying grace (*gratia gratum facientes*), but free will has the power to assent to preparation or refuse it. If free will assents to preparation and then receives the infusion of grace, the person is justified. The one who is justified must then cooperate with sanctifying grace in order to attain merit. The will that cooperates until the end earns the reward of eternal salvation.[74]

The sacraments are the means by which the grace of Christ is conferred. Bonaventure regards the seven sacraments as a sevenfold remedy for the disease of sin:

> First, because . . . the disease [here] is sevenfold, comprising three forms of sin, original, mortal, and venial, and four forms of penalty, ignorance, malice, weakness, and concupiscence; and because, as Jerome says, 'what heals the foot does not heal the eye'—therefore, seven different remedies are needed to expel completely this sevenfold disease. These are: Baptism, against original sin; Penance, against mortal sin; Extreme Unction, against venial sin; Orders, against ignorance; Holy Eucharist, against malice; Confirmation, against weakness; and Matrimony, against concupiscience, which it tempers and excuses.[75]

As seen in both Peter Lombard and Thomas Aquinas, baptism is the initiatory rite that transfers a person to a state of grace.[76] Penance is a 'second plank after shipwreck', a remedy for the restoration of grace, which is nothing other than the restoration of charity, after it has been lost through mortal sin.[77] Baptism is the occasion and instrumental cause of initiatory justification, and penance is the means by which justification is restored.

Bonaventure's soteriological pattern fits what has already been observed in Peter Lombard and Thomas Aquinas. Salvation is by grace, through the

---

[73] Bonaventure, *Breviloquium* 5.2.4 (Collegii St. Bonaventurae), 5, p. 254

[74] 'If therefore [free will] cooperates with it [grace] until the end, the *attainment* of eternal salvation is merited'. Bonaventure, *Breviloquium* 5.3.5 (Collegii St. Bonaventurae), 5, p. 255, emphasis original.

[75] Bonaventure, *Breviloquium* 6.3.2 (trans. de Vinck), pp. 230-31.

[76] Bonaventure, *Breviloquium* 6.7.4 (Collegii St. Bonaventurae), 5, p. 272.

[77] 'Concerning the sacrament of *penance* we must hold, that it is "a second plank after shipwreck", to which one who is shipwrecked through mortal sin is able to return, as long as he is in the state of this present life, whenever and however often he wills to implore divine mercy.' Bonaventure, *Breviloquium* 6.10.1 (Collegii St. Bonaventurae), 5, p. 275, emphasis original. On the restoration of the virtues (of which charity is the form) through penance, see Bonaventure, *Breviloquium* 5.4.1 (Collegii St. Bonaventurae), 5, p. 256.

instrumental cause of merit. Grace operates first as 'grace freely given', that which prepares the will for the reception of habitual grace. The infusion of the latter justifies a person by means of an inward transformation, enabling merit and the increase of grace until the attainment of eternal life. Bonaventure emphasizes the indispensable role of free will in consenting to grace, but this synergistic aspect of his soteriology does not negate the fact that salvation begins with the divine initiative that answers human limitations and is carried out by the effects of divine grace. A person may merit acceptance with God by grace. Given the fact that, like Peter Lombard and Thomas Aquinas, Bonaventure speaks of *sinners* meriting eternal life by their grace-empowered obedience, it is evident that for Bonaventure perfect obedience is not a divine demand. The formal cause of right standing with God is the ethical condition of the one who has been justified by grace, even though it necessarily falls short of perfection.

THE *VIA MODERNA*

Although theologians of the fourteenth and fifteenth-century movement known as the *via moderna* held to the same basic soteriological framework as their predecessors surveyed thus far (salvation by sacramental grace, which restores the soul and enables the accumulation of merit), they developed a doctrine of justification within the framework of a voluntarist theology, which simultaneously introduced both a new dimension of grace to the equation and a new role for human effort.[78] With the *via moderna*, divine grace takes on a covenantal dimension, establishing the framework within which one receives grace from God as a result of doing one's best to cease from giving assent to sin. Gabriel Biel (c. 1420-1495) will serve as the primary exemplar of this development.[79]

For theologians of the *via moderna*, the will of God is supreme over all; therefore, the nature of causality is subject to divine determination. There is no necessary connection between the infusion of grace and salvation. Works of charity are not intrinsically meritorious. God could save someone apart from the infusion of grace, and he could just as easily damn someone who had never

---

[78] John Duns Scotus is a transitional figure whose voluntarist theology anticipated that of the *via moderna*. For the purpose of this study, it is not necessary to survey his work here because the main contours of his thought were taken up by the *via moderna* and will, therefore, receive attention in this section. On Scotus' doctrine of justification, see McGrath, *Iustitia Dei*, 69-70, 123-24, 152, 165-67, 175-80, 195-97, 214-15.

[79] Biel is especially important for this study because of Luther's acquaintance with his work. On this connection, see Leif Grane, *Contra Gabrielem: Luthers Auseinandersetzung mit Gabriel Biel in der Disputatio contra scholasticam theologiam 1517* (Copenhagen: Gyldendal, 1962); Harry J. McSorley, 'Was Gabriel Biel a Semipelagian?' in *Warheit und Verkündigung: Michael Schmaus zum 70. Geburtstag*, (ed. Leo Scheffczyk, Werner Dettloff, and Richard Heinzmann; München: Ferdinand Schöningh, 1967), 2, pp. 1109-20.

sinned, if he so chose to act, for God cannot be a debtor to anyone.[80] The value of any meritorious act depends on God's free decision to count it as meritorious. Thus, merit depends, not on the intrinsic nature of any act, but on a covenant (*pactum*) that God has established with humanity, in which works of charity are deemed meritorious.[81] Included in the terms of this covenant is the assurance that God will give grace to the one who does what is in him (*facienti quod in se est*).[82] This formula refers to the human act of desisting from giving consent to sin.[83] Although the statement *facere quod in se est* preceded the *via moderna*, it took on a new significance within the context of the voluntarist theology of this school of thought. The doctrine that God will not deny grace to one who does what is in him succinctly expresses a unique synthesis between grace and human effort. Human effort has value, but only within the gracious framework established by God in the covenant.

In his sermon, 'The Circumcision of the Lord', Biel outlines three effects of grace. First, grace makes human nature acceptable to God, not intrinsically but according to the evaluation of God's free decision. Second, grace justifies, which consists of the remission of guilt and acceptance to eternal life. Third, grace makes the works of one who has been justified acceptable for eternal reward, though this applies only to works that are themselves prompted by grace.[84] Meritorious acts depend on both free will and grace, and free will can resist grace. However, grace is the principal cause of all meritorious acts, for 'grace is nothing other than infused love'.[85] God could have decided to accept human works as meritorious apart from the gift of grace, but instead 'God has

---

[80] 'God is able to accept someone in a purely natural state as worthy of eternal life without any habit of charity, and even to reprobate someone without any sin.' William of Ockham, *Quaestiones in Librum Tertium Sententiarum (Reportatio)* 9.1 (ed. Francis E. Kelley and Girard I. Etzkom, *OPT*), 6, pp. 279-80. 'And it is denied that God is able to be a debtor to anyone.' Gabriel Biel, *Collectorium circa Quattuor Libros Sententiarum* 2.27.1.2 (ed. Wilfred Werbeck and Udo Hofmann; Tübingen: Mohr Siebeck, 1984), 2, p. 515. All English translations from these works are my own.

[81] Biel, *Collectorium* 2.27.1.1 (ed. Werbeck and Hofmann), 2, pp. 510-12.

[82] 'God necessarily, immutably, and without falsehood gives grace to the one who does what is in him, since he has arranged to give grace immutably to the one who does what is in him.' Biel, *Collectorium* 2.27.1.3 (ed. Werbeck and Hofmann), 2, p. 523.

[83] 'Man is not able to remove the first [obstacle to grace], since sin with respect to guilt is not removed except through the remission of sin, which is from God alone, who nevertheless is prepared to remit the sins of the one who does what is in him. The sinner is said to be able to remove the obstacle in a second way, since he is able to cease from the consent and the act of sinning, indeed, to hate sin and to will not to sin.' Biel, *Collectorium* 2.27.1.3 (ed. Werbeck and Hofmann), 2, p. 524.

[84] Gabriel Biel, 'The Circumcision of the Lord', in Heiko A. Oberman (ed), *Forerunners of the Reformation: The Shape of Late Medieval Thought Illustrated by Key Documents* (New York: Holt, Rinehart, and Winston, 1966), pp. 168-69.

[85] Biel, 'The Circumcision of the Lord', p. 170.

established the rule [covenant] that whoever turns to Him and does what he can will receive forgiveness of sins from God. God infuses assisting grace into such a man, who is thus taken back into friendship.'[86] Salvation depends on the gracious covenantal framework established by God and on the grace of infused charity that is given within that framework to the one who does what he can on his own.

The *via moderna*'s doctrine of justification has been evaluated as Pelagian in nature.[87] In order to weigh the accuracy of this claim, it is necessary first to define Pelagianism. McGrath provides a suitable definition consisting of three tenets:

1) Adam's sin injured only himself, and his posterity sinned by imitation, not inheritance;
2) man's free will is autonomous, so that he can avoid sin by his own natural goodness;
3) eternal life can be merited without the need for interior (as opposed to exterior) grace, by due and proper use of the free will.[88]

The charge of Pelagianism has been related to the *via moderna*'s conceptions of both the absolute power of God (*potentia Dei absoluta*) and the ordained power of God (*potentia Dei ordinata*). On the one hand, this charge has been leveled at the *via moderna* because of its allowance for the possibility that God, in his absolute power, could have granted eternal life apart from the infusion of grace.[89] On the other hand, with regard to the ordained power of God, it has been argued that the mechanism of salvation that God has actually ordained is *de facto* Pelagian.[90] However, on both counts the charge is unwarranted. First, the fact that God could have ordained that eternal life be granted apart from the infusion of grace only means that for the *via moderna*, a Pelagian means of salvation exists in some possible world, but not this one. Within the covenant

---

[86] Biel, 'The Circumcision of the Lord', p. 173.

[87] Heiko A. Oberman, *The Harvest of Medieval Theology: Gabriel Biel and Late Medieval Nominalism*, 3rd ed. (Grand Rapids: Baker Academic, 2000), pp. 176-77.

[88] Alister E. McGrath, 'The Anti-Pelagian Structure of "Nominalist" Doctrines of Justification', *Epheremerides Theologicae Lovanienses* 57, no. 1 (1981), p. 118.

[89] McGrath ('Anti-Pelegian', pp. 112-13) notes such a conclusion drawn by a commission of six theologians against the works of William of Ockham in 1326.

[90] Oberman (*Harvest*, p. 177) writes, 'It is clear that the emphasis falls on "justification by works alone"; the concept of "justification by grace alone" is a rational outer structure dependent on the distinction between *potentia absoluta* and *potentia ordinata*. The outer structure is, of course, discernible by one who in pious meditation retraces God's revelation to its very sources, to that point where God could *de potentia absoluta* have decided otherwise. But the message preached and taught by the Church is the inner structure itself. An analysis of Biel's sermons proves that this is indeed the case. *It is therefore evident that Biel's doctrine of justification is essentially Pelagian*' (emphasis original).

that God has *de facto* established, salvation is invariably by grace. Second, while the slogan *facere quod in se est* does indicate an important human component prior to the reception of grace (and a departure from the Thomistic doctrine of a grace that prepares one to receive grace), it does not constitute a denial of the necessity of grace for salvation. Two important factors must be taken into account: (1) it is only within the terms of the covenant, which itself proceeds from the grace of God, that the *facere quod in se est* doctrine is operative at all;[91] (2) the person who does what is in himself prepares himself to receive interior grace, by which he will ultimately be saved; he does not render grace superfluous. This doctrine may represent a form of semi-Pelagianism, but it is certainly not Pelagian.[92]

It is evident that for the *via moderna*, perfect obedience is not a legal requirement for eternal life, for what is required is that human beings do their best in accord with their capacity as sinful creatures. Grace makes such people worthy of eternal life, not intrinsically but within the framework of the covenant. In this soteriological pattern one can see that grace is, again, the dominant theme. The framework within which merit is possible results from God's gracious decision, and eternal life can only be merited by the grace of infused charity. And yet the notion that eternal life is merited by works remains, both in the sense of the *facere quod in se est* doctrine and in the sense, already noted in earlier medieval theology, that works of charity performed in a state of grace accrue merit before God.

This survey of the soteriological patterns evident in the pre-Reformation Catholic scholastic tradition has revealed several noteworthy observations relevant to the question at hand. First, theologians of this period strongly affirm that salvation is by grace. Rooted in the freedom of God (whether understood as a decree of election or as also encompassing a covenant by which merit is made possible), salvation begins with the divine initiative toward humanity. Second, justification is a transformation from a state of sin to a state of righteousness that occurs by the infusion of habitual grace. Third, within this state of grace, it is possible to merit eternal life by works of charity. Whether this possibility is owing to the nature of charity itself or to the free decision of God to accept works of charity as meritorious, salvation is given on the basis of

---

[91] McGrath (*Iustitia Dei*, p. 147), writes of the *via moderna*'s soteriology: 'the moral abilities of humans are largely irrelevant, as the ultimate grounds of merit lie outside of humanity, in the extrinsic denomination of the divine acceptation'. The *facere quod in se est* doctrine really says more about God than it does about humanity.

[92] The defining characteristic of semi-Pelagianism is the idea that 'the first movement towards God is made by human efforts unaided by grace'. Alan Richardson and John Bowden, eds., *The Westminster Dictionary of Christian Theology* (Philadelphia: Westminster, 1983), s.v. 'Semi-pelagian', by E.J. Yarnold.   Semi-Pelagianism was condemned by the Second Council of Orange in 529, but the canons of this council appear to have been unknown in the late Middle Ages. For an argument that Biel was indeed a semi-Pelagian, see McSorley, 'Was Gabriel Biel a Semipelagian?'

a grace-wrought merit. Fourth, justification is connected to the sacramental system, particularly the sacraments of baptism and penance. The former is the instrumental cause of initial justification, and the latter restores justification once it has been lost through mortal sin. Fifth, perfect obedience is not a requirement for meriting eternal life. The gift of grace makes possible the fulfilling of divine demands to a sufficient degree that warrants the reward of the beatific vision. Final salvation, therefore, is the result of an inherent, though imperfect, righteousness. Any notion of an alien righteousness imputed to believers as necessary for the fulfillment of God's perfect standard does not enter the equation at all. The soteriological pattern is, as Michael Horton observes, monocovenantal in nature, meaning that it is a pattern that 'attempts to combine merit and grace, and the result is that both concepts are weakened. The place traditionally given in Reformed theology to Christ's full and meritorious obedience as our representative is eclipsed or even denied, while our own obedience (however weak) is seen as a condition of justification.'[93] The synthesis between merit and grace, demand and gift, law and gospel, is the primary aspect of Roman Catholic soteriology that gave rise to the Reformation doctrine of justification.

The Council of Trent

The pre-Reformation scholastics never encountered a doctrine of alien righteousness; it appears that the idea never occurred to them. But once the Reformation doctrine of justification came onto the scene in the sixteenth century, Rome responded by drawing on its pre-Reformation heritage and branding the notion of alien righteousness with the label of heresy, thereby rejecting a bicovenantal distinction between law and gospel and hardening in its commitment to a monocovenantal soteriology. The decree of the Council of Trent on justification represents the Catholic Church's official response to the Protestant doctrine. This section will focus on the council's decree in order to finish setting the background for an examination of the Reformation doctrine of justification.

The Council of Trent's decree on justification was issued on January 13, 1547, one of the results of its sixth session.[94] The decree was promulgated as a

---

[93] Michael S. Horton, 'Which Covenant Theology?' in R. Scott Clark (ed), *Covenant, Justification, and Pastoral Ministry: Essays by the Faculty of Westminster Seminary California*, (Phillipsburg, NJ: P & R, 2007), pp. 200-01. The term 'monocovenantal' does not have specific reference to the *pactum* of the *via moderna* but is simply a general description of a soteriological framework. In this context, when Horton speaks of the eclipse or denial of traditional Reformed theology, he has in view theologies of the present day, not pre-Reformation theology. Nevertheless, the rest of his statement is applicable to the soteriological pattern of this period.
[94] On the Council of Trent's decree on justification, see Hubert Jedin, *A History of the Council of Trent*, vol. 2, *The First Sessions at Trent, 1545-47* (trans. Dom Ernest Graf;

counter to the Protestant threat, offering an official ecclesiastical definition and exposition of the doctrine of justification. This doctrine stands in continuity with the theological tradition that preceded it, setting forth a grace-based soteriology that specifically rejects the innovative element of alien righteousness that had been introduced by the Reformers.[95]

The decree consists of sixteen chapters and thirty-three canons. The first four chapters establish a theological framework for the doctrine of justification by setting it in the context of redemptive history. Chapter 1 declares the need for justification by defining the plight of humanity as fallen in Adam and incapable of rising from this condition by the power of nature or even through the divine gift of the law. Although free will has not been obliterated by the fall, it is powerless on its own to lift any person from the state of sin.[96] The decree thus begins with a denial of Pelagianism and an affirmation of the necessity of grace for salvation. At the same time, it guards against the Protestant doctrine of the enslaved will, leaving some residual power to the human agent to be an active participant in his or her own justification. Chapter 2 describes the divine response to the human plight: the advent and atoning work of Jesus Christ, the objective ground of justification.[97] Chapter 3 then declares that, while Christ died for all, not all are justified by his death, but only those who are reborn by the merit of his passion. Significantly, this chapter, in good Augustinian fashion, equates justification with being made just.[98] Chapter

---

New York: Thomas Nelson, 1961), pp. 166-316; Heiko A. Oberman, 'The Tridentine Decree on Justification in the Light of Late Medieval Theology', *Journal for Theology and the Church* 3 (1967), pp. 28-54; Carl J. Peter, 'The Decree on Justification in the Council of Trent', in *Justification by Faith: Lutherans and Catholics in Dialogue VII*, (ed. George Anderson, T. Austin Murphy, and Joseph A. Burgess; Minneapolis: Augsburg, 1985), pp. 218-29; G.R. Evans, '*Vis Verborum*: Scholastic Method and Finding Words in the Debates on Justification of the Council of Trent', *Downside Review* 106 (1988), pp. 264-75; Marvin W. Anderson, 'Trent and Justification (1546): A Protestant Reflection', *Scottish Journal of Theology* 21, no. 4 (1968), pp. 385-406.

[95] I use the term 'innovative' here to represent Trent's perspective on alien righteousness, not to deny that the Reformation stands in some degree of continuity with the Patristic church on the doctrine of justification. On this question, see Thomas Oden, *The Justification Reader* (Grand Rapids: Eerdmans, 2002). Nevertheless, I do not wish to deny that the Reformation introduced new theological categories that clarified the debate significantly, categories of thought and language that had not been present before, even if the concept of alien righteousness had been implied before.

[96] Council of Trent 6.1 (ed. Tanner), p. 671.

[97] Ibid. 6.2 (ed. Tanner), p. 671

[98] '[S]o, if they were not born again in Christ, they never would be justified; seeing that, in that new birth, there is bestowed upon them, through the merit of His passion, the grace whereby they are made just [*iusti fiunt*].' *The Canons and Decrees of the Sacred and Oecumenical Council of Trent* (trans. J. Waterworth; London: Dolman, 1848), p. 32; Council of Trent 6.3 (ed. Tanner), 672. Unless otherwise indicated, English translations for this work are taken from Waterworth's translation, pp. 30-53.

4 then offers a more comprehensive definition of justification: '[A] transition from that state, in which man is born a son of the first Adam, to a state of grace and adoption of the sons of God, through the second Adam, Jesus Christ our savior.'[99] This transition cannot occur without 'the washing of regeneration' (*lavacro regenerationis*), which in this context refers to the sacrament of baptism.

Having set the theological framework, in the remaining chapters the council expounds on the nature of justification, including the components of preparation, justification proper, the ongoing aspects of justification, the restoration of justification that has been lost, and the accrual of merit for those who are justified. Chapters 5 and 6 address the issue of the preparation for justification in adults.[100] Chapter 5 affirms that preparation for grace is itself the result of prevenient grace, given without regard to merits. The person who receives this divine assistance toward the reception of habitual grace has the power to cooperate with it or refuse it, and at this point the significance of the residual power of free will declared in chapter 1 becomes obvious.[101] Trent affirms a synergistic doctrine of salvation, but it is a doctrine in which the priority of grace is affirmed; thus, semi-Pelagianism is denied: 'without the grace of God [man] is not able to move himself by free will toward justice in [God's] sight'.[102] The echoes of the Second Council of Orange, which by this time had been rediscovered, are prominent.[103] Chapter 6 affirms that the manner of preparation consists of a turning toward God in faith and a turning away from sin.[104]

Chapter 7 moves from preparation to actual justification, which includes both the forgiveness of sins and inward transformation, so that the one who is

---

[99] Council of Trent 6.3 (ed. Tanner, 672), my translation. As noted earlier, the word *homo* is translated 'man' because this English word can denote both humanity in general and a generic individual. In addition, the masculine noun *filius* further defines *homo* in this context.

[100] The decree contains no discussion of preparation in infants, presumably because the faith of the Catholic Church is sufficient for their justification through baptism; no preparation is necessary in that case. On the baptism of infants, see Council of Trent 7.13-14 (ed. Tanner), p. 686.

[101] 'The Synod furthermore declares, that in adults, the beginning of the said Justification is to be derived from the prevenient grace of God, through Jesus Christ, that is to say, from His vocation, whereby, without any merits existing on their parts, they are called; that so they, who by sins were alienated from God, may be disposed through His quickening and assisting grace, to convert themselves to their own justification, by freely assenting to and co-operating with that said grace.' Council of Trent 6.5 (trans. Waterworth), pp. 32-33.

[102] Council of Trent 6.5 (ed. Tanner), p. 672, my translation.

[103] Jedin (2, p. 241) remarks briefly about the use of the canons of the Second Council of Orange at the sixth session of Trent.

[104] Council of Trent 6.6 (ed. Tanner), pp. 672-73.

unjust becomes just.[105] The final cause of justification is the glory of God and of Christ and eternal life. The efficient cause is the mercy of God. The meritorious cause is Christ and his atoning work. The instrumental cause is baptism. The formal cause is the justice of God, not specifically in reference to his own character but to that by which he makes sinners just.[106] The unjust receive the merits of Christ by the infusion of the virtues of faith, hope, and charity through the Holy Spirit. By means of these infused virtues, the unjust are made just, and this inherent righteousness constitutes the legal basis of their salvation at the last judgment:

> Wherefore, when receiving true and Christian justice, they are bidden, immediately on being born again, to preserve it pure and spotless, as the first robe given them through Jesus Christ in lieu of that which Adam, by his disobedience, lost for himself and for us, that so they may bear it before the judgment-seat of our Lord Jesus Christ, and may have life everlasting.[107]

Although the decree does not use the terminology of 'final justification', the concept is clearly present here.

Chapters 8 and 9 further define the nature of faith in relation to justification. Chapter 8 addresses two aspects of the Pauline doctrine of justification: that it is by faith (Rom. 3:28) and that it is a free gift (Rom. 3:24). Trent affirms that faith is the beginning of salvation, and in this sense justification is by faith.[108]

---

[105] 'This disposition, or preparation, is followed by Justification itself, which is not remission of sins merely, but also the sanctification and renewal of the inward man, through the voluntary reception of the grace, and of the gifts, whereby man of unjust becomes just [*unde homo ex iniusto fit iustus*], and of an enemy a friend, that so he may be an heir according to hope of life everlasting.' Council of Trent 6.7 (trans. Waterworth), p. 34; (ed. Tanner), p. 673.

[106] Council of Trent 6.7 (ed. Tanner), p. 673.

[107] Council of Trent 6.7 (trans. Waterworth), pp. 35-36; (ed. Tanner), p. 674.

[108] '[W]e are therefore said to be justified by faith, because faith is the beginning of human salvation, the foundation, and the root of all Justification; without which it is impossible to please God, and to come unto the fellowship of His sons.' Council of Trent 6.8 (trans. Waterworth), p. 36. Oberman ('Tridentine Decree') argues that the use of the word *promereri* as opposed to *mereri* in this chapter has massive theological significance. He interprets *promereri* narrowly to refer only to strict merit (*meritum de condigno*), but not to congruous merit (*meritum de congruo*). If this is the case, then it appears that the council, by denying only the possibility of meriting justification *de condigno*, left room for justification on the basis of *meritum de congruo*, thereby aligning itself with the Scotist tradition (and semi-Pelagianism) as opposed to the Thomist tradition. In other words, the council may have deliberately safeguarded the *facere quod in se est* doctrine of the *via moderna*. Oberman's thesis, which hangs entirely on the meaning of one disputed word, faces at least two difficulties. First, it does not address chapter 5 of the decree, which discusses the preparation for grace and deliberately echoes the language of the Second Council of Orange. Oberman has not

The council further affirms that justification is a free gift because nothing that precedes justification, whether faith or works, can merit the grace of justification.[109] By tying faith and unmerited grace to the beginning aspect of salvation and not to its completion, the council interprets Paul's teaching in such a way that leaves room for a doctrine of merit in the ongoing process and culmination of justification. Having defined a proper role for faith in justification, the council proceeds in Chapter 9 to deny that faith alone can provide proper assurance of one's salvation.[110] Faith is necessary for justification, but these two chapters indicate a desire to refute the Protestant doctrine of *sola fide*.

Having addressed preparation for justification and actual justification, the council proceeds to define the ongoing aspects of justification in chapters 10-13. Chapter 10 affirms that those who are justified continue to increase in the righteousness they have received,[111] and Chapter 11 denies antinomianism, the perceived consequence of *sola fide*.[112] Of significance for this study is the affirmation of Chapter 11 that perfect obedience is impossible even for those who are most holy and just; nevertheless, venial sins do not result in the loss of the righteousness that one has received in justification.[113] This affirmation clearly fits the pattern that has been noted to this point, namely, that for late medieval Catholicism, perfect obedience is not a requirement for right standing with God. For the most part, however, the council's purpose in this chapter is to encourage the faithful to keep the commandments of God, for obedience to God's commands is possible in this life, even if it is never completely perfect. Chapter 12 briefly addresses the subject of the assurance of salvation by warning against the rash presumption that one definitely belongs to the company of those who have been predestined to life.[114] The council does not offer a detailed statement on the doctrine of predestination, but this chapter indicates a broadly Augustinian position that locates the divine initiative of

---

demonstrated how this chapter can be compatible with the *facere quod in se est* doctrine. Second, even if Oberman is correct, the most he demonstrates is that the council refused to deny the *facere quod in se est* doctrine, but this is a far cry from an affirmation of it. At most, Oberman can prove only that the Council of Trent left one aspect of its doctrine of justification sufficiently vague enough to encompass both the Thomist and Scotist schools of thought.

[109] '[W]e are therefore said to be justified freely, because that none of those things which precede justification-whether faith or works-merit the grace itself of justification.' Council of Trent 6.8 (trans. Waterworth), p. 36.

[110] Council of Trent 6.9 (ed. Tanner), p. 674.

[111] Council of Trent 6.10 (ed. Tanner), p. 675.

[112] Council of Trent 6.11 (ed. Tanner), pp. 675-76.

[113] 'For, although, during this mortal life, men, how holy and just soever, at times fall into at least light and daily sins, which are also called venial, not therefore do they cease to be just.' Council of Trent 6.11 (trans. Waterworth), p. 38.

[114] Council of Trent 6.12 (ed. Tanner), p. 676.

grace toward specific individuals in the eternal plan of God. Chapter 13 then addresses the gift of perseverance, ascribing it to the grace of God, yet encouraging wayfarers to commit themselves with all diligence to good works lest they fall away and come short of eternal life in the end. God gives the gift of perseverance, but those who neglect his grace will not receive it.[115]

For those who fall away from the state of grace, there is provision for the restoration of justification. Chapters 14 and 15 address this subject. Chapter 14 affirms the familiar metaphor of penance as a second plank after shipwreck.[116] When grace is lost through mortal sin, it can be restored by contrition, confession to a priest, absolution, and works of satisfaction. These works do not remit eternal punishment, which is remitted either through the sacrament of penance itself or the desire for the sacrament on the part of the one who has fallen. Rather, works of satisfaction remit temporal punishments for sin.[117] Chapter 15 affirms that, apart from the sin of apostasy, mortal sins do not result in the loss of faith. Therefore, it is possible for one to possess faith and yet still be cut off from the grace of Christ through mortal sin.[118] Although the chapter does not explicitly say so, it is evident that this kind of faith is that which is devoid of charity and is, therefore, dead.[119]

Having addressed preparation, actual justification, the ongoing aspects of justification, and the restoration of justification, the council proceeds to address in the final chapter the fruit of justification: merit that comes from good works. Those who are justified are enabled, by the grace of God, to perform meritorious works that result in eternal life. The reward of eternal life, therefore, can be attributed both to the grace of God and to the good works of the one who merits it.[120] The meritorious nature of good works is affirmed alongside the teaching that God alone is ultimately responsible for all good in us. Indeed, 'God forbid that a Christian should either trust or glory in himself, and not in the Lord, whose bounty towards all men is so great, that He will have the things which are His own gifts be their merits.'[121] This chapter exhibits

---

[115] 'For God, unless men be themselves wanting to His grace, as he has begun the good work, so will he perfect it, working (in them) to will and to accomplish.' Council of Trent 6.13 (trans. Waterworth), p. 40.

[116] '. . . for this manner of Justification is of the fallen the reparation: which the holy Fathers have aptly called a second plank after the shipwreck of grace lost.' Council of Trent 6.14 (trans. Waterworth), p. 41.

[117] Council of Trent 6.14 (ed. Tanner), p. 677.

[118] Council of Trent 6.15 (ed. Tanner), p. 677.

[119] On the nature of justifying faith, see Trent 6.7 (ed. Tanner), p. 673.

[120] 'And, for this cause, life eternal is to be proposed to those working well unto the end, and hoping in God, both as a grace mercifully promised to the sons of God through Jesus Christ, and as a reward which is according to the promise of God Himself, to be faithfully rendered to their good works and merits.' Council of Trent 6.16 (trans. Waterworth), pp. 42-43.

[121] Council of Trent 6.16 (trans. Waterworth), pp. 43-44.

the synthesis between gift and demand that has been evident throughout late medieval Catholic theology.

Particularly notable from Chapter 16 is the declaration that those who merit eternal life do so by fulfilling the law of God:

> [W]e must believe that nothing further is wanting to the justified, to prevent their being accounted to have, by those very works which have been done in God, fully satisfied the divine law according to the state of this life [*divinae legi pro huius vitae statu satisfecisse*], and to have truly merited eternal life, to be obtained also in its (due) time, if so be, however, that they depart in grace.[122]

The phrase 'according to the state of this life' indicates that those who merit eternal life have fulfilled the divine law in such a way that is fitting to fallen and redeemed humanity. It cannot be perfect obedience. The decree makes explicit here what has been implicit all along, namely, that God accommodates his standard of righteousness to the weakness of humanity, thereby creating the possibility for sinful human beings to merit eternal life by an imperfect obedience.

The canons that follow further refine the council's position on justification, and a selection of these is noteworthy for this study. Canons 1 and 2 reject any possibility that justification can occur apart from grace, thereby denying Pelagianism.[123] Canon 3 then rejects any possibility that one can be disposed to receive the grace of justification apart from grace, thereby denying semi-Pelagianism.[124] At the other end of the spectrum, in canons 4 and 5 the council anathematizes those who affirm the Protestant teaching on the bondage of the will.[125] Canons 9 and 12 deny *sola fide*, and canons 10 and 11 deny its

---

[122] Council of Trent 6.16 (trans. Waterworth), p. 43.

[123] 'CANON I.—If anyone saith, that man may be justified before God by his own works, whether done through the teaching of human nature, of that of the law, without the grace of God through Jesus Christ; let him be anathema.'
'CANON II.—If anyone saith, that the grace of God, through Jesus Christ, is given only for this, that man may be able more easily to live justly, and to merit eternal life, as if, by free will without grace, he were able to do both though hardly indeed and with difficulty; let him be anathema.' Council of Trent 6, Canons 1-2 (trans. Waterworth), p. 44.

[124] 'CANON III.—If any one saith, that without the prevenient inspiration of the Holy Ghost, and without his help, man can believe, hope, love, or be penitent as he ought, so as that the grace of Justification may be bestowed upon him; let him be anathema.' Council of Trent 6, Canon 3 (trans. Waterworth), p. 44.

[125] 'CANON IV.—If any one saith, that man's free will moved and excited by God, by assenting to God exciting and calling, nowise co-operates towards disposing and preparing itself for obtaining the grace of Justification; that it cannot refuse its consent, if it would, but that, as something inanimate, it does nothing whatever and is merely passive; let him be anathema.'

corollary: justification on the basis of the imputed righteousness of Christ.[126] Canon 23 denies two doctrines, one of which is the teaching that those who are justified can attain perfection in this life.[127] Canon 24 denies the Protestant teaching that good works are merely the evidence of justification and not the means of its increase.[128] On a similar theme, Canon 32 anathematizes those who do not adhere to the council's doctrine of merit.[129]

The Council of Trent's decree on justification stands squarely within the tradition that emerged from the broadly Augustinian teachings of pre-Reformation scholasticism. For Trent, justification occurs when one who has

---

'CANON V.—If any one saith, that, since Adam's sin, the free will of man is lost and extinguished; or, that it is a thing with only a name, yea a name without a reality, a figment, in fine, introduced into the Church by Satan; let him be anathema.' Council of Trent 6, Canons 4-5 (trans. Waterworth), p. 45.

[126] 'CANON IX.—If any one saith, that by faith alone the impious is justified; in such wise as to mean, that nothing else is required to co-operate in order to the obtaining the grace of Justification, and that it is not in any way necessary, that he be prepared and disposed by the movement of his own will; let him be anathema.'
'CANON X.—If any one saith, that men are just without the justice of Christ, whereby He merited for us to be justified; or that it is by that justice itself that they are formally just; let him be anathema.'
'CANON XI.—If any one saith, that men are justified, either by the sole imputation of the justice of Christ, or by the sole remission of sins, to the exclusion of the grace and the charity which is poured forth in their hearts by the Holy Ghost, and is inherent in them; or even that the grace, whereby we are justified, is only the favour of God; let him be anathema.'
'CANON XII.-If any one saith, that justifying faith is nothing else but confidence in the divine mercy which remits sins for Christ's sake; or, that this confidence alone is that whereby we are justified; let him be anathema.' Council of Trent 6, Canons 9-12 (trans. Waterworth), pp. 45-46.

[127] 'CANON XXIII.—If any one saith, that a man once justified can sin no more, nor lose grace, and that therefore he that falls and sins was never truly justified; or, on the other hand, that he is able, during his whole life, to avoid all sins, even those that are venial, except by a special privilege from God, as the Church holds in regard of the Blessed Virgin; let him be anathema.' Council of Trent 6, Canon 23 (trans. Waterworth), p. 47.

[128] 'CANON XXIV.—If any one saith, that the justice received is not preserved and also increased before God through good works; but that the said works are merely the fruits and signs of Justification obtained, but not a cause of the increase thereof; let him be anathema.' Council of Trent 6, Canon 24 (trans. Waterworth), p. 47.

[129] 'CANON XXXII.—If any one saith, that the good works of one that is justified are in such manner the gifts of God, as that they are not also the good merits of him that is justified; or, that the said justified, by the good works which he performs through the grace of God and the merit of Jesus Christ, whose living member he is, does not truly merit increase of grace, eternal life, and the attainment of that eternal life,—if so be, however, that he depart in grace,—and also an increase of glory; let him be anathema.' Council of Trent 6, Canon 32 (trans. Waterworth), pp. 48-49.

been prepared by actual grace receives the infusion of habitual grace through baptism. Perseverance in grace is a gift from God, and God has also made provision through the sacrament of penance for those who lose habitual grace through mortal sin. Justification enables the acquisition of merit through charity and good works, and thus final salvation is the result both of divine grace and of human merit. Trent affirms the power of free will to resist grace or to cooperate with it while also affirming a doctrine of predestination, and the coherence between these two teachings is never explained in detail. Where Trent moves beyond the scholastic theologians of previous centuries is with its explicit rejection of the Protestant teachings of the enslaved will, *sola fide*, the imputation of righteousness, and assurance of salvation. In the face of a bicovenantal soteriological pattern, which demands a perfect obedience for salvation and thus incorporates alien righteousness—as divine gift that answers divine demand—into the equation of justification, Rome hardened in its commitment to a monocovenantal scheme that blends grace and works together as a joint basis of final salvation.[130]

Conclusion

The Reformation doctrine of justification did not arise in a Pelagian context. For the emerging Roman Catholic theology of the late medieval and Reformation periods, Pelagianism was universally denied. With the exception of the *via moderna*, even semi-Pelagianism was widely denied. The soteriology of this tradition is undoubtedly based on grace.

Sanders' Judaism likewise exhibits a grace-based, monocovenantal pattern of religion. To be sure, medieval Catholicism and Second Temple Judaism according to Sanders are not parallel in every respect. It seems doubtful that the phrase 'covenantal nomism', as Sanders defines it, could be applied strictly to the former, lacking as it does the nationalistic features of Judaism's covenant theology. Nevertheless, similarities between the two are apparent. First, both traditions teach that 'getting in' is by divine grace. For Judaism, Israel's election is the basis of all salvific blessings. For Catholicism, the divine acts of predestination and unmerited preparatory grace bring sinners into the state of righteousness through baptism. Some theologians emphasize the power of free will to cooperate with or refuse preparatory grace, and some do not.

---

[130] Peter ('The Decree on Justification in the Council of Trent', p. 221) writes, 'For Trent, because of the divine promise in Christ, eternal salvation (heaven) is both a grace and a reward for the justified adult who hopes in God and perseveres to the end in good works. But justification is only a grace for the sinner, who has no merits; nowhere is it proposed as a reward for works of nature, free choice, or some combination of these with divine grace.' This distinction between justification and eternal salvation is crucial. For Trent, the legal aspect of final salvation includes personal merit, even if one is initially justified by grace alone.

Alternatively, the *via moderna* begins with a gracious divine decision to establish a covenant by which the one who does what is in him receives grace as a reward. In whatever form it comes, however, salvation is rooted in grace, not human effort. Second, both traditions teach that 'staying in' is a condition of final salvation and that it is accomplished by human effort working in conjunction with divine grace. For Sanders' Judaism, Israelites must strive to keep the law, but the law itself contains provision for their inevitable failures through the sacrificial system. For Catholicism, those who are justified must, by cooperating with grace, persevere and increase in grace, thereby accruing merit that results in eternal life. Those who commit mortal sin along the way have the gracious provision of the sacrament of penance to restore them. Finally, both traditions implicitly deny the necessity of perfect obedience as the legal basis of right standing with God, and this in turn accounts for their monocovenantal soteriological patterns. For Sanders' Judaism, 'All those who are maintained in the covenant by obedience, atonement and God's mercy belong to the group which will be saved.'[131] The synthesis between divine provision and human effort here exemplified is quite similar to that of late medieval Catholicism, where those who are righteous by grace, yet imperfectly so, bring their grace-wrought merits before the judgment seat of God and receive eternal life as a reward.

This chapter has set the background for an exposition of the doctrine of justification that arose during the Reformation and that was refined in the post-Reformation period, thereby becoming the theological hallmark of the 'old perspective' on Paul. It has demonstrated that such a doctrine did not arise in a Pelagian, or strictly legalistic, context. If the Reformers and their heirs did not define their doctrine of justification in opposition to a Pelagian foil, what then distinguishes their doctrine from that of Rome? Chapters 3 and 4 will pursue an answer to this question by surveying the works of three prominent Reformers and the traditions that succeeded them.

---

[131] E.P. Sanders, *Paul and Palestinian Judaism: A Comparison of Patterns of Religion* (Minneapolis: Fortress, 1977), p. 422.

CHAPTER 3

Three Prominent Reformers on Justification

What does it mean to be Protestant? If the doctrine of justification is the material principle of the Reformation, the article by which the church stands or falls, what unique aspect of the Protestant doctrine of justification distinguishes it from that of Rome? As McGrath points out and as the foregoing chapter has demonstrated, it cannot be merely Protestantism's anti-Pelagian character: 'Such [anti-Pelagian] doctrines of justification can be adduced from practically every period in the history of doctrine, particularly in the later medieval period'.[1] The Protestant doctrine of justification, the hallmark of the 'old perspective' on Paul, is certainly an anti-Pelagian doctrine, but this fact alone does not make it Protestant. That which truly distinguishes Protestantism from Rome on this question is the doctrine of alien righteousness, or the location of the legal basis of right standing with God outside of, rather than intrinsic to, the believer. The issue of grace *per se* is not in dispute. Both sides agree that salvation is by grace. Where they differ is over the question of how grace operates for the purpose of granting sinful human beings a favorable verdict before the judgment seat of God. Does God render this verdict because he sees that his grace has accomplished an effective, though not yet perfect, transformation of the sinner? Or does God count the believer righteous with regard to an alien righteousness imputed to him or her? This issue is the real dividing line between two major streams of Christendom.[2]

Historically, although not every proponent of the doctrine of alien righteousness went on to spell out its important theological corollaries, it will be argued here that, within Protestantism as a whole and especially in its most theologically developed expressions, two significant theological issues, noted

---

[1] Alister E. McGrath, *Iustitia Dei: A History of the Christian Doctrine of Justification*, 3rd ed. (New York: Cambridge University Press, 2005), p. 209.

[2] McGrath, *Iustitia Dei*, pp. 209-10: 'The notional distinction, necessitated by a forensic understanding of justification, between the external act of God in pronouncing sentence, and the internal process of regeneration, along with the associated insistence upon the alien and external nature of justifying righteousness, must be considered to be the most reliable *historical* characterisation of Protestant doctrines of justification. As the Osiandrist controversy made clear, an anti-Pelagian doctrine of justification could still be rejected as unrepresentative of the Reformation *if justifying righteousness was conceived intrinsically*', emphasis original.

already in previous chapters, are tied to this doctrine. First is the divine demand for perfect obedience. Because God demands perfection, no member of Adamic humanity can ever attain justification on the basis of an inherent righteousness, for no matter what degree of righteousness one might attain, it would all be nullified by the presence of even one sin. Given that sin is a universal human condition, the hope of an intrinsic righteousness that justifies before God is a false hope. The second theological corollary of alien righteousness is the necessity of a clear distinction between law and gospel, that is, between the principles of divine demand and divine provision, or the contrast between doing and receiving. Those who seek justification on the basis of an inherent righteousness place some measure of confidence in their ability to obey the law, at least in a manner that is satisfactory enough for a God who does not require perfection. To be sure, it is the gospel that supplies the grace that makes this obedience possible, but that is precisely the point: law and gospel have been synthesized into a monocovenantal scheme. However, those who seek justification on the basis of an alien righteousness place no trust in the law to justify them. They must look instead to one who has fulfilled the law on their behalf. Thus, the law retains its integrity as an unwavering standard of perfection, and the gospel gives entirely by grace what the law demands. There is an additional theological corollary of the doctrine of alien righteousness, but it is one that remains rather implicit in the works of the Reformers and their heirs, and thus it will be noted briefly but not traced out in detail. That corollary is the eschatological nature of justification. In its Roman Catholic expression, justification is not a present anticipation of the final judgment. It is a transformation that heals the fallen nature of the sinner and puts him or her in a position to merit eternal life. It is by no means irreversible, for when mortal sin drives out the infused virtue of charity, one is no longer justified. Justification must then be re-appropriated through the sacrament of penance. By contrast, the forensic nature of the Protestant doctrine places justification within an eschatological courtroom setting, where the final judgment is anticipated in the present as sinners are justified by faith on the basis of the imputation of Christ's righteousness.[3] Therefore, even though the believer is a sinner in the present, he

---

[3] Berndt Hamm unpacks this idea further: 'Since in Reformation thinking justification is the *unconditional* acceptance of the sinner, for Christ's sake and not because of any previous, present or future quality in his life and morals, and is always founded outside us in God himself—since that is the case, justification acquires an eschatological meaning in the Reformation that is foreign to it in Catholic theology. In scholastic thinking, as we have seen, man's acceptance into grace and righteousness in justification, and his acceptance into sanctification at the Last Judgment, are two separate things, divided by the way of life inherent in obedience to the law and the principles of satisfaction and merit. Man's morality is the prerequisite of his final acceptance. Reformation unconditionality brought the two aspects together: the sinner has already been accepted for salvation through his justification and in advance of his new life and good works, despite the enduring power of sin. This is the eschatological

has already been declared righteous before God: *simul iustus et peccator.*

These are the theological categories and nuances that define the Reformation doctrine of justification. Within the context of a grace-based system of salvation, the Reformers and their successors set forth an opposing view of the nature of grace and proclaimed, in truth, a different understanding of the gospel. Whatever one may conclude about E.P. Sanders' portrayal of Second Temple Judaism, it should be evident that the existence of a grace-based soteriological pattern among Jews in the first century does not warrant the kind of hermeneutical presupposition that new perspective proponents have developed in Sanders' wake, anymore than the historical reality of a grace-based soteriological pattern in the late medieval Catholicism renders absurd the kind of polemic that the Reformers and their successors produced. Sanders' thesis leaves untouched the categories that have, historically, defined the Reformation doctrine of justification.

The purpose of this chapter and of the following one is to demonstrate the veracity of the claim made above, namely, that alien righteousness, and not grace *per se*, is the defining characteristic of the Protestant doctrine. The 'old perspective' on Paul that has been enshrined in the theology of mature Protestantism has its roots in the teachings of three prominent Reformers: Martin Luther, Philip Melanchthon, and John Calvin.[4] It is to their work that we now turn.

---

final validity of justification. Through the acceptance of the sinner, his entering into the righteousness of Christ, something final has taken place; it cannot be superseded even by the Last Judgment, but will then be brought out of concealment into the revelation of bliss.' Berndt Hamm, 'What Was the Reformation Doctrine of Justification?' in C. Scott Dixon (ed), *The German Reformation: Essential Readings* (Malden, MA: Blackwell, 1999), pp. 73-74.

[4] These three figures have been chosen because they, more than any of the other first or second-generation Reformers, were responsible for setting the trajectory of the historic Protestant doctrine of justification by the imputation of Christ's righteousness. To be sure, there are differences among them, as the subsequent discussion will show, but the main contours of the 'old perspective' on Paul are common to all three men. It can hardly be disputed that Luther and Melanchthon are the two towering figures that stand at the head of the Lutheran tradition. It may be asked, then, why Calvin, a second-generation Reformer, should be the only representative of the Reformed tradition in this chapter. The answer is that the doctrine of justification that became standard in the Reformed tradition is that of Calvin. Major first-generation Reformers such as Ulrich Zwingli and Martin Bucer did not develop a doctrine of justification that has endured in Reformed circles down to this day. For a discussion, see McGrath, *Iustitia Dei*, pp. 248-58.

Martin Luther[5]

The turn toward alien righteousness as the legal basis of right standing with God began with Martin Luther (1483-1546), whose importance for Reformation theology is universally acknowledged, even though his own doctrine of justification and its relationship to subsequent Protestant theology is debated. The best way to proceed with an investigation of Luther's most significant writings on this theme is to do so chronologically, taking note of the fact that 'Luther's doctrine of justification was one thing in 1513 and became another by 1536'.[6] The evidence indicates that Luther underwent a gradual theological development in the period 1513-1521, during which time the main contours of his mature doctrine of justification were being formed.[7] Thus, a fair assessment of his theology will take note of the fact that, especially in the years leading up to his decisive break with Rome after the 1521 Diet of Worms, Luther's theology was still in process. At the tail-end of this discussion, it will be necessary to interact with a contrary understanding of Luther's doctrine, particularly the claim made by the Finnish School that Luther's doctrine of justification was primarily theotic instead of forensic.

LUTHER'S EARLY THOUGHT, 1513-1521

In his first lecture series through the Psalms (1513-1514), it is clear that Luther, who had studied the works of Gabriel Biel, was still an adherent to the theology of the *via moderna*. In his comments on Psalm 51:4, Luther argues that human works are intrinsically nothing before God, and yet God has determined, according to the terms of his freely ordained covenant (*pactum*), that faith and

---

[5] Some of the material from this section and the following section on Melanchthon appeared previously in 'Luther and Melanchthon on justification: continuity or discontinuity?' in Michael Parsons (ed), *Since We Are Justified by Faith: Justification in the Theologies of the Reformation* (Milton Keynes, UK: Paternoster, 2012), pp. 30-43.

[6] R. Scott Clark, '*Iustitia Imputata Christi*: Alien or Proper to Luther's Doctrine of Justification?' *CTQ* 70 (2006), p. 273.

[7] Timothy George, 'Martin Luther', in Jeffery P. Greenman and Timothy Larsen (eds), *Reading Romans through the Centuries: From the Early Church to Karl Barth* (Grand Rapids: Brazos, 2005), pp. 101-19. This understanding of a gradual development stands in contrast to what Heiko Oberman called the 'romantic' and 'unrealistic' view of a definitive Reformation breakthrough that occurred all at once. Heiko A. Oberman, *The Two Reformations: The Journey from the Last Days to the New World* (ed. Donald Weinstein; New Haven, CT: Yale University Press, 2003), pp. 47-48. Others who argue that Luther's development was gradual throughout this period include Lowell C. Green, 'Faith, Righteousness, and Justification: New Light on Their Development Under Luther and Melanchthon', *Sixteenth Century Journal* 4, no. 1 (1973), pp. 65-86; Alister E. McGrath, *Luther's Theology of the Cross: Martin Luther's Theological Breakthrough* (Malden, MA: Blackwell, 1985), pp. 93-147.

baptism will result in salvation.[8] His comments on Psalm 115:1 are more explicit, for here he indicates full agreement with the principle of *facere quod in se est*. Speaking of the necessity of preparation to receive grace, Luther writes,

> Hence the teachers correctly say that to a man who does what is in him [*facienti quod in se est*] God gives grace without fail, and though he could not prepare himself for grace on the basis of worth [*de condigno*], because the grace is beyond compare, yet he may well prepare himself on the basis of fitness [*de congruo*] because of this promise of God and the covenant of His mercy. . . . Therefore He bestows everything gratis and only on the basis of the promise of His mercy, although He wants us to be prepared for this as much as lies in us [*quantum in nobis est*]. Hence, as the Law was the figure and preparation of the people for receiving Christ, so our doing as much as is in us [*quantum in nobis est*] disposes us toward grace.[9]

In accord with the *via moderna*, Luther's theology at this point has a strong anti-Pelagian character, for he insists repeatedly on the inherent worthlessness of human works and constantly exalts the mercy and free promise of God as the only hope for sinners. And yet, within the framework of God's merciful covenant, there is room for some to distinguish themselves by doing what is in them to prepare themselves for grace. In other words, the promise of grace is a conditional promise that leaves room for congruous merit.

Luther's struggle with the phrase 'the righteousness of God' found in Romans 1:17 is well-known from his 1545 preface to his Latin works: 'For I had hated that phrase "the righteousness of God" which, according to the use and custom of all the doctors, I had been taught to understand philosophically, in the sense of the formal or active righteousness (as they termed it), by which God is righteous, and punishes unrighteous sinners.'[10] McGrath has advanced a probable hypothesis about how Luther would have conceived of the righteousness of God in the years prior to 1515. Given his theological context, it is likely that the early Luther understood God's righteousness to refer to his strict, impartial equity in the administration of the terms of the covenant (*pactum*): God is righteous precisely because he is no respecter of persons but

---

[8] 'For we are still unrighteous and unworthy before God, so that whatever we can do is nothing before Him. Yes, even faith and grace, through which we are today justified, would not of themselves justify us if God's covenant did not do it. It is precisely for this reason that we are saved: He made a testament and covenant with us that whoever believes and is baptized shall be saved.' Martin Luther, *First Lectures on the Psalms I: Psalms 1-75*, *LW* 10, pp. 236-37 (*WA* 3, p. 289).

[9] Martin Luther, *First Lectures on the Psalms II: Psalms 76-126*, *LW* 11, pp. 396-97.

[10] The English translation is McGrath's, cited in *Luther's Theology of the Cross*, p. 96. The original may be found in *WA* 54:185-86.

rewards impartially with grace those who do what is in them and condemns those who do not fulfill this covenant stipulation. Thus, 'justification can only be based upon merit' as God, the impartial judge, allows human beings to distinguish themselves by their deeds.[11] It must be kept in mind that the kind of merit in view is entirely congruous, for it is only by free grace that God has determined to accept any human work as meritorious. Nevertheless, because of the conditionality of the *pactum*, the decisive element in justification comes from the human side of the equation. The young Luther would have struggled to understand how this notion of righteousness could be good news for the sinner (as stated in Rom. 1:17) when it was impossible to know whether one had truly done what was in him (*quod in se est*). McGrath observes,

> The 'righteousness of God' thus remains an unknown quality, the impersonal attribute of an utterly impartial and scrupulously just judge, which stands over and against man, and ultimately justifies or condemns him on the basis of a totally unknown quality—and is thus the cause of much *Anfechtungen*! To someone such as Luther, who appears to have become increasingly uncertain about his own moral qualities as the *Dictata* progress, it must have seemed inevitable that God, in his righteousness, would condemn him.[12]

And so the theology of the *via moderna* provides a quite plausible context within which to understand Luther's struggle over the righteousness of God.

McGrath further argues that a major breakthrough occurred in 1515 that set Luther on a trajectory toward a very different understanding of justification. Adducing evidence from Luther's 1515-1516 lectures on Romans, he argues that by this time Luther's theology has taken an Augustinian turn.[13] Significantly, Luther has changed course on the principle of *facere quod in se est*. In his Romans lectures he regards the idea as a Pelagian notion, even though he acknowledges that 'there are now no Pelagians by profession and title'.[14] Pelagianism was universally condemned as a heresy, but by 1515 Luther detects it in the theology he once espoused. Luther's evaluation is technically incorrect, as was argued in the previous chapter. The *via moderna* was not a Pelagian movement, for it espoused a soteriology in which God takes the initiative by graciously establishing the terms of the *pactum* for fallen humanity, whose works are intrinsically nothing before him. Nevertheless, this example illustrates the kind of rhetoric the Reformers used to brand their opponents. In this rhetorical, non-technical sense, even a kind of Pelagianism can exist within a grace-based theological context.

---

[11] McGrath, *Luther's Theology of the Cross*, p. 109.

[12] McGrath, *Luther's Theology of the Cross*, pp. 110-11.

[13] The discussion that follows draws on the insights of McGrath, *Luther's Theology of the Cross*, pp. 128-36.

[14] Martin Luther, *Lectures on Romans*, *LW* 25, p. 496 (*WA* 56, p. 502).

Whereas Luther had previously viewed God's righteousness as his impartial administration of the terms of the *pactum*, resulting in a doctrine of justification by (congruous) merit, the Romans lectures indicate a decisive shift toward a more Augustinian view of salvation. No longer does he urge his listeners to do what is in them in order to attain grace. Instead, he argues that one must receive the first grace passively,[15] and this is directly related to the fact that the will is enslaved to sin and cannot, apart from grace, will anything good.[16] Luther explicitly repudiates his earlier view that the human will is decisive in salvation.[17] He espouses instead an Augustinian doctrine of predestination.[18] Necessarily, this new understanding of the particularity of grace entails that God's righteousness can no longer consist in his impartial administration of a covenant that allows human beings to distinguish themselves by their deeds. God's righteousness, he notes in his comments on Romans 1:17, does not consist in his personal rectitude; it is, rather, that by which he makes us righteous.[19] Divine righteousness is opposed to human righteousness, for the latter arises from works but the former precedes them.

Even at this early stage Luther begins to move beyond Augustine by teaching a doctrine of alien righteousness. Several observations will demonstrate this claim. First, when commenting on Romans 1:17, Luther contrasts the righteousness of humanity, which is the result of works, with the righteousness of God, which is 'by faith alone, by which the Word of God is

---

[15] 'To the first grace as well as to the glory we always adopt a passive attitude, as a woman does toward conception. For we are also the bride of Christ. Therefore even though we pray and beg for grace, yet when grace does come and the soul is to be impregnated with the Spirit, it ought neither pray nor act, but only be still.' Martin Luther, *Lectures on Romans*, *LW* 25, p. 368 (*WA* 56, p. 378).

[16] 'The free will without grace has absolutely no power to achieve righteousness, but of necessity it is in sin. Therefore blessed Augustine is correct in his book *Against Julian* when he calls it "a bound will rather than a free will". For when we possess grace, then the will is actually made free, especially with respect to salvation. To be sure it is always free in a natural way, but only with respect to those things which are under its power and lower than itself, but not with respect to the things above it, since it is captive in sin and now cannot choose that which is good in God's eyes.' Luther, *Romans*, *LW* 25, p. 375 (*WA* 56, p. 385).

[17] '[T]hat salvation takes place or does not take place because of our own will. I myself once understood it in this sense.' Luther, *Roman*, *LW* 25, p. 372 (*WA* 56, p. 382).

[18] Luther, *Romans*, *LW* 25, pp. 373-78 (*WA* 56, pp. 383-88).

[19] 'And here again, by the righteousness of God we must not understand the righteousness by which He is righteous in Himself but the righteousness by which we are made righteous by God. This happens through faith in the Gospel. Therefore blessed Augustine writes in chapter 11 of *On the Spirit and the Letter*: "It is called the righteousness of God because by imparting it He makes righteous people, just as 'Deliverance belongs to the Lord' refers to that by which He delivers".' Luther, *Romans*, *LW* 25, pp. 151-52 (*WA* 56, p. 172).

believed'.[20] In the Catholic scholastic tradition, faith is only effective insofar as
it is formed by charity. Thus, it is viewed as a grace-wrought virtue that
commends the sinner to God by means of an inward moral transformation. This
particular understanding of faith makes the expression 'faith alone'
nonsensical, for it is only by means of its conjunction with charity that faith has
any saving value. For Luther to use the expression 'faith alone',[21] and then to
define faith as that which believes the word of God, is to shift the locus of
divine saving action from within the sinner to the external promise of God.[22]

Second, commenting on Romans 4:7, Luther makes his doctrine of alien
righteousness explicit and links it specifically to Christ:

> Therefore, I was correct when I said that all our good is outside of us
> [*Extrinsecum nobis*], and this good is Christ, as the apostle says (1 Cor. 1:30):
> 'God made Him our wisdom, our righteousness, and sanctification, and
> redemption.' And none of these things are in us except through faith and hope in
> Him. Hence all the praise of the church in the Song of Solomon belongs to
> Christ, who dwells in His church through faith, just as all the light of the earth
> does not belong to the earth but to the sun which sheds its light upon it. Thus in
> the Song of Solomon the church confesses that she is often naked and described
> as having no other desire than for her Bridegroom, saying (Song of Sol. 1:4):
> 'Draw me after Thee, we will run to the odor of Thine ointments.' Always she
> seeks, always she desires, always she praises her Bridegroom. And thereby she
> shows that she herself is empty and poor in herself, and that only outside of
> herself [*extra se*] is her fullness and righteousness.[23]

Luther speaks of both the alien character of our righteousness, which lies

---

[20] Luther, *Romans*, *LW* 25, p.151 (*WA* 56, pp. 171-72).

[21] Green ('Faith, Righteousness, and Justification', pp. 69-77) argues that in the Romans
lectures Luther was still operating with a Catholic understanding of *fides* as a shorthand
for the theological virtues faith, hope, and love. However, this claim does not sit well
with Luther's explicit affirmation in his comments on Romans 1:17 that the
righteousness of God is given to us by faith alone. In fact, Green himself argues (p. 75)
that Luther's new view of faith first becomes evident in the 1518 *Acta Augustana*, and
he basis this argument in part on the fact that Luther writes, 'Sola fides iustificat' (*WA* 2,
p. 14). It appears that there is no material difference between this statement and the
earlier one in the Romans lectures that attributes the righteousness of God to faith alone.
The evidence indicates that Luther came to a new understanding of faith earlier than
Green imagines. Yet even if Green's argument stands, there is still clear evidence that
Luther espoused a doctrine of alien righteousness as early as the Romans lectures.

[22] See Bayer's discussion of promise as a key Reformation breakthrough in Luther's
theology in Oswald Bayer, *Martin Luther's Theology: A Contemporary Interpretation*
(trans. Thomas H. Trapp; Grand Rapids: Eerdmans, 2008), pp. 44-58.

[23] Luther, *Romans*, *LW* 25, p. 267 (*WA* 56, p. 279). Here Luther adopts the allegorical
interpretation of Song of Solomon, which was widespread until more recent times.

outside of us in Christ, and also of our possession of it through faith, by which 'these things are in us'. He does not deny, but rather affirms, the necessity of the sinner having righteousness in himself. Yet this righteousness does not arise through grace-wrought works but through possession of Christ by faith.

Third, commenting on Romans 5:19, Luther ties the notion of alien righteousness specifically to the obedience of Christ counted to sinners. In particular, commenting on the nature of the 'gift' mentioned in this verse, Luther argues, 'This gift is "by the grace of that one Man", that is, by the personal merit and grace [*merito et gratia personali*] of Christ, by which He was pleasing to God [*qua Deo placuit*], so that He might give this gift to us.'[24] He further specifies that the 'gift' of Romans 5:19 is the righteousness that has been given to us.[25] If this gift of righteousness is that which comes to us by the personal merit and grace of Christ, the merit and grace that render him pleasing to the Father, it is fair to conclude that only Christ's righteousness, counted to us, is that which renders us pleasing to the Father. Luther is articulating here a nascent doctrine of the imputation of Christ's righteousness to the believer.

Alien righteousness appears in other writings from this period. In his sermon 'Two Kinds of Righteousness' (1519), Luther articulates a distinction between the righteousness that comes from outside of us and that which is properly our own. Alien righteousness is 'instilled [*infusa*] from without'.[26] While the use of the word *infusa* indicates that Luther is not speaking the exact language of later Protestant orthodoxy, he is nevertheless beginning to articulate concepts that would later develop into the Protestant doctrine. That some notion of imputation is present here is evident from the context, for Luther goes on to argue that the person who has received this alien righteousness can justly claim, 'Mine are Christ's living, doing, and speaking, his suffering and dying, mine as much as if I had lived, done, spoken, suffered, and died as he did.'[27] It is impossible to account for this kind of transfer of Christ's obedient life to the believer without at least a nascent doctrine of imputation. Luther employs the metaphor of marriage to make sense of the transfer. Just as a husband and wife possess all things in common because they are united together as one flesh, so does the church possess all that belongs to Christ because they are one spirit.[28]

Luther does not, however, speak of alien righteousness as received all at once. He says that the righteousness of Christ is given in baptism as well as anytime a person is truly repentant. Furthermore, he speaks of a progression in

---

[24] Luther, *Romans*, *LW* 25, p. 306 (*WA* 56, p. 318).

[25] Luther, *Romans*, *LW* 25, p. 306 (*WA* 56, p. 318).

[26] Martin Luther, 'Two Kinds of Righteousness', *LW* 31, p. 297 (*WA* 2, p. 145).

[27] Luther, 'Two Kinds of Righteousness', *LW* 31, p. 297 (*WA* 2, p. 145).

[28] 'Just as a bridegroom possesses all that is his bride's and she all that is his—for the two have all things in common because they are one flesh [Gen. 2:24]—so Christ and the church are one spirit [Eph. 5:29-32].' Luther, 'Two Kinds of Righteousness', *LW* 31, p. 297 (*WA* 2, p. 145).

this righteousness: 'Christ daily drives out the old Adam more and more in accordance with the extent to which faith and knowledge of Christ grow. For alien righteousness is not instilled all at once, but it begins, makes progress, and is finally perfected at the end through death.'[29] Luther is not referring here to the believer's growth in personal righteousness, that is, the righteousness of good works. That is the second kind of righteousness, a subject that he has not yet addressed at this point in the sermon. What Luther is apparently referring to here as a growth in alien righteousness is progress in faith. In fact, only a few lines earlier Luther had virtually identified faith with Christ's righteousness.[30] As faith, which is God's work within the believer, continues to grow and progress, so does the believer's possession of alien righteousness. It is then from the root of alien righteousness that our own proper righteousness, that of good works, grows.[31] Alien righteousness must always precede our own proper righteousness.

Several quotations above indicate that Luther still conceives of righteousness as in some sense infused into the believer. How does this differ from the standard Roman Catholic teaching? In what sense can Luther uphold an alien righteousness together with the concept of infusion? Luther differs from Rome on this point by linking infused righteousness to Christ's obedience in such a way that what Christ has done is counted to the believer. The believer's righteousness is nothing other than Christ himself, who has been united to the believer like a husband is united to his wife. This righteousness is alien in that it belongs properly to Christ, and the believer has done nothing to warrant acceptance in God's sight. The believer's only hope is in the righteousness of another. Yet this righteousness is also infused through the divine work of faith, by which Christ himself is present within.[32] This doctrine

---

[29] Luther, 'Two Kinds of Righteousness', *LW* 31, p. 299 (*WA* 2, p. 146).

[30] 'In many passages of the Psalter, faith is called "the work of the Lord', "confession", "power of God", "mercy", "truth", "righteousness". All these are names for faith in Christ, rather, for the righteousness which is in Christ.' Luther, 'Two Kinds of Righteousness', *LW* 31, p. 299 (*WA* 2, p. 146).

[31] 'This [second] righteousness is the product of the righteousness of the first type, actually its fruit and consequence.' Luther, 'Two Kinds of Righteousness', *LW* 31, p. 300 (*WA* 56, p. 147).

[32] Paul Althaus (*The Theology of Martin Luther*, [trans. Robert C. Schultz; Philadelphia: Fortress, 1966], p. 231) describes aptly the twin dynamic of alien righteousness and the internal work of God: 'It is not enough, however, to say either that faith receives justification or that man receives justification *in* faith. Luther's thought must be expressed more definitely. Justification is received *with* faith, that is, in the form of faith. Faith is the work and gift of God. God justifies a man by giving him faith. Christ is the righteousness of men and to this extent this righteousness is outside of us. But Christ is my righteousness only if I appropriate him and make him my own. Faith is the only way in which Christ can give himself to me. Only the Christ who is appropriated in faith, that is, the Christ who lives in my heart through faith, is my righteousness. Christ

stands in stark contrast to the grace-empowered cultivation of a righteousness of works proclaimed by Rome. And so, while Luther does not break away from infusion as an aspect of justification as later Protestantism would, he nevertheless articulates a doctrine of alien righteousness that is significantly different from the prevailing understanding of justification in his own context.

In the 1519 lectures on Galatians, Luther speaks of two ways of being justified, and these two ways correspond to the law-gospel distinction that would become a hallmark of Lutheran theology. The first is the way of works, which leads to justification before men but is damnable in the sight of God. The second way is the way of faith, wherein a person views his or her own former righteousness as nothing and trusts only in the mercy of God in Christ.[33] Luther speaks of alien righteousness again in this context, arguing that Christ's righteousness and that of the Christian are one and the same. Just as all have become sinners by the sin of another, so do all become righteous because of the righteousness of another.[34] Furthermore, that he clearly regards his view of justification as antithetical to the prevailing theology and practice of his day is evident from his polemic against 'the great mass of sententiarists' who teach remission of sins through human acts associated with penance.[35] It is important to remember that in Catholic theology the sacrament of penance is a gracious provision of God, an accommodation to human weakness, much like the sacrificial system was for Israel. And yet, compared to the righteousness that comes by faith, Luther saw it as an empty, merely human attempt to procure righteousness by moral effort. For Luther, the gift of a passive righteousness of faith revealed in the gospel so eclipses the grace of the medieval sacramental system that the latter is reduced to a paltry form of Pelagianism by comparison.

Commenting on Galatians 3:10, Luther implicitly affirms the criterion of perfect obedience as necessary for divine approval. He acknowledges the tension between Paul's quotation of Deuteronomy 27:26, which pronounces a

---

is not only the "object" of faith but is himself present in faith. Through faith Christ is present with and in a man. The believing heart holds fast to Christ just as the setting of a ring grasps the jewel: we have Christ in faith. Only in faith are Christ and man so joined together, so made one, that man in God's judgment participates in Christ's righteousness.' See also Mark A. Seifrid, 'Luther, Melanchthon and Paul on the Question of Imputation', in Mark Husbands and Daniel J. Treier (eds), *Justification: What's at Stake in the Current Debates* (Downers Grove, IL: InterVarsity, 2004), pp. 137-52; Gerhard Ebeling, *Luther: An Introduction to His Thought*, trans. R. A. Wilson (Philadelphia: Fortress, 1970), pp. 159-74.

[33] Martin Luther, *Lectures on Galatians 1519*, *LW* 27, pp. 219-22 (*WA* 2, pp. 489-90).

[34] 'Indeed, since [this righteousness] is directed toward Christ and His name, which is righteousness, the result is that the righteousness of Christ and of the Christian are one and the same, united with each other in an inexpressible way. . . . Thus it comes about that just as all became sinners because of another's sin, so by Another's righteousness all become righteous.' Luther, *Galatians 1519*, *LW* 27, p. 222 (*WA* 2, p. 491).

[35] Luther, *Galatians 1519*, *LW* 27, p. 222 (*WA* 2, p. 491).

curse on all who *do not* do the works of the law, and Paul's explicit argument that those who *are* of the works of the law are, therefore, cursed.[36] At first the opposite conclusion might seem to follow: because the law curses those who do not fulfill its demands, therefore, we ought to perform the works of the law in order to avoid the curse. Yet Luther argues that Paul's logic moves in a different direction because of his presupposition that no one can fulfill the law. Perfect obedience is an impossible standard for sinful human beings to attain. For this reason, all who place themselves under the law are, *de facto*, cursed: 'The result is that with this word Moses has forced all men under the curse; and when he says: "Cursed be everyone, etc.", he means exactly what he would mean if he were to say: "No man will do these things that are written; therefore all will be cursed and in need of Christ as Redeemer".'[37] Thus, Luther draws a line in the sand to separate the law from the gospel. The former can only condemn sinful humanity, and thus sinners must seek righteousness in Christ alone.

The same themes emerge in the 1520 treatise *The Freedom of a Christian*, published at a time when a break with Rome was imminent, though Luther still retained the hope that separation would not be necessary.[38] Here Luther argues that only the Word of God can bring righteousness, and it must be received by faith, not works.[39] He then expounds three effects of faith. First, faith alone justifies.[40] This argument is dependent on the distinction between commands and promises, a distinction that would later be formulated in terms of law and gospel. The law demands perfect obedience, an obedience that no human being can render, as Luther states:

> Now when a man has learned through the commandments to recognize his helplessness and is distressed about how he might satisfy the law—since the law must be fulfilled so that not a jot or tittle shall be lost, otherwise man will be condemned without hope—then, being truly humbled and reduced to nothing in his own eyes, he finds in himself nothing whereby he may be justified and saved. Here the second part of Scripture comes to our aid, namely, the promises of God which declare the glory of God, saying, 'If you wish to fulfill the law and not covet, as the law demands, come, believe in Christ in whom grace,

---

[36] Luther, *Galatians 1519*, *LW* 27, pp. 255-56 (*WA* 2, p. 513).

[37] Luther, *Galatians 1519*, *LW* 27, p. 256 (*WA* 2, p. 513).

[38] Luther's prefatory address to Pope Leo X indicates both his extremely low estimation of the current condition of the Roman Church but also his desire to remain in submission to the pope in hope of bringing at least some measure of reform. Martin Luther *The Freedom of a Christian*, *LW* 31, pp. 334-43.

[39] 'One thing, and only one thing, is necessary for Christian life, righteousness, and freedom. That one thing is the most holy Word of God, the gospel of Christ.' Martin Luther, *The Freedom of a Christian*, *LW* 31, p. 345 (*WA* 7, p. 50).

[40] Luther, *Freedom*, *LW* 31, p. 348 (*WA* 7, p. 52).

righteousness, peace, liberty, and all things are promised you. If you believe, you shall have all things; if you do not believe, you shall lack all things.'[41]

The law exposes the sinfulness of humanity, thereby revealing the emptiness of works and demonstrating that justification must be by faith alone. Thus the law is preparatory for the gospel.

The second effect of faith is that it truly fulfills the law of God. By ascribing to God truthfulness and reliability, faith fulfills every divine demand.[42] Unlike Calvin and the Reformed tradition, Luther does not speak of faith as something empty in and of itself. For Luther, faith is the righteousness of a Christian.[43] The third effect of faith 'is that it unites the soul with Christ as a bride is united with her bridegroom'.[44] Herein lies the doctrine of alien righteousness, for the sinner's wickedness and damnation now belong to Christ, and Christ's righteousness now belongs to the sinner. The doctrine of imputation flows from the faith-union that a believer shares with Christ. It is out of the righteousness that comes by faith that good works grow naturally like fruit from a tree.[45]

LUTHER'S MATURE THOUGHT, 1522-1545

The main contours of Luther's doctrine of justification have already been established in the foregoing discussion. In the years after his break from Rome, Luther apparently did not undergo any major theological shifts comparable to his discovery of the true meaning of the righteousness of God and the corresponding theological developments that grew out of it from the period already discussed.[46] The most notable development in his theology during this time is that the doctrine of justification became the center and organizing principle of his whole theology.[47] This fact is evident as early as 1522, where in his 'Preface to the New Testament' Luther clearly articulates a law-gospel

---

[41] Luther, *Freedom*, *LW* 31, pp. 348-49 (*WA* 7, pp. 52-53).

[42] 'Is not such a soul most obedient to God in all things by this faith? What commandment is there that such obedience has not completely fulfilled? What more complete fulfillment is there than obedience in all things? This obedience, however, is not rendered by works, but by faith alone.' Luther, *Freedom*, *LW*, 31, p. 350 (*WA* 7, p. 54).

[43] 'Therefore faith alone is the righteousness of a Christian and the fulfilling of all the commandments.' Luther, *Freedom*, *LW* 31, p. 353 (*WA* 7, p. 56). This does not mean that faith has become a surrogate work by which the one who believes performs a meritorious act before God. Faith is the work of the gospel, and its righteousness consists in the fact that Christ is present in it. Like the Reformed tradition, Luther ties righteousness ultimately to Christ, but unlike the Reformed, he does not thereby remove the quality of righteousness from faith itself.

[44] Luther, *Freedom*, *LW* 31, p. 351 (*WA* 7, pp. 54-55).

[45] Luther, *Freedom*, *LW* 31, p. 361 (*WA* 7, p. 61).

[46] On which see McGrath, *Luther's Theology of the Cross*.

[47] McGrath, *Iustitia Dei*, p. 223.

distinction as a hermeneutical axiom. The command-promise dichotomy previously mentioned in *The Freedom of a Christian* now becomes the key to faithful interpretation of Scripture: '. . . no one any longer knows what is gospel or law, New Testament or Old. Necessity demands, therefore, that there should be a notice or preface, by which the ordinary man can be rescued from his former delusions, set on the right track, and taught what he is to look for in this book, so that he may not seek laws and commandments where he ought to be seeking the gospel and promises of God.'[48] The reason Luther considers it so important for the ordinary reader of Scripture to recognize the difference between law and gospel is for the sake of justification: 'Hence it comes that to a believer no law is given by which he becomes righteous before God . . . because he is alive and righteous and saved by faith.'[49] Justification by the free grace of God, given in the gospel, determines his approach to Scripture as a whole.[50]

In 1525 Luther published what has widely been regarded as his greatest work, *The Bondage of the Will*,[51] a response to Erasmus of Rotterdam's *The Free Will*.[52] In the conclusion of this work, Luther commends Erasmus for being the only theological opponent to cut through extraneous matters and address the main issue of contention between Luther and Rome.[53] This comment indicates the importance of the doctrine of the bound will for Luther, a doctrine that requires in turn a monergistic work of grace to result in salvation. Although monergism and alien righteousness are not identical concepts, for Luther they necessarily go together, so that Luther's doctrine of the bound will becomes a succinct expression of his doctrine of justification.[54]

---

[48] Martin Luther, 'Preface to the New Testament', *LW* 35, p. 357.

[49] Luther, 'Preface to the New Testament', *LW* 35, p. 361.

[50] Luther's doctrine of justification is what led him to elevate certain books of Scripture (John, Romans, Galatians, Ephesians, 1 Peter) over other books (the Synoptic Gospels and the letter of James). Justification by faith became for him the criterion by which to determine a canon within the canon. See Luther, 'Preface to the New Testament', *LW* 35, p. 362 and his 'Preface to the Epistles of St. James and St. Jude', *LW* 35, pp. 395-98.

[51] Martin Luther, *The Bondage of the Will*, *LW* 33, pp. 3-295 (*WA* 18, pp. 551-787). For an analysis of Luther's argument, see Gerhard O. Forde, *The Captivation of the Will: Luther vs. Erasmus on Freedom and Bondage* (ed. Steven Paulson; Grand Rapids: Eerdmans, 2005).

[52] Desiderius Erasmus, *De libero arbitrio*, in *Desiderii Erasmi Opera Omnia* (New York: Georg Olms Verlag, 2001), 9, pp. 1215-47; idem, *The Free Will*, in *Discourse on Free Will*, (ed. and trans. Ernst F. Winter; New York: Frederick Ungar, 1961).

[53] Luther, *Bondage*, *LW* 33 p. 294. Among the extraneous matters are the Papacy, purgatory, and indulgences.

[54] McGrath (*Iustitia Dei*, p. 231), rightly argues, 'Essential to his understanding of justification is the concept of *iustitia Christi aliena*, which is not necessarily implied by the doctrine of the unfree will. If human free will is enslaved, it is certainly true that humans cannot justify themselves—but this does not place God under any obligation to

Whereas the early Luther conceived of the righteousness of God as a personal attribute by which he upholds the terms of the *pactum* and so allows human beings to distinguish themselves by their own free will, the mature Luther regarded such a notion as antithetical to the gospel and instead conceived of the righteousness of God as a divine gift given through the gospel to the elect. There is and can be no human preparation for justification. It is the work of God, who creates faith by means of the gospel. The act of creating faith in the hearer of the gospel is the act of justification, for the faith that apprehends Christ thereby possesses him as righteousness.

The close link between these two concepts—monergism and alien righteousness—is apparent when Luther, with a rhetorical flourish, criticizes Erasmus' view of merit for being worse than Pelagianism. He argues that Erasmus' doctrine of congruous merit attempts to leave room for grace but nevertheless ultimately ascribes the distinction between the saved and the lost to the free will of humanity instead of to grace, thereby amounting to a form of condign merit.[55] Therefore, Luther prefers Pelagianism to Erasmus' view, first because Pelagianism is honest about its doctrine of merit, and second because at least Pelagianism allows for the purchase of grace at a worthy price, whereas Erasmus' view cheapens grace by ascribing it to moral efforts that are, intrinsically, of little or no worth. Luther, on the other hand, eliminates all merit from consideration, whether condign or congruous, and ascribes justification completely to the grace of God.

Although the subject of imputation arises rarely in this work, Luther does speak of justification, in line with Romans 4:2-3, as a forensic reckoning of righteousness.[56] Because, according to Paul, righteousness is reckoned not to the one who works but to the one who does not work, justification cannot result from a synthesis of grace and merit, faith and works, law and gospel. One must either work or not work in order to attain justification:

> In short, Paul sets the one who works and the one who does not work alongside
> each other, leaving no room for anyone between them; and he asserts that

---

justify them by means of an extrinsic righteousness, provided the source of justifying righteousness is conceded to be none other than God himself. That the will of humans is enslaved is one matter; that God should choose to justify them in one specific manner as a result is quite another.' It is true that outside the context of Luther's theology there is no *necessary* theological link between these two concepts. Nevertheless, for Luther they cannot be separated. God's monergistic work of salvation consists of the gift of faith given in the gospel, and since faith that is created by the gospel cannot exist apart from Christ and his righteousness, alien righteousness thereby becomes a necessary component of a monergistic doctrine of salvation.

[55] Luther, *Bondage*, *LW* 33, pp. 266-70.

[56] 'Notice how Paul dwells on the word "reckoned", how he stresses, repeats, and insists on it. . . . He repeats the word "reckon" nearly ten times in this chapter'. Luther, *Bondage*, *LW* 33, p. 271 (*WA* 18, p. 772).

righteousness is not reckoned to the former, but that it is reckoned to the latter provided he has faith. There is no way of escape for free choice here, no chance for it to get away with its endeavoring and striving. It must be classed either with the one who works or with the one who does not work. If it is classed with the former, so you are told here, it does not have any righteousness reckoned to it, whereas if it is classed with the latter—the one who does not work but has faith in God—then it does have righteousness reckoned to it. But in that case it will no longer be a case of free choice at work, but of being created anew through faith.[57]

Luther's problem with Erasmus is not that the latter lacks any conception of grace.[58] It is, rather, that by failing to understand the true nature of justifying grace, Erasmus has sought a middle ground between grace and works. For Luther, this error entails the nullification of grace, replacing the gospel with a kind of moralism comparable to the error of the Pelagians, or even worse.

Luther's 1535 commentary on Galatians reiterates the centrality of justification. In his summary of the letter's argument, he asserts that the whole of true Christian doctrine hangs on this one article.[59] Justification does not occur through the active righteousness of works, the righteousness that operates on the earthly plane among human beings.[60] Rather, justification results from the passive righteousness of faith, the righteousness that is Christ himself, seated in heaven at the right hand of the Father: 'Sin cannot happen in this Christian righteousness; for where there is no Law, there cannot be any transgression (Rom. 4:15).'[61] Faith alone takes hold of Christ in heaven and his righteousness, in spite of the fact that the sinner remains on earth under the condemnation of the law.[62] The believer is, therefore, simultaneously just and a sinner (*simul iustus et peccator*), a sinner in this earthly sphere but righteous in Christ. It is, therefore, essential that these two kinds of righteousness be distinguished, and this distinction corresponds to that between law and gospel,

---

[57] Luther, *Bondage, LW* 33, p. 271.
[58] On Erasmus' doctrine of grace, see *The Free Will*, sections 20, 44, 48-50, 52, 56.
[59] 'For if the doctrine of justification is lost, the whole of Christian doctrine is lost.' Martin Luther, *Lectures on Galatians 1535, LW* 26, p. 9 (*WA* 40/1, p. 48).
[60] Luther, *Galatians 1535, LW* 26, pp. 4-6 (*WA* 40/1, pp. 40-42). Clark (*Iustitia Imputata*, p. 294) oversteps the evidence when he argues that *iustitia activa* 'is that accomplished by Christ'. Luther does not mention Christ's own righteousness in this context.
[61] Luther, *Galatians 1535, LW* 26, p. 8 (*WA* 40/1, p. 47).
[62] 'Thus as long as we live here, both remain. The flesh is accused, exercised, saddened, and crushed by the active righteousness of the Law. But the spirit rules, rejoices, and is saved by passive righteousness, because it knows that it has a Lord sitting in heaven at the right hand of the Father, who has abolished the Law, sin, and death, and has trodden over them in Himself (Col. 2:15).' Luther, *Galatians 1535, LW* 26, p. 9 (*WA* 40/1, p. 48).

a distinction that is absolutely necessary to a proper understanding of justification.

A particularly striking contrast between Luther and Rome appears in his comments on Galatians 2:16. Whereas Rome attributes the formal righteousness of faith to the virtue of charity that animates it, Luther attributes the justifying power of faith to Christ himself.[63] Faith 'takes hold of Christ in such a way that Christ is the object of faith, or rather not the object but, so to speak, the One who is present in the faith itself'.[64] This contrast constitutes a succinct expression of the major difference between Rome and Luther on the question of justification. For Rome, faith derives its significance from an infused virtue, and Christ's atoning work is relegated to the position of a necessary precondition for the infusion of grace. For Luther, faith justifies because the crucified Christ is present in it, and he constitutes the believer's righteousness. The former locates the legal basis of right standing with God in a grace-wrought virtue intrinsic to the believer; the latter locates it outside of the believer, in Christ, who is possessed by faith.

Perhaps the best place to end this survey of Luther's work is where it began, namely, with a glance toward his 1545 recounting of his struggle over the righteousness of God.[65] Recalling his encounter with Augustine's *On the Spirit and the Letter* sometime after his own understanding of God's righteousness had changed, Luther recounts the pleasant surprise that it was to him to find that Augustine had also taken 'the righteousness of God' in Romans 1:17 as a divine gift, not a personal attribute. Yet in a passing comment given only as a minor qualification, Luther speaks volumes about his own doctrine of justification: 'And although this [Augustine's interpretation] is expressed somewhat imperfectly, and he does not explain everything about imputation clearly, it was nevertheless pleasing to find that he taught that the "righteousness of God" is that, by which we are justified.'[66] That the Reformation was an Augustinian movement is undeniable. But it is instructive to note where the Reformers themselves offer a critique of Augustine's

---

[63] 'But where they [the scholastics] speak of love, we speak of faith. And while they say that faith is the mere outline but love is its living colors and completion, we say in opposition that faith takes hold of Christ and that He is the form that adorns and informs faith as color does the wall. Therefore Christian faith is not an idle quality or an empty husk in the heart, which may exist in a state of mortal sin until love comes along to make it alive. But if it is true faith, it is a sure trust and firm acceptance in the heart.' Luther, *Galatians 1535*, *LW* 26, p. 129 (*WA* 40/1, pp. 228).

[64] Luther, *Galatians 1535*, *LW* 26, p. 129 (*WA* 40/1, pp. 228-29).

[65] Of course, many other works in the voluminous Luther corpus could be cited. For a discussion of a 1536 disputation over the relationship of works and justification in which Luther was a participant, see Seifrid, 'Luther, Melanchthon, and Paul'; cf. Clark, '*Iustitia Imputata*', pp. 301-06.

[66] Translation provided in McGrath, *Luther's Theology of the Cross*, p. 97 (*WA* 54, p. 186).

soteriology. Luther acknowledges that the great Western father held to a doctrine of justification that was deficient in one respect: it did not include an adequate explanation of imputation. This brief comment, published in the year prior to Luther's death, is a testimony to the centrality of alien righteousness for his doctrine of justification.

SUMMARY: LUTHER'S DOCTRINE OF JUSTIFICATION

For Luther, the Reformer, the article of justification is the cornerstone of Christian theology, for it alone expresses what is required for sinful humanity to be made right with God. Although there is a civic righteousness that any human being can attain by works, before God there are no human works that can justify, for the sinful human being is a bad tree that can only bear bad fruit. In order to bring forth good fruit, the tree must first be made good, and this is what happens in justification. In the particularity of his grace, God creates faith in his elect by means of the gospel. Faith justifies because it takes hold of Christ, who is the righteousness of the sinner. God's act of justifying is essentially his act of evoking faith through the effective power of his Word, so that faith is not so much the condition of justification as it is the means by which God justifies. For Luther, unlike Calvin and the Reformed tradition, justification is completely unconditional.[67]

Luther does not draw a distinction between justification and sanctification, as later Protestantism would.[68] Instead, he regards the divine transformative work as an aspect of the declaration of righteousness given in justification. Nevertheless, this link between the forensic and the transformative aspects of salvation does not follow the same lines as the Roman Catholic doctrine. For Rome, the legal basis of one's right standing with God is the grace-wrought righteousness that inheres within the believer. There is a logical priority of personal righteousness over legal standing, for the former is determinative of the latter. At the final judgment, God evaluates the human being for what he or she is intrinsically. For Rome, the salvific term 'justification' refers to a transformative event that imparts habitual grace to its recipient, an event that is disconnected from God's final legal evaluation. As for the final judgment itself, the Roman position is essentially one that entails the justification of the godly.

---

[67] As will be discussed below, for the Reformed tradition, faith is a precondition of justification. Election to salvation is unconditional, and effectual calling and regeneration arise from God's unconditional decree of election, thereby creating faith in the elect. But faith is still a condition that must be met in order for the elect to be justified.

[68] Peter A. Lillback, 'Calvin's Development of the Doctrine of Forensic Justification: Calvin and the Early Lutherans on the Relationship of Justification and Renewal', in K. Scott Oliphint (ed), *Justified in Christ: God's Plan for Us in Justification* (Fearn, UK: Mentor, 2007), pp. 51-80; Olli-Pekka Vainio, *Justification and Participation in Christ: The Development of the Lutheran Doctrine of Justification from Luther to the Formula of Concord (1580)* (Boston: Brill, 2008), pp. 36-42.

For Luther, by contrast, Christ's righteousness alone is the legal basis of right standing with God. The believer's own proper righteousness, then, has no determinative bearing on his legal standing before God. The believer's good works are simply the natural product of what he has become in Christ: a new creation. Alien righteousness retains a logical priority even when the forensic and transformative aspects of salvation are not clearly distinguished. Justification is not merely an event in which grace is received. It is itself a present anticipation of the final judgment, so that it may be truly said that God justifies the ungodly by creating faith within them.

Crucial to this doctrine is the distinction between law and gospel, in contrast to the Roman Catholic synthesis. The law demands perfect obedience, and without the hope of offering such to God, the sinner's only recourse is to the gospel. God does not offer eternal life as a reward for grace-wrought merit. He gives it freely and unconditionally through his Son, whose righteousness belongs to the sinner by faith.

In recent years some, most notably those associated with the so-called 'Finnish School', have argued that Luther's doctrine of justification is essentially a theotic, rather than a forensic, doctrine.[69] Tuomo Mannermaa, for example, speaks of a 'communication of attributes' between the believer and the indwelling Christ, and he writes of the Christian 'participating in God's essence' and 'becoming a partaker of the properties of this essence'.[70] According to this line of thought, the true significance of justification for Luther lies not in the alien righteousness of Christ imputed to us but rather in our own ontological participation in the divine essence through the divine-human person of Christ. Insofar as this interpretation of Luther displaces alien righteousness as the key dividing line between him and Rome, it threatens the thesis of this section.[71] It is, therefore, necessary to interact with the Finnish School, if only briefly.

The methodology of the Finnish School has been subjected to devastating

---

[69] Tuomo Mannermaa, *Christ Present in Faith: Luther's View of Justification* (Minneapolis: Fortress, 2005); Carl E. Braaten and Robert W. Jenson (eds), *Union with Christ: The New Finnish Interpretation of Luther* (Grand Rapids: Eerdmans, 1998). Although he does not belong to the Finnish School and his aims are different, Stephen Strehle (*The Catholic Roots of the Protestant Gospel: Encounter Between the Middle Ages and the Reformation* [New York: Brill, 1995], pp. 66-85) offers some similar arguments in an attempt to tie Luther more closely to Osiander than to Melanchthon.
[70] Tuomo Mannermaa, 'Justification and *Theosis* in Lutheran-Orthodox Perspective', in Carl E. Braaten and Robert W. Jenson (eds), *Union with Christ: The New Finnish Interpretation of Luther* (Grand Rapids: Eerdmans, 1998), pp. 32, 34.
[71] Of course, even if the arguments of the Finnish School are granted, it would not ultimately threaten the overall thesis of this work, for it can still be established that Protestantism as a whole, whether with Luther or against Luther, developed its doctrine of justification on the basis of an alien righteousness.

criticism.[72] The root problem of their thesis is that it reads theosis into Luther without warrant. For example, in their interpretations of Luther, these scholars often load words and phrases with unwarranted theological freight. A few examples will suffice to illustrate the point.[73] Addressing the matter of union with Christ, a central theological category for the Finnish School, Trueman notes, 'the Finnish case rests not so much upon the idea that union with Christ is central to Luther's articulation of justification but rather upon the use of realistic language to describe the union and its effects'.[74] In other words, while it is undeniable that union with Christ constitutes a central aspect of Luther's theology, it is simply illegitimate to presuppose that this union is ontological in nature without adequate warrant. So, for example, one finds Mannermaa quoting from a sermon in which Luther refers to participation in the divine nature (a reference to 2 Pet. 1:4), followed by a claim on Mannermaa's part that this means that the Christian 'becomes a partaker of the properties of this [divine] essence'.[75] But Mannermaa does not offer any contextual justification for this radical interpretation. Instead, he merely reads a theological presupposition into Luther's language. The same phenomenon occurs when Mannermaa imports the concept of the communication of attributes from Christology to soteriology, claiming that Luther upholds a realistic conception of the exchange between Christ and the believer.[76] This kind of theologically weighted language is simply misleading, for it reads the doctrine of theosis into Luther by assuming that any reference to the concepts of union, participation, and exchange necessarily constitute ontological realities. Furthermore, it applies to soteriology a theological concept normally restricted to the doctrine of the hypostatic union, which constitutes a claim of massive significance. And Mannermaa makes this claim without providing a shred of evidence that Luther ever spoke this way about the *communicatio idiomatum*.[77] The Finnish School, because of its theological presuppositions, appears to fall prey to the error of

---

[72] Timothy J. Wengert, review of Carl E. Braaten and Robert W. Jenson (eds), *Union with Christ: The New Finnish Interpretation of Luther*, *Theology Today* 56 (1999), pp. 432-34; Carl R. Trueman, 'Is the Finnish Line a New Beginning? A Critical Assessment of the Reading of Luther Offered by the Helsinki Circle', *WTJ* 65, no. 2 (2003), pp. 231-44; Clark, '*Iustitia Imputata*', pp. 307-10; Mark Seifrid ('Paul, Luther, and Justification in Gal 2:15-21', *WTJ* 65, no.2 [2003], pp. 215-30) offers a more modest critique.

[73] See Trueman, 'Finnish Line', for a more detailed discussion.

[74] Trueman, 'Finnish Line', 235.

[75] Mannermaa, 'Justification and *Theosis*', p. 34.

[76] Mannermaa, 'Justification and *Theosis*', p. 32.

[77] Leaving aside at this point the unique features of the Lutheran doctrine of the communication of attributes, one wonders how the claim that there is a communication of attributes (however that may be conceived) between Christ and the believer might impact the uniqueness of the incarnation itself. If this doctrine is not unique to the hypostatic union, in what sense does Christ retain his unique personhood?

eisegesis in its reading of Luther, and these examples are not isolated.[78]

The Finnish School and its supporters have been open about their ecumenical motivation.[79] Unfortunately, it appears that this motive has led to shoddy historical work, resulting in a distorted picture of Luther. Wengert's final appraisal is worth noting:

> In short, this book will help readers to know what Finnish theologians think of their own tradition. Here one sees what happens when modern ecumenical agendas and old-fashioned pietism become the chief spectacles through which to view an historical figure. If readers want to understand Luther's radical approach to justification by faith alone, this book will finally disappoint.[80]

The evidence presented throughout this section indicates that Luther's doctrine of justification stands in basic continuity with that of Protestantism in general. To be sure, there are some notes of discontinuity between Luther and later Protestant theologians.[81] However, Luther's shift to a doctrine of alien righteousness as the legal basis of right standing with God has defined justification for Protestantism as a whole. The untenable claims of the Finnish School do not threaten this assessment.

Philip Melanchthon

Scholarly discussion surrounding Luther's theology in relation to that of Philip Melanchthon (1497-1560) sometimes suggests that Melanchthon departed radically from the teachings of his colleague and subsequently led Lutheranism as a whole down a faulty path, one that essentially buried Luther's rich, life-

---

[78] Trueman, Wengert, and Clark all note the historical insensitivity of the volume *Union with Christ*, displayed in its overreliance on sources from Luther's early, transitional period, as well as a number of citations that reveal little awareness of context.

[79] 'Now of course the Finnish theses may seem so evident to me because I so want them to be true. My interest in Luther is not that of a *Lutherforscher*, but that of a systematic theologian and ecumenist. As a systematician, I have found I can *do* very little with Luther as usually interpreted. And the sort of Lutheranism that constantly appeals to that Luther has been an ecumenical disaster. With Luther according to the Finns, on the other hand, there can be much systematically and ecumenically fruitful conversation.' Robert W. Jenson, 'Response to Tuomo Mannermaa, "Why Is Luther So Fascinating?"' in *Union with Christ*, p. 21.

[80] Wengert, review of *Union with Christ*, p. 434.

[81] As mentioned before, Luther did not draw a hard distinction between the legal and transformative aspects of salvation. He did not hesitate to affirm that faith itself is righteousness. His doctrine of justification is completely unconditional, in contrast to the Reformed doctrine of justification based on the condition of faith.

giving teaching under the dry soil of legal fiction.[82] This 'Luther against the
Lutherans' thesis should be rejected, but not before it has been mined for some
nugget of truth. Especially in his later writings, Melanchthon did depart from
Luther on some issues related to justification, developing ideas in ways that
Luther never did. And yet, Luther continued to speak approvingly of
Melanchthon's work, granting high praise to the 1535 edition of the *Loci
Communes*, the first revision in which Melanchthon's independence had started
to show:

> If anybody wishes to become a theologian, he has a great advantage, first of all,
> in having the Bible. This is now so clear that he can read it without any trouble.
> Afterward he should read Philip's *Loci Communes*. This he should read
> diligently and well until he has its contents fixed in his head. If he has these two
> he is a theologian, and neither the devil nor a heretic can shake him. . . .
>
>   There's no book under the sun in which the whole of theology is so compactly
> presented as in the *Loci Communes*. If you read all the fathers and sententiaries
> you have nothing. No better book has been written after the Holy Scriptures than
> Philip's.[83]

At the very least, the thesis that Melanchthon departed significantly from
Luther becomes hard to sustain in the light of such statements on Luther's part.
Yet the polar opposite conclusion, namely, that Luther and Melanchthon
formulated the exact same doctrine of justification, does not necessarily follow
either. It is better to allow that there are some aspects of discontinuity between
Luther and Melanchthon within an overall shared theological context that
revolves around the doctrine of justification by free grace on the basis of an
alien righteousness. Of greatest significance for this study is the fact that,
whatever theological alterations Melanchthon may have made and however
they might have influenced Lutheranism as a whole, he never departed from
that foundational point of division from Rome.

CONTINUITY WITH LUTHER

The 1521 edition of the Melanchthon's *Loci Communes* may best be described

---

[82] After tying Luther's view to that of Osiander, Strehle (*Catholic Roots*, pp. 82-83)
writes, 'No matter how one might feel about this matter or other details of Osiander's
system we must at least recognize that the church has become greatly impoverished in
adopting Melanchthon's one-dimensional concepts to the exclusion of other tensions in
Luther's thought—tensions that Osiander had hoped to bring forth.' See also
Mannermaa, *Christ Present in Faith*, pp. 4-6; Seifrid ('Luther, Melanchthon and Paul',
p. 143), who is generally more nuanced in his arguments, writes, 'In any case, it is clear
that Melanchthon and Luther differ dramatically from one another on the question of
justification because they proceed from radically different perspectives.'
[83] Martin Luther, *Table Talk*, *LW* 54, pp. 439-40. This comment is dated in the winter of
1542-1543. Melanchthon's first edition of the *Loci Communes* was published in 1521.

as an organized arrangement of Luther's theology. On point after point Melanchthon follows closely on the heels of his Wittenberg colleague. He affirms that all things happen by necessity and that, therefore, there is no such thing as free will.[84] He draws a clear distinction between law and gospel, attributing justification solely to the mercy of God to the exclusion of all human merit.[85] He critiques the scholastic understanding of grace, arguing that in Scripture grace is divine favor rather than a quality imparted to the soul.[86] He affirms that faith itself is righteousness and that it is not within the power of human nature.[87] He argues that the law's proper function is 'to reveal sin and especially to confound the conscience'.[88]

The main contours of Luther's doctrine of justification would remain in place throughout all of Melanchthon's subsequent works. In the 1521 *Loci* he affirms repeatedly that the law demands the impossible,[89] a conviction that remained unchanged by the time he published his 1543 edition:

> There is no doubt that the law of God demands both inner and outward obedience, as it says, 'You shall love the Lord your God with all your heart', Deut. 6:5. But since this corrupted nature of men cannot produce perfect obedience, as Paul so clearly testifies in Romans 7-8, and since this sin remains in us in this life in the form of doubt, lack of faith and insufficient fear and love of God, and countless desires which run counter to the law of God, it follows

---

[84] 'Since all things that happen, happen necessarily according to divine predestination, our will (*voluntas*) has no liberty.' Philip Melanchthon, *Loci Communes Theologici* [1521], LCC 19, p. 24 (CR 21, pp. 87-88).

[85] 'Generally speaking, there are two parts to Scripture, law and gospel. The law shows sin, the gospel grace. The law indicates disease, the gospel points out the remedy.' Melanchthon, *Loci Communes* [1519], LCC 19, pp. 70-71 (CR 21, pp. 139).

[86] 'Grace is nothing else, if it is to be most accurately defined, than God's goodwill toward us, or the will of God which has mercy on us. Therefore, the word "grace" does not mean some quality in us, but rather the very will of God, or the goodwill of God toward us.' Melanchthon, *Loci Communes* [1521], LCC 19, p. 87 (CR 21, p. 158).

[87] 'But FAITH alone in the mercy and grace of God in Christ Jesus is our RIGHTEOUSNESS. . . . I commend these two passages [Rom. 4:5; Gen. 15:6] to you very highly so that you may understand that faith is properly called righteousness. For the Sophists are offended by this kind of speech—when we say that faith is righteousness.' Melanchthon, *Loci Communes* [1519], LCC 19, p. 89 (CR 21, pp. 159-60).

[88] Melanchthon, *Loci Communes* [1521], LCC 19, p. 118; see idem, *Paul's Letter to the Colossians* (trans. D.C. Parker; Sheffield, UK: Almond, 1989), pp. 64-66 for an exposition of a twofold use the law. The latter work was originally published in 1527. The third use of the law would not make its appearance in Melanchthon until 1534.

[89] 'The law demands the impossible, and the conscience, convicted of sin, is assailed in all directions.' Melanchthon, *Loci Communes* [1521], LCC 19: p. 85 (CR 21, p. 156).

that men are not pronounced righteous, that is, accepted before God by reason of the Law.[90]

It is the theological reality of divine justice, a justice that cannot be compromised by an easing of the law's demand, combined with the anthropological reality of sinful corruption, that drives Melanchthon to affirm that justification must be on account of Christ (*propter Christum*) as opposed to on account of the law (*propter Legem*).[91] Human righteousness must be radically distinguished from the righteousness that avails before God.[92] Contrary to the Roman doctrine, the atoning work of Christ is not the prerequisite for a gift of grace that enables sinners to attain right standing with God by law.[93] On the contrary, for Melanchthon, Christ's righteousness is our righteousness, and the blessing of justification is given by God's free grace alone, apart from all works or merits.[94] Given the divine demand for perfection, it could be no other way. The bicovenantal theology of Luther, a dividing line drawn between himself and Rome, remains intact for Melanchthon from beginning to end. If, as Luther said, the ability to distinguish between the law and the gospel is the mark of a true theologian, it is no wonder that Luther held Melanchthon in such high esteem.[95]

At this point it is worth noting the inappropriateness of the charge, brought forth by Strehle, that Melanchthon's doctrine of justification is essentially voluntaristic. With Melanchthon in view, Strehle writes, 'And so, the doctrine of forensic justification arises, not so much from the seminal ideas of Protestantism, but from the Nominalists' concept of God. It is based upon their

---

[90] Philip Melancthon *Loci Communes 1543* (trans. J. A. O. Preus; St. Louis: Concordia, 1992), p. 72; Idem, *Tertia Aetas Locorum Theologicorum ab Ipso Melanthone Editorum* 4, CR 21, p. 716.

[91] 'For this reason he is the mediator, so that we might be righteous on account of him, since we are not righteous by the law.' Melanchthon, *Tertia Aetas* 4 (CR 21, p. 664), my translation.

[92] Melanchthon, *Colossians*, pp. 38-42, 46-57.

[93] Melanchthon (*Loci Communes* [1521], LCC 19, pp. 74-77) criticizes the medieval teaching that the gospel is the 'new law', a republication of divine demand that focuses on inward obedience instead of merely external obedience. For Melanchthon, not only does this teaching obscure the nature of the Mosaic Law (which addressed inward obedience as well), but it also conflates law and gospel, thereby obscuring the glory of God's provision of free justification in his Son.

[94] '[A]nd we cling to Christ in faith, not doubting in the least that the righteousness of Christ is our righteousness, that the satisfaction Christ wrought is our expiation, and that the resurrection of Christ is ours.' Melanchthon, *Loci Communes* [1521], LCC 19, pp. 88-89 (CR 21, p. 159).

[95] 'Therefore whoever knows well how to distinguish the Gospel from the Law should give thanks to God and know that he is a real theologian.' Luther, *Galatians 1535*, LW 26, p.115.

presupposition that the will of God is free from any sense of absolute righteousness and can declare the black white or white black in accordance with its desires.'[96] On the contrary, it is precisely Melanchthon's commitment to the uncompromising justice of God that drives him to a doctrine of imputation. If the will of God were severed from any sense of absolute righteousness, then why would the law require perfect obedience? Why couldn't God count less than perfect obedience as acceptable, as in the theology of the *via moderna*? Melanchthon's doctrine of imputation is not rooted in a voluntaristic doctrine of God. Rather, it is rooted in a doctrine of divine righteousness that is absolute and uncompromising, combined with a divine provision in Jesus Christ that meets the standard of righteousness. For Melanchthon, perfect obedience is required for justification. Imputation makes justification possible in a fallen world, and the most natural place to look as a source for Melanchthon's doctrine of imputation is Scripture, particularly Paul's arguments in Romans 4:1-8 and 2 Corinthians 5:21, not to the writings of medieval Nominalists.

ELEMENTS OF DISCONTUINITY WITH LUTHER

In the 1530s Melanchthon began to forge his own path on certain issues, although none of these theological developments threatened the central reality of alien righteousness or the law-gospel distinction. Three particular issues related to the doctrine of justification are worthy of mention.

First, Melanchthon eventually modified Luther's doctrine of free will and necessity. Whereas the first edition of the *Loci Communes* sounds virtually identical to Luther's later work, *The Bondage of the Will*, by 1535 Melanchthon had made some adjustments to his former view. In later editions of the *Loci Communes* he denies that all things happen by necessity and affirms that human beings have some measure of free will in relation to external, or civic, righteousness.[97] However, he continues to maintain that humanity's fallen condition renders the will incapable of pleasing God, and so the will is still bound in some sense.[98] Scheible notes, 'With this didactic he proved himself to be a genuine student of Luther. But it is so formulated that Erasmus could also

---

[96] Strehle, *Catholic Roots*, p. 70.

[97] 'However, let us first speak of the cause of sin, on account of which, when it stands firm that God is not the cause of sin, it will then be easily reckoned to be contingent, or that not all things happen by absolute necessity.' Philip Melanchthon, *Secunda Aetas Locorum Theologicorum ab Ipso Melanthone Editorum* 18a, CR 21, p. 271; 'Therefore the human will is able in its own strength, without renovation, to do some kinds of external works of the law.' Idem, *Tertia Aetas* 4 (CR 21, p. 654), my translations. See also idem, *Colossians*, pp. 39-42.

[98] 'Now truly in this weakness, inward movements suitable to the law of God are not kindled without the Holy Spirit.' Melanchthon, *Tertia Aetas* 4, CR 21, p. 663, my translation.

agree. Melanchthon "transcended" the conflict over the freedom of the will.'[99]
There is no evidence that Luther opposed Melanchthon on this score, but it is
important to note that the transition involved here constitutes an embrace of
some form of synergism. This fact is evident from a passage in the 1543 *Loci*:

> The free choice in man is the ability to apply oneself toward grace, that is, our
> free choice hears the promise, tries to assent to it and rejects the sins which are
> contrary to conscience. . . . Further, these points become clearer when the
> promise is considered. Since the promise is universal and since in God there are
> not conflicting wills, it is necessary that there is some cause within us for the
> difference as to why Saul is rejected and David received, that is, there must be a
> different action on the part of the two men.[100]

Seeing a universal salvific will in God and refusing to allow for a hidden,
discriminating decree behind the promise that has been revealed, Melanchthon
is driven to the conclusion that something in the individual constitutes the
decisive cause of his or her salvation or damnation. The distinction between
David and Saul is finally owing to David's assent to grace and Saul's obstinacy
toward it. Such an idea is foreign to Luther's doctrine of unconditional
justification. For Luther, God justifies by creating faith in his elect; justification
is a monergistic divine work. For the mature Melanchthon, the two issues of
alien righteousness and monergism become separated, as he upholds the former
but ultimately denies the latter. Melanchthon gives free will a decisive role in
salvation, but he consistently maintains that justifying righteousness is alien,
rather than intrinsic to, the sinner.

A second way that the mature Melanchthon modified his earlier view is with
his description of the nature of faith. Like Luther, the early Melanchthon did
not hesitate to affirm that faith itself is righteousness. By 1543 Melanchthon no
longer speaks with such terminology. Instead, he locates righteousness in Christ
and affirms that faith is merely an instrument that grasps Christ, and, as such, is
intrinsically unworthy in itself:

> [W]e are righteous by faith, that is, through mercy for the sake of Christ we are
> righteous, not because faith is a virtue which merits the remission of sins by its
> own worthiness. . . . Therefore we do not say that we are righteous by faith in the
> sense that this is a worthiness of such great power that it merits remission, but in
> the sense that there must be some instrument in us by which we lay hold upon
> our Mediator who intercedes for us, and on account of whom the eternal Father

---

[99] Heinz Scheible, 'Philip Melanchthon (1497-1560)', in Carter Lindberg (ed), *The
Reformation Theologians: An Introduction to Theology in the Early Modern Period*
(Malden, MA: Blackwell, 2002), p. 71.
[100] Melanchthon, *Loci Communes 1543*, p. 44.

is favorable toward us.[101]

For Luther, Christ and faith are tied so closely together that it is difficult to distinguish between them. Melanchthon, on the other hand, offers some refinement on this question and argues for a conceptual distinction between Christ and faith. In doing so, he guards against the charge that faith is nothing more than a surrogate work, a charge that would reduce his gospel to another kind of law. For the mature Melanchthon, Christ alone is the sinner's righteousness. Even faith cannot stand in his place. But faith is necessary to take hold of Christ, and thus the doctrine of justification by faith means that God's imputation of righteousness occurs when the sinner, by the work of God's grace and the assent of free will, meets the condition of faith and so grasps Christ and his righteousness.

Third, contrary to Luther, Melanchthon promoted a third use of the law.[102] Highly motivated to defend his gospel against the charge of antinomianism, Melanchthon began to argue by 1534 that the law has an ongoing function in the lives of believers, namely, to aid them in the practice of obedience.[103] In the 1543 *Loci* Melanchthon argues that believers have been freed from the law's condemnation, but nevertheless the law must continue to be preached to the regenerate in order to point out the remnants of sin in them and to inform them of what God demands.[104] It is evident in his argument that his concern is to safeguard an objective standard of righteousness for believers so that they will not seek to worship God on the basis of their own imaginations but will adhere to what he has revealed.[105] Some have argued or implied, with some degree of plausibility, that the rise of the third use in Melanchthon resulted from a

---

[101] Melanchthon, *Loci Communes 1543*, p. 109.

[102] The historical context and origin of this doctrine in Melanchthon is explained in Timothy J. Wengert, *Law and Gospel: Philip Melanchthon's Debate with John Agricola of Eisleben over* Poenientia (Grand Rapids: Baker, 1997).

[103] Wengert, *Law and Gospel*, pp. 195-96.

[104] 'Meanwhile the law, which points out the remnants of sin, must nevertheless be taught, so that the knowledge of sin and repentance might grow, and the gospel of Christ might sound forth at the same time, so that faith might grow. Likewise, the law therefore must be set forth, so that it might teach certain works, to which God wills us to exercise obedience.' Melanchthon, *Tertia Aetas* 6, CR 21, p. 719, my translation. The mere preaching of the law to believers does not constitute a third use of the law in and of itself. Because believers remain sinners before God, the law's role of pointing out remaining sin in them to drive them continually to the gospel pertains to its second use. However, Melanchthon's affirmation in the last sentence of the above quote goes beyond this role to one of educating and forming believers for obedience to God, and this use of the law, which is uniquely for believers, constitutes a third use.

[105] Melanchthon, *Tertia Aetas* 6, CR 21: p. 719.

truncated doctrine of the effectiveness of justification.[106] While this may indeed be the case, it must be kept in mind that the mature Melanchthon explicitly and consistently separated the believer's obedience to the law from the ground of justification, and in this crucial sense, maintained the law-gospel distinction that separated Luther from Rome. Insofar as right standing with God is concerned, Melanchthon stands with Luther in his assertion that the law has no bearing on the issue, that faith alone justifies, and that justifying righteousness is alien to the sinner.

SUMMARY: MELANCHTHON'S DOCTRINE OF JUSTIFICATION

For Philip Melanchthon, justification consists of the remission of sins and the imputation of righteousness, namely, the righteousness of Jesus Christ to the sinner. This divine declaration occurs when the sinner takes hold of Christ by faith. Although revealing some measure of discontinuity with Luther, Melanchthon shares a basic theological framework that sets the two Reformers apart from the Roman Catholic doctrine of justification. Even more explicitly and consistently than Luther, Melanchthon affirms that the law demands of sinners that which is impossible: perfect obedience. For this reason, and contra Rome, divine grace cannot be merely an aid that enables one to fulfill the law in a satisfactory, though incomplete, manner. Instead, the gospel must be clearly distinguished from the law so that the divine provision of righteousness through Jesus Christ might be given to sinners by faith alone. With Luther, Melanchthon stands apart from Rome not because he affirms a grace-based soteriology in opposition to Pelagianism, but rather because he affirms a bicovenantal doctrine, tied to his understanding of the divine demand and provision, as opposed to a monocovenantal scheme that blurs the distinction between law and gospel, resulting in the absorption of gospel into law. This is no small matter, for the gospel itself and the glory of Christ are at stake: 'And so those who deny that faith justifies, teach nothing but the law by abolishing the gospel and by abolishing Christ.'[107]

John Calvin

For John Calvin (1509-1564), the doctrine of justification is 'the main hinge on which religion turns'.[108] With Luther and Melanchthon, Calvin's doctrine

---

[106] Seifrid ('Luther, Melanchthon, and Paul', p. 142) writes, 'Since "justification" no longer had an effective dimension, the Law (in its "third use") moved in to fill the vacuum left behind.' Wengert, *Law and Gospel*, pp. 190-91, hints very strongly at a similar evaluation.

[107] Philip Melanchthon, *Apologia Confessionis Augustanae* [1531], CR 27, p. 39, my translation.

[108] John Calvin, *Institutes of the Christian Religion* 3.11.1, LCC 20, p. 726. Discussions of Calvin's view of justification may be found in Wilhelm Niesel, *The Theology of*

depends on the bicovenantal distinction between law and gospel, rooted in a divine demand for perfection and resulting in a doctrine of alien righteousness. The two issues of imputation and monergism, though inextricably bound for Luther and separated by Melanchthon, are for Calvin two distinguishable issues that nevertheless belong together. Monergism locates the basis of the whole of salvation outside the sinner; God alone is responsible for salvation.[109] Imputation locates the legal basis of justification outside the sinner; Christ alone is the believer's hope for righteousness. Both doctrines nullify human effort and magnify the grace of God. In his polemic against the Roman Catholic doctrine of justification, Calvin often attacks the distinguishable concepts of free will and inherent righteousness as the basis of right standing with God. When Calvin's doctrine of alien righteousness is viewed as one aspect of his monergistic soteriology, his appeal to both doctrines as polemic against the Roman view makes good sense. For Calvin, alien righteousness is more central to the doctrine of justification than is monergism, serving to distinguish his view even from that of Augustine; nevertheless, the two doctrines mutually support and illuminate one another.

The following survey will demonstrate that what distinguishes Calvin's doctrine of justification from that of Rome is a doctrine of alien righteousness within the overall context of a monergistic soteriology. This survey will trace Calvin's doctrine as it is developed in the *Institutes of the Christian Religion*, followed by an examination of a few polemical treatises, then concluding with

---

Calvin (Philadelphia: Westminster, 1956), pp. 130-39; François Wendel, *Calvin: Origins and Development of His Religious Thought* (Durham, NC: Labyrinth, 1987), pp. 255-63; Karl Barth, *The Theology of John Calvin* (Grand Rapids: Eerdmans, 1995), pp. 166-67, 277-78; McGrath, *Iustitia Dei*, pp. 253-57; T.H.L. Parker, 'Calvin's Doctrine of Justification', *EQ* 24 (1952), pp. 101-07; Pierre Marcel, 'The Relation Between Justification and Sanctification in Calvin's Thought', *EQ* 27 (1955), pp. 132-45; Thomas Coates, 'Calvin's Doctrine of Justification', *Concordia Theological Monthly* 34 (1963), pp. 325-34; W. Stanford Reid, 'Justification by Faith According to John Calvin', *WTJ* 42 (1980), pp. 290-307; Trevor Hart, 'Humankind in Christ and Christ in Humankind: Salvation as Participation in Our Substitute in the Theology of John Calvin', *SJT* 42 (1989), pp. 67-84; Jonathan H. Rainbow, 'Double Grace: John Calvin's View of the Relationship of Justification and Sanctification', *Ex Auditu* 5 (1989), pp. 99-105; Craig B. Carpenter, 'A Question of Union with Christ? Calvin and Trent on Justification', *WTJ* 64 (2002), pp. 363-86.

[109] A salvation that is monergistic in nature does not entail absolute passivity on the part of the believer in every respect. While some aspects of the application of salvation (e.g., regeneration) may occur without any act on the part of the recipient, salvation as a whole may be conceived of as monergistic if its application to any particular individual is determined infallibly and unconditionally by God in eternity past and executed in time effectually, even though some aspects of salvation (e.g., sanctification) involve the believer's active participation. In this sense, even though Calvin predates the development of a full-fledged *ordo salutis* in his tradition, his soteriological doctrine is, on the whole, monergistic.

some gleanings from exegetical works.

INSTITUTES OF THE CHRISTIAN RELIGION

Although Calvin's section on justification in the *Institutes* underwent major developments in length and organization between 1536 and 1559, the basic theological substance of his doctrine remained intact from the beginning.[110] The 1536 edition sets the doctrine of justification against the background of the divine demand for perfect obedience. The law demands absolute perfection. To argue otherwise is to despise the righteousness of God.[111] Therefore, it is vain to trust that one's own works might serve as even a partial basis of justification. Nor can works of satisfaction and supererogation compensate for human weakness and thereby meet the standard of God's righteousness.[112] As Scripture testifies, whoever has broken the law at even one point is guilty of breaking the whole.[113] There is absolutely no hope for sinful humanity to attain righteousness by law. For this reason, justification must be sought, not from an

---

[110] In fact, in the 1536 edition there is no separate heading for justification, but the subject is treated under the heading of the law. In his translation of the 1536 edition, Battles identifies two sections that directly address the doctrine of justification, which total about eleven pages combined (John Calvin, *Institutes of the Christian Religion* [1536], revised ed., trans. Ford Lewis Battles [Grand Rapids: Eerdmans, 1986], pp. 29-35, 37-41). By contrast, the 1559 edition translated by Battles contains over one-hundred pages on the subject of justification (LCC 20, pp. 725-833).

[111] 'Also God's righteousness is despised where it is not recognized as such and so perfect, that nothing is accepted by him except what is whole and perfect, and uncorrupted of any filth. But if this is so, all our works, if judged by their own worth, are nothing but corruption and filth.' Calvin, *Institutes* [1536] 1.28 (trans. Battles), p. 31 (*OS* 1, p. 57).

[112] 'But we do not gabble about what many are accustomed today to boast of. After they have been compelled to confess that it is an impossibility for them to achieve perfect and ultimate righteousness through the merit of works, since they never fulfill the law, they indeed confess it. But lest they seem deprived of all glory, that is, to have yielded completely to God, they claim they have kept the law in part and are, in respect to this part, righteous. What is lacking they contend has been made up and redeemed by satisfactions and works of supererogation. They consider this to be compensation for their lack. Forgetfulness of their own true nature, contempt of God's justice and ignorance have plunged them into this error.' Calvin *Institutes* [1536] 1.27 (trans. Battles), p. 31 (*OS* 1, p. 56).

[113] 'Next, even if it were possible for us to have some wholly pure and righteous works, yet, as the prophet says, one sin is enough to wipe out and extinguish every memory of that previous righteousness [Ezek. 18:24]. James agrees with him: "Whoever," he says, "fails in one point, has become guilty of all" [James 2:10]. Now since this mortal life is never pure or devoid of sin, whatever righteousness we might attain [Prov. 24:16; 1 John 1:8], when it is corrupted, oppressed and destroyed by the sins that follow, could not come into God's sight or be reckoned to us as righteousness.' Calvin, *Institutes* [1536] 1.28 (trans. Battles), p. 32 (*OS* 1 p. 57).

infusion of grace that sends us back to the law better equipped, but rather completely apart from the law: 'The fact, then, remains that through the law the whole human race is proved subject to God's curse and wrath, and in order to be freed from these, it is necessary to depart from the power of the law and, as it were, to be released from its bondage into freedom.'[114] And lest one imagine that the exclusion of the law pertains only to an initial act of justification but not to the maintenance of one's right standing with God, Calvin rules out that possibility as well.[115] The extent of human depravity renders justification completely unattainable, from beginning to end, by the law. Instead, sinners must look elsewhere, to a perfect righteousness that is alien to them and is made theirs by faith:

> But Christ's righteousness, which alone can bear the sight of God because it alone is perfect, must appear in court on our behalf, and stand surety for us in judgment (Heb. 11:6; Rom. 8:34). Received from God, this righteousness is brought to us and imputed to us, just as if it were ours. Thus in faith we continually and constantly obtain forgiveness of sins.[116]

Thus it is the doctrine of the imputation of Christ's righteousness that meets the uncompromising standard of divine perfection, so that the sinner stands before God as if he has fulfilled the law in its entirety.

By 1559 Calvin's argument, now greatly expanded, follows much the same pattern.[117] Calvin acknowledges that there are two ways of righteousness, that is, two paths by which to obtain justification before God: the way of faith and the way of works.[118] Since the way of works entails perfection, and sin has rendered perfection unattainable, all people must seek righteousness by faith,

---

[114] Calvin, *Institutes* [1536] 1.30 (trans. Battles), p. 33 (*OS 1*, p. 58).

[115] 'But God does not, as many stupidly believe, once for all bestow on us this forgiveness of sins in order that, having obtained pardon for our past life, we may afterward seek righteousness in the law; this would be only to lead us into false hope, to laugh at us, and mock us. For since no perfection can come to us so long as we are clothed in this flesh, and the law moreover announces death and judgment to all who do not achieve perfect righteousness in works, it will always have grounds for accusing and condemning us unless, on the contrary, the Lord's mercy counters it, and by continual forgiveness of sins repeatedly acquits us.' Calvin, *Institutes* [1536] 1.30 (trans. Battles), p. 33 (*OS* 1, p. 59).

[116] Calvin, *Institutes* [1536] 1.32 (trans. Battles), p. 35 (*OS* 1, p. 61).

[117] See Wendel, *Calvin*, pp. 257-58 for a brief explanation of small developments that occurred in intervening editions of the *Institutes*.

[118] '[F]irst let us explain what these expressions mean: that man is justified in God's sight, and that he is justified by faith or works. He is said to be justified in God's sight who is both reckoned righteous in God's judgment and has been accepted on account of his righteousness.' John Calvin, *Institutes of the Christian Religion* [1559] 3.11.2, LCC 20, p. 726 (*OS* 4, p. 182).

and 'faith righteousness so differs from works righteousness that when one is established the other has to be overthrown'.[119] This claim stands in opposition, not to a doctrine of works-righteousness, but rather to the prevailing medieval doctrine of righteousness by a mixture of faith and works, where grace is the dominant note. Calvin's doctrine of justification, like those of Luther and Melanchthon, hinges on the absolute dichotomy between doing and receiving. Law and gospel, as pathways to justification, are mutually exclusive and cannot be blended together.

Echoing Melanchthon, Calvin defines justification as divine acceptation, consisting of the two components of the forgiveness of sins and the imputation of Christ's righteousness.[120] For Calvin, this divine reckoning is dependent on union with Christ, which results from faith.[121] Against Luther, Calvin does not speak of faith as righteousness but defines it rather as an empty vessel that receives Christ.[122] The phrase 'justification by faith' means that once the sinner has met the condition of faith (this in itself being a gift of divine grace), he is so joined to Christ that all of his sins are counted to Christ, and Christ's righteousness is counted to him. Union with Christ is, for Calvin, the soteriological reality that makes possible the application of his benefits to the believer:

---

[119] Calvin, *Institutes* [1559] 3.11.13, LCC 20, p. 743 (*OS* 4, p. 197).

[120] 'Therefore, we explain justification simply as the acceptance with which God receives us into his favor as righteous men. And we say that it consists in the remission of sins and the imputation of Christ's righteousness.' Calvin, *Institutes* [1559] 3.11.2, LCC 20, p. 727 (*OS* 4, p. 183).

[121] 'I confess that we are deprived of this utterly incomparable good until Christ is made ours. Therefore, that joining together of Head and members, that indwelling of Christ in our hearts—in short, that mystical union—are accorded by us the highest degree of importance, so that Christ, having been made ours, makes us sharers with him in the gifts with which he has been endowed. We do not, therefore, contemplate him outside ourselves from afar in order that his righteousness may be imputed to us but because we put on Christ and are engrafted into his body—in short, because he deigns to make us one with him.' Calvin, *Institutes* 3.11.10, LCC 20, p. 737 (*OS* 4, p. 191).   Brian J. Vickers (*Jesus' Blood and Righteousness: Paul's Theology of Imputation* [Wheaton: Crossway, 2006], p. 36) writes, 'In Calvin we find an example of how it is not a matter of *either* imputation *or* union, but that the two ideas work together. Christ's righteousness is imputed to the believer in the context of the believer's union with Christ.' Carpenter ('A Question of Union with Christ?') likewise notes the importance of union with Christ in Calvin's theology, but his extreme conclusions overreach the evidence.

[122] 'We compare faith to a kind of vessel; for unless we come empty and with the mouth of our soul open to seek Christ's grace, we are not capable of receiving Christ. From this it is to be inferred that, in teaching that before his righteousness is received Christ is received in faith, we do not take the power of justifying away from Christ.' Calvin, *Institutes* [1559] 3.11.7, LCC 20, p. 733 (*OS* 4, p. 188).

First, we must understand that as long as Christ remains outside of us, and we are separated from him, all that he has suffered and done for the salvation of the human race remains useless and of no value for us. Therefore, to share with us what he has received from the Father, he had to become ours and to dwell within us.[123]

Union with Christ and imputation do not stand at odds with one another. Rather, the imputation of Christ's righteousness to the believer represents the legal aspect of union with Christ. Calvin clearly distinguishes between the transformative and legal aspects of salvation, treating the former in chapters 1-10 of Book III of the *Institutes* and the latter in chapters 11-18. Nevertheless, both realities proceed from union with Christ.[124] Contra the claims of some, however, Calvin does not envision the legal and the transformative as two parallel branches growing side-by-side.[125] Rather, strong evidence suggests that, with regard to justification and sanctification (or, frequently, 'regeneration' in Calvin's terminology), Calvin ascribes logical (though not temporal) priority to justification, making the legal aspect of union with Christ the foundation for the believer's transformation. The beginning of Calvin's extended discussion on justification (*Institutes* 3.11-18) makes this logical and organic relationship between the benefits of union with Christ plain:

Christ was given to us by God's generosity, to be grasped and possessed by us in faith. By partaking of him, we principally receive a double grace: namely, that being reconciled to God through Christ's blamelessness, we may have in heaven instead of a Judge a gracious Father; and *secondly*, that sanctified by Christ's spirit we may cultivate blamelessness and purity of life. Of regeneration, indeed, the *second* of these gifts, I have said what seemed sufficient. The theme of justification was therefore more lightly touched upon [in Book II, chapters 16-17] because it was more to the point to understand first how little devoid of good works is the faith, through which alone we obtain free righteousness by the mercy of God; and what is the nature of the good works of the saints, with which

---

[123] Calvin, *Institutes* [1559] 3.1.1, LCC 20, p. 537.

[124] Although Calvin does not yet have his own 'Finnish School', there is some current debate about his doctrine of justification in relation to union with Christ. See, for example, Carpenter, 'A Question of Union with Christ?'; Hart, 'Humankind in Christ'; Thomas L. Wenger, 'The New Perspective on Calvin: Responding to Recent Calvin Interpretations', *JETS* 50, no. 2 (2007), pp. 311-28; Marcus Johnson, 'New or Nuanced Perspective on Calvin? A Reply to Thomas Wenger', *JETS* 51, no. 3 (2008), pp. 543-58; Thomas L. Wenger, 'Theological Spectacles and a Paradigm of Centrality: A Reply to Marcus Johnson', *JETS* 51, no. 3 (2008), pp. 559-72.

[125] So argues Wendel, *Calvin*, p. 257; Rainbow, 'Double Grace', p. 103. Wenger ('New Perspective') argues that such an interpretation of Calvin arises from an attempt to read Calvin through a paradigm of centrality while ignoring Calvin's own statements about the relationship between justification and sanctification.

part of this question is concerned. Therefore we must now discuss these matters thoroughly. And we must so discuss them as to bear in mind that this is *the main hinge on which religion turns*, so that we devote the greater attention and care to it. For unless you *first of all* grasp what your relationship to God is, and the nature of his judgment concerning you, you have neither a *foundation* on which to establish your salvation nor one on which to build piety toward God.[126]

Thus, while union with Christ is the source of a double grace that is both legal and transformative, Calvin has no trouble affirming an order of causation among distinguishable aspects of salvation.[127]

Chapter 11 of Book 3 of the 1559 *Institutes* is quite polemical in nature, taking aim at both Osiander and scholastic theology and refuting both for their synthesizing of law and gospel. First, Calvin argues that Osiander's doctrine of justification by the indwelling divine righteousness of Christ shatters the assurance of faith by making justification dependent on an imperfect righteousness that is essential to us.[128] Given the law's requirement for perfection, it is impossible that moral regeneration can become the legal basis for righteousness before God. Second, Calvin rejects the error of the 'sophists' and the 'Schoolmen' that attributes righteousness before God in some measure

---

[126] Calvin, *Institutes* 3.11.1, LCC 20, pp. 725-26, emphasis added. Johnson ('New or Nuanced Perspective?', p. 553) asks why Calvin would lightly touch upon justification (2.16-17), discuss sanctification in full (3.1-10), and then return to a full treatment of justification (3.11-18) if justification held a place of logical priority for him. The answer appears to be in Calvin's own words quoted above. In the context of discussing faith, 'it was more to the point to understand first how little devoid of good works is the faith, through which alone we obtain free righteousness by the mercy of God'. In other words, Calvin treats sanctification in full first because it naturally complements his prior discussion of faith and heads off any charge that his gospel is antinomian in character. It has nothing to do with an indifference on his part to the logical order of these benefits in salvation.

[127] Bruce McCormack ('What's at Stake in Current Debates over Justification? The Crisis of Protestantism in the West' in Mark Husbands and Daniel J. Treier [eds], *Justification: What's at Stake in the Current Debates* [Downers Grove, IL: IVP, 2004], pp. 100-01), Pierre Marcel ('Justification and Sanctification', pp. 133-34), and Thomas Wenger ('The New Perspective on Calvin', pp. 321-25) all discern a logical priority for justification in Calvin's thought. Wenger adds the additional argument that Calvin's doctrine of double justification—justification of believers and of their works (discussed below)—clearly indicates a logical order between legal standing in Christ and holiness in the believer, such that the believer's legal standing in union with Christ is the foundation of his or her transformation in union with Christ

[128] 'No portion of righteousness sets our consciences at peace until it has been determined that we are pleasing to God, because we are entirely righteous before him.' Calvin, *Institutes* [1559] 3.11.11, LCC 20, p. 739 (*OS* 4, p. 194).

to meritorious works.[129] He responds with an anthropological argument: 'Now we confess with Paul that the doers of the law are justified before God; but, because we are all far from observing the law, we infer from this that those works which ought especially to avail for righteousness give us no help because we are destitute of them.'[130] This error represents 'a sort of Pelagianism', not identical to the universally condemned heresy, but akin to it in its corruption of the gospel. Even Augustine does not escape this section unscathed, for though Calvin approves of Augustine's attribution of all credit for salvation to divine grace, the revered Western father does not articulate a doctrine of alien righteousness.[131]

Thus, Calvin's discussion of justification in his greatest theological work revolves around the question of what God demands of us and how that demand may be met. Because God demands perfection, and we are incapable of providing it, we must receive, in union with Christ by faith, the perfect righteousness of Jesus Christ counted to us. In the 1559 edition the discussion of justification takes place within a context in which Calvin has already affirmed a monergistic soteriology,[132] though he has not yet addressed the doctrine of election itself.[133] His doctrine of alien righteousness fits neatly into this monergistic context, even if the question of free will and the effectiveness of grace does not come into view often in the course of discussing justification. The two issues—monergism and alien righteousness—become intermingled more often in some of Calvin's polemical treatises, to which this study will

---

[129] Calvin, *Institutes* [1559] 3.11.14-15, LCC 20, pp. 744-45. The 'Schoolmen' are referred to in the 1560 French edition as 'les theologiens Sorboniques'.

[130] Calvin, *Institutes* [1559] 3.11.15 (LCC 20, p. 745).

[131] 'The schools have gone continually from bad to worse until, in headlong ruin, they have plunged into a sort of Pelagianism. For that matter, Augustine's view, or at any rate his manner of stating it, we must not entirely accept. For even though he admirably deprives man of all credit for righteousness and transfers it to God's grace, he still subsumes grace under sanctification, by which we are reborn in newness of life through the Spirit.' Calvin, *Institutes* [1559] 3.11.15, LCC 20, pp. 745-46 (*OS 4*, pp. 199-200). This observation strongly confirms the thesis of this study, demonstrating that alien righteousness is the central dividing line between the Reformers and Rome. Without question, Calvin saw very significant differences between Augustine and the 'Schoolmen' of his day. Nevertheless, that he felt the need to criticize both along similar lines in the exposition of his doctrine of justification indicates that there was at least some major continuity that ran from Augustine, through the Middle Ages, and into the Reformation period among Catholic theologians.

[132] Calvin, *Institutes* 2.4 (LCC 20, pp. 309-16).

[133] Calvin treats the doctrine of election in 3.21-24 (LCC 21, pp. 920-87). Richard A. Muller (*The Unaccommodated Calvin: Studies in the Foundation of a Theological Tradition* [New York: Oxford University Press, 2001], pp. 118-39) demonstrates that Calvin's arrangement of topics intentionally follows Melanchthon's *Loci Communes*, which in turn was based on the order that Melanchthon perceived in Paul's letter to the Romans.

now turn.

POLEMICAL WORKS

Calvin's polemical treatises are especially helpful in the present study because they indicate sharply the primary points at which he conceived his own views to differ from those of his contemporary opponents. Therefore, they shine helpful light on the precise categories that define the Protestant doctrine of justification over against Rome.[134] Three particular works are worthy of investigation here: Calvin's 'Reply to Sadoleto', his reply to articles drawn up by the theological faculty of Paris, and his *Acts of the Council of Trent, with the Antidote.*

In March of 1539, after Calvin's dismissal from Geneva, Cardinal Jacopo Sadoleto wrote to the city's magistrates and citizens, inviting them to return to Rome. In this letter, he argues, 'we obtain this blessing of complete and perpetual salvation by faith alone in God and in Jesus Christ'. However, he immediately goes on to explain that this faith is not 'a mere credulity and confidence in God' that one's sins have been forgiven by the work of Christ. This kind of faith may be the beginning of justification, but 'we must also bring a mind full of piety towards Almighty God, and desirous of performing whatever is agreeable to him'. Ultimately, Sadoleto affirms that 'in this very faith love is essentially comprehended as the chief and primary cause of our salvation'.[135] He also briefly discusses lapses into sin, arguing that they are covered by 'whatever expiations, penances, and satisfactions, she [the Church] tells us that our sin is washed away, and we (always by the grace and mercy of God) restored to our former integrity, these methods of expiation and satisfaction we have recourse to employ—trusting, when we do so, to find a place of mercy and pardon with God'.[136] Clearly, Sadoleto affirms the necessity of grace and faith in justification, and he calls upon his audience to entrust themselves to the mercy of God. Yet he does so within a synergistic framework that places emphasis on one's inherent righteousness.

Calvin viewed Sadoleto's appeal as a spiritual danger to the people of Geneva, and in spite of his recent dismissal from the city, he published a response to Sadoleto in August of 1539 in order to protect those who had been (and would soon be again) his flock. In his polemical treatises he never argues that his Roman Catholic opponents misunderstand justification by basing it entirely on works as opposed to grace. Instead, he argues that they misunderstand the true nature of grace and mix together two mutually exclusive

---

[134] They also demonstrate the strong continuity between Calvin's contemporary opponents and the scholastic tradition, surveyed in the previous chapter, that preceded them.

[135] Jacopo Sadoleto, 'Letter to the Genevans', in John C. Olin (ed), *A Reformation Debate* (Grand Rapids: Baker, 2002), pp. 35-36 (*OS* 1, p. 447).

[136] Sadoleto, 'Letter to the Genevans', p. 37.

principles: the righteousness of faith and the righteousness of works. Addressing justification in his response to Sadoleto, he argues, first, that the law pronounces all people guilty, humbles them, and casts away all self-confidence, so that sinners can find 'the only haven of safety' in God's mercy.[137] The only hope for sinners is the righteousness of Jesus Christ:

> As all mankind are, in the sight of God, lost sinners, we hold that Christ is their only righteousness, since, by his obedience, he has wiped off our transgressions; by his sacrifice, appeased the divine anger; by his blood, washed away our stains; by his cross, borne our curse; and by his death, made satisfaction for us. We maintain that in this way man is reconciled in Christ to God the Father, by no merit of his own, by no value of works, but by gratuitous mercy. When we embrace Christ by faith, and come, as it were, into communion with him, this we term, after the manner of Scripture, the righteousness of faith.[138]

Calvin does not use the language of imputation here, but the concept is unmistakable, rooted in the sinner's faith-embrace of Christ, which establishes a union that entails imputation. He then goes on to explain how works relate to justification. Works have no basis in the justification of the sinner, which is based solely on the free imputation of righteousness, as evidenced by the meaning of the word 'justify' in Scripture.[139] However, good works are the evidence of justification and always accompany it because, wherever Christ is, there his Spirit is as well; whoever has taken hold of Christ by faith for justification has also been regenerated by the work of the Holy Spirit. Justification and sanctification may be distinguished, but never separated.[140]

In 1543 the theological faculty of the Sorbonne published twenty-five articles rejecting Reformation teachings as a means of defending the university from heresy. This document carried the weight of the endorsement of King Francis I.[141] In 1544 Calvin published a response to these articles. This work, entitled *Articles Agreed upon by the Faculty of Sacred Theology of Paris: With the Antidote*, walks through each article in a three-step manner. First, Calvin quotes the article in its entirety. Second, he includes a section entitled 'Proof'

---

[137] John Calvin, 'Reply to Sadoleto', in John C. Olin (ed), *A Reformation Debate* (Grand Rapids: Backer, 2002), p. 66.

[138] Calvin, 'Reply to Sadoleto', p. 67 (*OS* 1, p. 469).

[139] '[I]f you would attend to the true meaning of the term *justifying* in Scripture, you would have no difficulty. For it does not refer to a man's own righteousness, but to the mercy of God, which contrary to the sinner's deserts, accepts of a righteousness for him, and that by not imputing his unrighteousness.' Calvin, 'Reply to Sadoleto, p. 67 (*OS* 1, p. 470).

[140] Calvin, 'Reply to Sadoleto', p. 68; cf. Rainbow, 'Double Grace', pp. 102-03; Marcel, 'Justification and Sanctification', pp. 132-45.

[141] Wulfert De Greef, *The Writings of John Calvin: An Introductory Guide*, expanded ed. (Louisville: Westminster John Knox, 2008), p. 146.

for each article, a section in which he impersonates his opponents and constructs absurd proofs for their arguments, employing irony as an argument against them. Finally, he responds with his own 'Antidote' to each article. In his antidote to an article concerning free will, Calvin clearly affirms human inability and a corresponding monergistic doctrine of salvation:

> [W]e again conclude with Augustine, that the children of God are actuated by his Spirit to do whatever is to be done. Also, that they are drawn by him, so as out of unwilling to be made willing. Also, that since the fall it is owing only to the grace of God that man draws near to him, and that it is owing only to the same grace that he does not recede from him.[142]

When he comes to address the doctrine of justification directly, particularly the claim by the faculty that justification is based on faith and good works, Calvin's 'Proof' section indicates the bicovenantal theology that drives his doctrine of justification by the imputation of Christ's righteousness. Impersonating his opponents in order to expose their elevation of philosophy above Scripture, Calvin writes the following:

> First, by a philosophic reason; righteousness is a quality, and therefore no man is righteous out of himself, but on account of the quality of his works. Again, the ratio of part to part is the same as that of whole to whole. But perfect obedience of the law is righteousness. Therefore, partial obedience is a portion of righteousness. But when the Lutherans place the righteousness of faith in the predicament of a relation, saying that we are righteous merely because God accepts us in Christ, according to what Paul teaches the Ephesians, they act contrary to the whole system of philosophy. Again, when they deny that the principle of proportion between the whole and the part applies to this subject, because God promises the reward to none but those who fulfil his law, pronouncing those cursed who offend in any one point, I answer, that one who denies first principles is not to be argued with.[143]

The antidote that immediately follows this section brings forth numerous Pauline statements that separate the righteousness of faith from works and the law (Rom. 3:21-23; 4:4-7, 14, 16; Eph. 2:8-9), further affirming Calvin's bicovenantal framework. Of course, Calvin's opponents were well aware of these passages, but they harmonized them with their own theology by interpreting them in reference to the ceremonial law only. This hermeneutical

---

[142] John Calvin, *Articles Agreed Upon by the Faculty of Sacred Theology of Paris in Reference to Matters of Faith at Present Controverted; with The Antidote*, in Thomas F. Torrance (ed), *Tracts and Treatises on the Reformation of the Church* (Grand Rapids: Eerdmans, 1958) 1, p. 77.

[143] Calvin, *Articles of the Faculty of Paris*, p. 80.

move is virtually identical to the new perspective's identification of 'works of the law' with ceremonial boundary markers. Calvin responds to this interpretation with further exegetical comments and then concludes the section by affirming that all glory belongs to God in justification; humanity has no grounds whatsoever for boasting, for human works form no part of our righteousness before God.[144]

The Council of Trent's decree on justification was discussed in the previous chapter. Calvin published a response to this decree in 1547 entitled *Acts of the Council of Trent: With Antidote*.[145] In his response, Calvin first expresses disdain toward Trent's anthropology. The Council erred in assigning some power to the free will of fallen humanity to choose good. By contrast, Calvin affirms on the basis of Paul's teaching that the will 'is not only prone to sin, but it is made subject to sin'.[146] This argument paves the way for Calvin's affirmation of a monergistic soteriology. Because the human will is completely enslaved to sin, no person can contribute anything to salvation from himself; salvation is ultimately and entirely God's work. God's grace is effectual in transforming the will: 'Scripture . . . makes God the author of a good will.'[147]

Next Calvin addresses justification directly. Responding to the seventh chapter of the decree,[148] Calvin criticizes Trent for confusing justification with sanctification. He argues on the basis of Romans 4:6 and 2 Corinthians 5:19 that justification consists of the forgiveness of sins but not inward transformation. Justification and sanctification belong together, just like the light and heat of the sun, but they are not the same thing.[149] To confuse them is

---

[144] Calvin, *Articles of the Faculty of Paris*, p. 82.

[145] For a discussion of the Council of Trent on justification and Calvin's response to it, see Carpenter; Theodore W. Casteel, 'Calvin and Trent: Calvin's Reaction to the Council of Trent in the Context of His Conciliar Thought', *Harvard Theological Review* 63 (1970), pp. 91-117.

[146] John Calvin, *Acts of the Council of Trent, with the Antidote*, in Thomas F. Torrance (ed), *Tracts and Treatises on the Reformation of the Church* (Grand Rapids: Eerdmans, 1958) 3, p. 109.

[147] Calvin, *Acts of the Council of Trent*, p. 111.

[148] Because Calvin regarded the introduction to the decree as the first chapter, his references to Trent's chapter numbers are always one number higher than the actual chapter numbers of the decree. References to chapter numbers in this section do not correspond to Calvin's numbering system but to the actual chapter numbers of Trent's decree.

[149] Calvin was fond of the metaphor of light and heat to refer to the legitimate distinction between justification and sanctification without implying that they are ever separated. He employs this metaphor against Chapter 7 of Trent's decree and against Canon 11. See Calvin, *Acts of the Council of Trent*, pp. 116, 152. The latter reference reads, 'It is therefore faith alone which justifies, and yet the faith which justifies is not alone: just as it is the heat alone of the sun which warms the earth, and yet in the sun it is not alone, because it is constantly joined with light.' He uses the same metaphor against Osiander in *Institutes* [1559] 3.11.6, LCC 20, pp. 731-33.

to bring one's own righteousness into justification and thereby mix the righteousness of faith with the righteousness of works:

> The whole dispute is as to The Cause of Justification. The Fathers of Trent pretend that it is twofold, as if we were justified partly by forgiveness of sins and partly by spiritual regeneration; or, to express their view in other words, as if our righteousness were composed partly of imputation, partly of quality. I maintain that it is one, and simple, and is wholly included in the gratuitous acceptance of God. I besides hold that it is without [outside] us, because we are righteous in Christ only.[150]

In this passage forgiveness of sins is basically equated with imputation, although Calvin does distinguish the two concepts elsewhere.[151] Their equation here is probably owing to the fact that both concepts are forensic as opposed to regenerative, and Paul's argument in Romans 4:6-8 (a passage Calvin had recently quoted) basically equates the two. Furthermore, in the last sentence Calvin beautifully expresses the concept of alien righteousness ('without us') in connection with union with Christ ('because we are righteous in Christ only'), thereby guarding against any distortion of the gospel through the mixing of faith and works or the partitioning of justification to Christ's objective work and our own inherent righteousness.

With regard to the continual aspect of justification, Calvin responds to chapter 8 by arguing 'that the completion, not less than the commencement of justification, must be ascribed to faith'.[152] This comes in response to the Council's teaching that faith begins justification but does not complete it. In this way, the Council supposed that it could affirm the Pauline teaching that justification is by faith and not by works by relegating those particular passages to the beginning of justification. Calvin will have none of it, arguing instead that justification is, from beginning to end, by faith alone; there can be no mixing of faith and works as the ground of one's righteousness before God. In response to the teaching that justification increases through faith and good works (Chapter 10), Calvin again affirms imputation as the sole basis of righteousness. Here he also introduces the idea of double justification, which signifies the justification of both a person and that person's works: 'In short, I affirm, that not by our own merit but by faith alone, are both our persons and works justified; and that the justification of works depends on the justification of the person, as the effect on the cause.'[153] In Calvin's thought, the justification

---

[150] Calvin, *Acts of the Council of Trent*, p. 116 (CR 35, p. 448).
[151] Calvin, *Institutes* [1559] 3.11.2, LCC 20, pp. 725-27.
[152] Calvin, *Acts of the Council of Trent*, p. 122; see also *Institutes* [1559] 3.14, a chapter entitled, 'The Beginning of Justification and Its Continual Progress', LCC 20, pp. 768-88.
[153] Calvin, *Acts of the Council of Trent*, p. 128 (CR 35, p. 458).

of a believer's good works rests not on their own intrinsic worth but on the believer's connection to Christ.[154]

In response to chapter 14, Calvin vehemently denies any scriptural basis for the sacrament of penance. Not only is it a mere human decree, he argues, it is one that detracts from the sufficiency of Christ: 'They lay upon me the burden of satisfaction, ordering me to provide at my own hand that which Christ shews me is to be sought from his blood alone.'[155] While much more could be said about Calvin's response to Trent, the basic contours of his thought have been outlined here: (1) a monergistic soteriology in response to Trent's faulty anthropology and (2) the imputation of Christ's righteousness as the sole basis of justification from beginning to end in response to Trent's doctrine of inherent righteousness obtained through a process of divine-human cooperation. The second point, driven by a bicovenantal theology, makes best sense within the wider framework of the first.

EXEGETICAL WORKS

Because Calvin reserved theological disputations primarily for the *Institutes*, his commentaries focus much more on verse-by-verse exposition and show restraint when it comes to polemics.[156] However, on occasion he does interact with theological opponents in the commentaries. Commenting on Paul's statement that no one will be justified by the law (Rom 3:20), Calvin argues that to be a sinner is to be deprived of righteousness altogether. This means that it is frivolous 'to invent, as the sophists do, a half-righteousness, so that works in part may justify'.[157] He further expounds this view of his opponents in his comments on verse 21, where Paul writes of 'the righteousness of God' that is revealed apart from the law. He argues that they have illegitimately mixed the righteousness of faith with the righteousness of works. To pursue righteousness by faith means to pursue it by faith alone. Although he does not specifically mention the imputation of Christ's righteousness in this section, he clearly alludes to the concept when he writes, 'We are, therefore, *in Christ*, because we

---

[154] 'Therefore, as we ourselves, when we have been engrafted in Christ, are righteous in God's sight because our iniquities are covered by Christ's sinlessness, so our works are righteous and are thus regarded because whatever fault is otherwise in them is buried in Christ's purity, and is not charged to our account.' Calvin, *Institutes* 3.17.10, LCC 20, p. 813.

[155] Calvin, *Acts of the Council of Trent*, p. 139.

[156] On Calvin's methodological aims for the *Institutes* and his commentaries, see Muller, *The Unaccommodated Calvin*, pp. 118-58.

[157] John Calvin, *The Epistles of Paul the Apostle to the Romans and to the Thessalonians*, Calvin's Commentaries (ed. David W. Torrance and Thomas F. Torrance; Grand Rapids: Eerdmans, 1961), p. 70; cf. Calvin's treatment of Romans 3:28 in *Romans*, p. 79. See H. Paul Santmire, 'Justification in Calvin's 1540 Romans Commentary', *Church History* 33 (1964), pp. 294-313, for a discussion of this subject.

are out of ourselves.'[158] To seek justification by faith is, for Calvin, to go outside of oneself to the alien righteousness of Christ, which is possessed by being 'in Christ'. Having gone out of oneself, it is illegitimate to seek to return to the law, to human effort, to human righteousness, as even a partial basis of justification.

Calvin's comments on 2 Corinthians 5:19 further illumine his understanding of justification. Here he accuses the 'Papists' of misunderstanding Paul's statement that God has committed to ministers of the gospel the ministry of reconciliation. They regard it as 'a pretext to provide some shadow of warrant for the altogether ungodly and execrable traffic they conduct over the salvation of souls'. More specifically, 'the Papists . . . shut up the forgiveness of sins in lead or marble statues or connect it with fictitious and frivolous superstitions'. The various Roman ceremonies, including the sacrament of penance, are probably here in view, although a reference to indulgences may not be far from Calvin's mind. He then adds, 'Beware of placing any confidence at all in anything but the Gospel.'[159] Here he does not attack the claim that justification is based partly on good works in fulfillment of the moral law but the claim that it is based on anything other than Christ alone. The whole Roman system of absolution was predicated on the idea of grace, specifically, the grace that forgives sins. However, this grace was perverted because it led sinners to place their faith in something other than Christ. For Calvin, justification by faith alone answers not only the heresy of merit theology; it answers any system of salvation that denies the sufficiency of Christ and directs sinners to look elsewhere, no matter how full of grace that system may be. Ultimately, Calvin envisions no significant distinction between the attempt to be justified partly on the basis of good works or partly on the basis of fulfillment of certain ceremonial requirements. Both ideas detract from the glory of Christ and ultimately reduce to a form of justification by works.

Calvin makes a similar argument in his comments on Galatians 2:15. Again he is at pains to deny that Paul's polemic against 'works of the law' pertains only to Jewish ceremonies and not to good works in general. He grants that Paul's particular focus in Galatians is the ceremonial aspects of the Jewish law, but he argues that even ceremonial observances can lead one away from Christ and thereby threaten justification by faith alone. He draws a parallel between the ceremonial observances Paul argued against in Galatians with those of the Roman Catholic Church:

> Paul was worried not so much about ceremonies being observed as that the confidence and glory of salvation should be transferred to works. Just as, in the

---

[158] Calvin *Romans*, p. 72.

[159] John Calvin, *The Second Epistle of Paul the Apostle to the Corinthians and the Epistles to Timothy, Titus, and Philemon*, Calvin's Commentaries (ed. David W. Torrance and Thomas F. Torrance; Grand Rapids: Eerdmans, 1964), p. 79.

dispute over forbidding flesh [meat] on certain days, we do not so much regard the importance of the prohibition itself as the snare which is set for consciences. Paul therefore is not wandering from the point when he begins a disputation on the law as a whole, whereas the false apostles were arguing only about ceremonies.[160]

Further down he makes explicit his 'all or nothing' view of justification: 'we cannot be justified through the righteousness of Christ unless we are poor and destitute of our own righteousness. Consequently, we have to ascribe either nothing or everything to faith or to works.'[161] Calvin engages his Catholic opponents in other significant passages pertaining to justification, including Ephesians 2:8-9, Philippians 3:9, and Titus 3:5.[162] However, the main substance of his polemic and its implications for the doctrine of justification has been given here.

SUMMARY: CALVIN'S DOCTRINE OF JUSTIFICATION

Calvin unfolds his doctrine of justification consistently in opposition to the Roman Catholic doctrine of faith and works as a joint basis for righteousness, a mixing together of law and gospel. Affirming that the law demands perfection and that perfection is out of the reach of Adamic humanity, Calvin argues that works can be no part of the legal basis of right standing with God. Instead, sinners can only be declared righteous before God on the basis of the imputed righteousness of Christ, which is given to those in union with Christ by faith. Faith in itself is intrinsically nothing; it is an empty vessel that receives Christ, who alone is the sinner's righteousness. Alien righteousness, therefore, is the heart of Calvin's doctrine, situated aptly within a wider monergistic soteriology.

Conclusion

Surveying the theological landscape of the sixteenth-century Catholic Church, Luther, Melanchthon, and Calvin did not observe rampant Pelagianism; they did not articulate the doctrine of justification by faith as a foil to Pelagianism, properly defined. The Catholic Church did not proclaim that unaided human ability could keep the law of God and so attain righteousness by works. Its soteriology was rooted in grace, as was demonstrated in the previous chapter.

---

[160] John Calvin, *The Epistles of Paul the Apostle to the Galatians, Ephesians, Philippians and Colossians*, Calvin's Commentaries (ed. David W. Torrance and Thomas F. Torrance; Grand Rapids: Eerdmans, 1965), p. 39. See also idem, *Sermons on Galatians* (Audobon, NJ: Old Paths, 1995), 218-40.

[161] Calvin, *Galatians*, pp. 39-40.

[162] Calvin, *Galatians*, pp. 144-45, 274-75; idem, *Second Corinthians, Timothy, Titus, and Philemon*, pp. 381-82.

What the Reformers encountered was a grace-based, monocovenantal soteriology where the purpose of grace is to provide necessary assistance for the keeping of the law, at least in a satisfactory manner. Those who were justified by grace were infused with the ability to merit eternal life, if they cooperated with grace and availed themselves of the gracious provisions of the sacraments (particularly penance) when necessary. Final salvation was indeed a reward for works, but the whole scheme took place within a gracious, though law-driven, framework.

The Reformers responded to this soteriological pattern with a bicovenantal theology. By distinguishing between the law and the gospel, they affirmed that reliance on the law and works must be completely renounced, and the sinner must in turn fully rely on Jesus Christ. Any measure of reliance on the law is ineffective, for the law demands absolute perfection, which is out of the reach of sinful humanity. Rather than misplacing one's hope in the law and works (even if only in part), the Reformers argued that only the righteousness of Christ is sufficient to grant sinners right standing before God. Therefore, the gospel requires abandoning all trust in the law for justification. To attribute righteousness to both grace and works is to nullify the sufficiency of Christ's atoning work and to put one's hope in something other than the gospel.

Theologically, the Reformation doctrine of justification can be traced back to a conflict in understanding over the nature of God and what he requires. Catholic theologians were by no means unified on this question, but that they did not share the Reformers' adherence to perfection as the divine demand is evident. Merit theology, whether that of the Thomist or Scotist variety, ultimately conflicts with the view of God held by the Reformers, namely, a view that regards his holy transcendence so highly that nothing short of perfection can be received into his favor. For the Reformers, God's righteousness cannot be accommodated to the weakness of man in justification, nor can it be subjected to the compromised standard of the slogan 'To those who do what is in them, God will not deny grace' (*Facientibus quod in se est Deus non denegat gratiam*). Righteousness before God may only be received as it is counted on the basis of the obedience of the one who has attained perfection, Jesus Christ. And so the bicovenantal theology of the Reformers safeguards the integrity of both the law and the gospel by maintaining both the uncompromising standard of divine demand and the corresponding glory of the gift of God given through his Son in the gospel to those who are unworthy of his grace.

It should be evident at this point how this historical-theological observation intersects with the new perspective on Paul. The hermeneutical presupposition that has arisen in the wake of Sanders' *Paul and Palestinian Judaism* assumes that a grace-based soteriology cannot serve as a foil to the Reformation doctrine of *sola fide*. As some have argued, Paul must be freed from the Lutheran shackles imposed on him during the sixteenth century in order to read his polemic appropriately, and that means avoiding the conclusion that his polemic has much, or even anything, to do with legalism. If anything has been proven in these last two chapters, it is that a grace-based soteriology, namely, that of the late medieval Catholic Church, serves quite well as a foil to the Reformation doctrine of *sola fide*. The reason for this is because the Reformation doctrine is predicated, not on the antithesis of salvation by grace and salvation by works, but rather on the bicovenantal distinction between law and gospel and the monocovenantal synthesis of the two. Sanders' Judaism, whatever its merits may or may not be in terms of historical analysis, simply does not alter the categories of this debate. Monocovenantalism remains fully intact once Sanders' covenantal nomism is expounded. For Sanders, first-century Jews may not have attempted to earn salvation by good works, but they certainly maintained that adherence to the law was necessary to remain in the covenant and that one's faithfulness to the law was at least partly determinative of one's standing at the final judgment. That Paul could have opposed this teaching with a bicovenantal doctrine of justification is entirely conceivable and should not be ruled out *a priori*. In fact, exegetical arguments will be presented in Chapter 5 indicating that Paul argued in precisely this kind of way. But before these arguments are presented, it is necessary to conclude this historical survey by noting some theological developments that pertain to the doctrine of justification in the post-Reformation period.

CHAPTER 4

Justification in the Post-Reformation Period

The previous chapter has established that the Reformation doctrine of justification stands opposed to that of Rome because of its adherence to a divine demand for perfect obedience, its bicovenantal structure, and its corresponding doctrine of alien righteousness. The present chapter will demonstrate that post-Reformation theology[1] retained the same themes and, in some cases, refined and nuanced them, thereby giving shape to the historic Protestant doctrine of justification.[2] The goal of this chapter is not to provide a detailed survey of any particular theologian's work. It is, rather, to trace the three previously mentioned themes in a representative sample of confessions and theologians of the post-Reformation period. Because the 'old perspective'

---

[1] A number of confessions of faith have been chosen as representative samples of historic Protestant teaching on the doctrine of justification because of their value in assessing, not merely the views of an individual, but of an entire tradition. In addition, some prominent theologians of the post-Reformation period are consulted as well for the following reasons: first, in order to broaden the scope of the survey and further confirm the presentation of the historic Protestant doctrine that I aim to set forth here; second, in order to probe deeper into theological issues that are typically not addressed in confessions due to their brevity. While the Lutheran and Reformed streams of Protestantism did not develop identical doctrines of justification, there is sufficient overlap between them to speak in broad terms of one single, historic Protestant doctrine of justification, namely, justification by the imputation of Christ's righteousness through faith. Aspects that are unique to the Reformed tradition will be noted in the discussion below.

[2] As will be demonstrated below, the most significant theological developments to the doctrine of justification during this period pertain to the rise of covenant theology among the Reformed, on which see Alister E. McGrath, *Iustitia Dei: A History of the Christian Doctrine of Justification*, 3rd ed. (New York: Cambridge University Press, 2005), pp. 265-77; William Klempa, 'The Concept of the Covenant in Sixteenth- and Seventeenth-Century Continental and British Reformed Theology', in Donald K. McKim (ed), *Major Themes in the Reformed Tradition* (Grand Rapids: Eerdmans, 1992), 94-107; J. Mark Beach, *Christ and the Covenant: Francis Turretin's Federal Theology as a Defense of the Doctrine of Grace* (Göttingen: Vandenhoeck and Ruprecht, 2007). For more general discussions of justification during this time period, see G.C. Berkouwer, 'Justification by Faith in the Reformed Confessions', trans. Lewis B. Smedes, *Major Themes in the Reformed Tradition*, pp. 132-41.

on Paul encompasses both the theology of the historic Lutheran and Reformed traditions, confessions and theologians of these two traditions will be treated together.

The Demand for Perfect Obedience

As the previous chapter has demonstrated, the doctrine of justification cannot be abstracted from the doctrine of God. What is the nature of God's righteousness? Is it such that he will condescend to the weakness of sinners and allow them to merit eternal life by grace through an imperfect, yet ever-increasing obedience? Or is God's standard one of immutable perfection, requiring full vicarious satisfaction for those who have fallen short? The Reformers clearly advocated the latter, which had major implications for their doctrine of justification, transferring the locus of righteousness from inside the sinner (who could never, by a perfect standard, measure up) to the alien righteousness of Jesus Christ. Post-Reformation theologians followed the lead of their predecessors by insisting on the same divine standard of perfection. Without a perfect righteousness, there can be no justification.

Justification cannot have a partial basis in good works because all good works performed by fallen human beings are stained with sin and are, therefore, imperfect and in violation of the divine standard. So argues Zacharias Ursinus (1534-1583) in both the *Heidelberg Catechism* and in his *Commentary on the Heidelberg Catechism*, the latter of which contains the following statement:

> We must now refute the false doctrine of the Papists, according to which we are justified by works; or partly by faith, and partly by works. This is the argument which we employ; It is necessary that that righteousness which will stand in the judgment of God must be absolutely perfect, and conformable to the law in every respect. But our best works in this life are imperfect, and defiled with sin. Therefore our best works cannot be the whole, nor even a part of our righteousness before God.[3]

Significantly, Ursinus opposes his own Reformed view not only to a doctrine of justification by works but also to a doctrine that blends faith and works into a

---

[3] Zacharias Ursinus, *Commentary on the Heidelberg Catechism* 62 (trans. G.W. Williard; Grand Rapids: Eerdmans, 1954), p. 333. Question 62 of the catechism reads, 'But why cannot our good works be our righteousness before God, or at least a part of it?' The answer reads, 'Because the righteousness which can stand before the judgment of God must be absolutely perfect and wholly in conformity with the divine law. But even our best works in this life are all imperfect and defiled with sin.' *The Heidelberg Catechism* (1563), in Jaroslav Pelikan and Valerie Hotchkiss (eds), *Creeds and Confessions of Faith in the Christian Tradition* (New Haven, CT: Yale University Press, 2003), 2, p. 441.

monocovenantal scheme, and he does so precisely because the divine demand
for perfection cannot cohere with either doctrine. If perfect obedience is the
standard, it matters little whether one seeks justification by works or by some
combination of faith and works. In either case, the standard of perfection
cannot be met, and so the grace-based soteriology of Rome remains a suitable
foil for the theology of the post-Reformation.

The great Lutheran theologian Martin Chemnitz (1522-1586) likewise
affirms the demand for perfect obedience, expounding the doctrine of
justification in connection with God's unchanging character:

> But God has revealed His will in the Law, and this cannot be annulled. For it is
> easier for heaven and earth to pass away than for the least jot or tittle of the Law
> to be done away with so that it is not fulfilled.
>
> Therefore, in keeping with His revealed will, God does not will to justify a
> person without righteousness, that is, not unless satisfaction has been made for
> sin in keeping with the Law and unless the Law has been fulfilled by perfect
> obedience. . . . But God has set forth His Son as our Mediator, made under the
> Law, for which He has made satisfaction both by bearing our sins and by His
> perfect obedience.[4]

Elsewhere he writes the following:

> We do not teach that God out of some kind of capriciousness without any basis
> imputes righteousness to believers, but we affirm from the Word of God that
> there must be the firm, solid, entirely pure, and totally complete and perfect
> foundation of the free imputation, so that even the righteousness which dwelt in
> Abraham and David cannot be the foundation of this relationship and
> imputation. . . . But it was necessary that the Son of God become incarnate and
> be 'born under the Law' in order that His completely pure satisfaction and
> perfect obedience might be the firm, solid, and immovable 'basis' of this
> imputation.[5]

Chemnitz's denial of a divine capriciousness represents a denial of any kind of
voluntarist theology that would divorce God's justifying verdict from his

---

[4] Martin Chemnitz, *Justification: The Chief Article of Christian Doctrine as Expounded
in* Loci Theologi, (trans. J.A.O. Preus, ed. Delpha Holleque Preus; St. Louis: Concordia,
1985); see also idem, *Examination of the Council of Trent* 1.8-9 in Eric Lund (ed),
Documents from the History of Lutheranism 1517-1750 (Minneapolis: Fortress, 2002),
pp. 232-34.   On justification in Lutheran orthodoxy, see Robert D. Preus, 'The
Justification of a Sinner before God as Taught in Later Lutheran Orthodoxy', in Klemet
I. Preus (ed), *Doctrine Is Life: Essays on Justification and the Lutheran Confessions* (St.
Louis: Concordia, 2006), pp. 39-53; idem, 'The Doctrine of Justification in the
Theology of Classical Lutheran Orthodoxy', in *Doctrine Is Life*, pp. 79-96.
[5] Chemnitz, *Justification*, p. 86.

immutably holy character. The affirmation of the necessity for perfect obedience thereby fortifies his position against the charge of a legal fiction, an arbitrary decree of God that is completely disconnected from reality. Instead, God's decree of justification is based on the perfect obedience of Christ imputed to the believer.

The Synod of Dort (1618-1619) specifically rejects the Arminian affirmation that the new covenant consists of a withdrawal of the divine demand for perfection and a reckoning of faith and its imperfect obedience as a perfect fulfillment of the law:

> [T]he synod rejects the errors of those. . . [w]ho teach that what is involved in the new covenant of grace which God the Father made with men through the intervening of Christ's death is not that we are justified before God and saved through faith, insofar as it accepts Christ's merit, but rather that God, having withdrawn his demand for perfect obedience to the law, counts faith itself, and the imperfect obedience of faith, as perfect obedience to the law, and graciously looks upon this as worthy of the reward of eternal life.[6]

It is noteworthy that Dort rejects, not a doctrine of justification by works (which did not exist in Arminianism), but rather a doctrine of gracious condescension on God's part that would compromise his commitment to uphold the law. Such a doctrine shifts the locus of saving efficacy from Christ, the object of faith, to faith itself.[7] Unlike the Remonstrant tendency—expressed in the governmental theory of the atonement—toward a sundering of God's law and his person, post-Reformation theologians held tenaciously to the teaching that God's law brooks no violations without consequence.[8]

Perfect obedience is often tied to a prelapsarian covenant between God and

---

[6] *The Canons of the Synod of Dort*, in Jaroslav Pelikan and Valerie Hotchkiss (eds), *Creeds and Confessions of Faith in the Christian Tradition* (New Haven, CT: Yale University Press, 2003), 2, p. 582. The Latin text is available in Philip Schaff (ed), *The Creeds of Christendom*, 4th ed. (New York: Harper and Brothers, 1877), vol. 3.

[7] The previous chapter demonstrated that Luther regarded faith as righteousness. However, it is important to distinguish Luther's view from the view rejected by Dort. For Luther, faith and Christ are tied so intimately together that it may be said that faith itself is Christ in the believer. In addition, faith is a divine act that is created by the gospel alone. Luther certainly did not conceive of faith as a human act that measures up to a lower-level divine standard.

[8] The classic exposition of the governmental theory is Hugo Grotius, *Defensio Fidei Catholicae de Satisfactione Christi Adversus Faustum Socinum Senensem*, in Edwin Rabbi (ed), *Opera Theologica* (Assen, The Netherlands: Van Gorcum, 1990), 1, pp. 1-277; see also Herman Bavinck, *Reformed Dogmatics*, vol. 3, *Sin and Salvation in Christ* (Grand Rapids: Baker Academic, 2006), pp. 349-50, 358; Louis Berkhof, *Systematic Theology* (Grand Rapids: Eerdmans, 1996), pp. 388-89; Roger E. Olson, *Arminian Theology: Myths and Realities* (Downers Grove, IL: IVP Academic, 2006), pp. 221-41.

Adam, the fulfillment of which would have resulted in the attainment of eternal life. What later came to be known as the 'covenant of works' finds expression in the 1615 *Irish Articles*:

> Man being at the beginning created according to the image of God (which consisted especially in the wisdom of his mind and the true holiness of his free will), had the covenant of the law ingrafted in his heart, whereby God did promise unto him everlasting life upon condition that he performed entire and perfect obedience unto his commandments, according to that measure of strength wherewith he was endued in his creation, and threatened death unto him if he did not perform the same.[9]

As the doctrine of the covenant of works took hold in Reformed orthodoxy, it became a theological premise for the Reformed doctrine of justification by the imputation of Christ's perfect obedience. By tying eternal life in the prelapsarian state to perfect obedience to the law, Reformed theologians developed a new dimension to the Adam-Christ typology of Scripture. For Reformed orthodoxy, Christ fulfilled the covenant of works that Adam transgressed, thereby making eternal life available to all who are clothed in his righteousness. The perpetuity of the covenant of works becomes explicit by the time of the Westminster divines (1647), who argue that, even during the Mosaic dispensation of the covenant of grace, the covenant of works was republished as a divine demand for perfect obedience, to which was attached the promise of eternal life, even though it was unattainable for fallen humanity:

> God gave to Adam a law, as a covenant of works, by which he bound him and all his posterity to personal, entire, exact, and perpetual obedience, promised life upon the fulfilling, and threatened death upon the breach of it, and endued him with power and ability to keep it.
>
> This law, after his fall, continued to be a perfect rule of righteousness, and, as such, was delivered by God upon Mount Sinai, in ten commandments, and written in two tables: the first four commandments containing our duty towards God; and the other six our duty to man.[10]

---

[9] *The Irish Articles* 21, in Jaroslav Pelikan and Valerie Hotchkiss (eds), *Creeds and Confessions of Faith in the Christian Tradition* (New Haven, CT: Yale University Press, 2003), 2, p. 556.

[10] *The Westminster Confession of Faith* 19.1-2, in Jaroslav Pelikan and Valerie Hotchkiss (eds), *Creeds and Confessions of the Christian Tradition* (New Haven, CT: Yale University Press), 2, pp. 628-29. For a recent exegetical defense of the doctrine of republication, see Bryan D. Estelle, J.V. Fesko, and David VanDrunen, (eds), *The Law Is Not of Faith: Essays on Works and Grace in the Mosaic Covenant* (Phillipsburg, NJ: P & R, 2009).

For the Reformed, God's mercy to the elect cannot be conceived in such a way that it could possibly detract from his justice, and thus the requirement for perfect obedience remains a crucial component of the doctrine of justification into the period of Reformed orthodoxy, as it was incorporated into the covenant of works.

And yet, the demand for perfect obedience in the covenant of works does not entail the denial of any divine condescension toward man in his prelapsarian state. On the contrary, the covenant of works itself represents a free promise of God that only obligates him to reward perfect obedience with eternal life on the conditions he has freely set forth in his covenant (*ex pacto*), as Francis Turretin (1623-1687) argues:

> By his own right, God could indeed have prescribed obedience to man (created by him) without any promise of reward. But in order to temper that supreme dominion with his goodness, he added a covenant consisting in the promise of a reward and the stipulation of obedience. As he wished to assert more strongly his own right over man, so he demonstrated the highest benignity in this—that he (himself in need of nothing) willed to invite to a nearer communion with him (and more powerfully allure by that bond of love and mutual obligation), the creature (already subject to him by right of creation and owing him all things from natural obligation) by entering into a covenant with him, so that man now excited by the promise of God can certainly expect happiness, not from his mere philanthropy alone, but also from a covenant (on account of his truthfulness and fidelity).[11]

While this free, divine condescension may echo the voluntarist theology of the *via moderna*, it must be kept in mind that for the Reformed, the divine promise of eternal life is attached only to the condition of perfect obedience. Thus, in contrast to the principle of *facere quod in se est*, it specifically excludes eternal life as a merited reward for any fallen creature. The covenant of works, therefore, represents a doctrine of divine condescension that steadily maintains a commitment to a divine demand for perfect obedience, one that is rooted not only in the free condescension of God to his creatures but also in his uncompromising holiness.

Against the Roman doctrine of final justification on the basis of grace-empowered merit, theologians of the post-Reformation period continued to affirm, with Luther, Melanchthon, and Calvin, that God will accept nothing less than perfect obedience to the law. Since perfect obedience cannot be attained by a sinner, the law cannot be the sinner's means of justification.

---

[11] Francis Turretin, *Institutes of Elenctic Theology* 8.3.2 (Phillipsburg, NJ: P & R, 1992), 1, p. 574. See also Beach, *Christ and the Covenant. The Westminster Confession* (7.1) also speaks of the covenant of works as a divine condescension.

Bicovenantalism

As has been demonstrated already in the Reformation period, the divine demand for perfect obedience within the context of universal human sinfulness entails a bicovenantal soteriological framework wherein the way of the law must be abandoned and the way of the gospel embraced.[12] Justification must be received by faith alone and not attained by any mixture of faith and works. The mutual exclusivity of the two covenants finds continued affirmation during the post-Reformation period.

The Belgic Confession (1561) asserts that salvation is by faith alone because it is found in Christ alone. To add anything to Christ would be to make him a half Savior.[13] *The Second Helvetic Confession* (1566) concurs, arguing explicitly that justification cannot be attributed partly to Christ and partly to human merits, as in the Roman doctrine.[14] The Lutheran *Formula of Concord* (1577) makes the following affirmation, which indicates the mutual exclusivity of law and gospel with respect to justification:

> We believe, teach, and confess that it is necessary to teach with special diligence the *particulae exclusivae* for the preservation of the pure doctrine about the righteousness of faith before God. We mean the *exclusive particles*, that is, the following words of the holy apostle Paul, by which Christ's merit is entirely

---

[12] This statement should not be taken to imply antinomianism. For most theologians of this period, the law-gospel distinction pertains only to the legal basis of justification. One must seek justification either by the law or by the gospel, but one cannot do both. How the law functions for a believer aside from the question of justification is another matter.

[13] 'We believe that for us to acquire the true knowledge of this great mystery the Holy Spirit kindles in our hearts a true faith that embraces Jesus Christ, with all his merits, and makes him its own, and no longer looks for anything apart from him. For it must necessarily follow that either all that is required for our salvation is not in Christ or, if all is in him, then he who has Christ by faith has his salvation entirely. Therefore, to say that Christ is not enough but that something else is needed as well is a most enormous blasphemy against God—for it then would follow that Jesus Christ is only half a Savior. And therefore we justly say with Paul that we are justified "by faith alone" or by faith "apart from works". However, we do not mean, properly speaking, that it is faith itself that justifies us—for faith is only the instrument by which we embrace Christ, our righteousness. But Jesus Christ is our righteousness in making available to us all his merits and all the holy works he has done for us and in our place. And faith is the instrument that keeps us in communion with him and with all his benefits. When those benefits are made ours they are more than enough to absolve us of our sins.' *The Belgic Confession* 22, in Jaroslav Pelikan and Valerie Hotchkiss (eds), *Creeds and Confessions of Faith in the Christian Tradition* (New Haven, CT: Yale University Press, 2003), 2, p. 416.

[14] *Confessio Helvetica Posterior* 15.5, in Philip Schaff (ed), *The Creeds of Christendom* (New York: Harper and Brothers, 1877), 3, p. 267.

separated from our works and the honor is given to Christ alone. For the holy apostle Paul writes, 'Of grace', 'without merit', 'without Law', 'without works', 'not of works'. All these words together mean that we are justified and saved through faith alone in Christ.[15]

The *Formula* likewise denies the following teachings:

Faith has the first place in justification, yet renewal and love also belong to our righteousness before God in a particular way. Although renewal and love are not the chief cause of our righteousness, nevertheless our righteousness before God is not entire or perfect without such love and renewal.

Believers are justified before God and saved jointly by Christ's righteousness credited to them and by the new obedience begun in them. Or, believers are justified in part by the credit of Christ's righteousness, but in part also by the new obedience begun in them.[16]

The *Formula* affirms the absolute necessity of distinguishing between faith and personal merits, or between the principles of doing and receiving. Because the essence of the law is that it commands performance, the distinction between law and gospel hinges on the distinction between faith and personal obedience. The two cannot be mixed together as a joint basis for right standing with God, for they make opposite demands.

Johannes Andreas Quenstedt (1617-1688) echoes the teaching of the *Formula of Concord*:

On our part it is this faith alone which justifies us and effects (*influit*) our justification. Whatever merely embraces and apprehends to itself the promises of grace, the forgiveness of sins and the merit of Christ does so without any admixture of works. . . . Thus we are said to be justified by faith exclusively without the deeds of the Law, Rom. 3.28. Eph. 2.8, 9. True, faith is never alone, never all by itself and isolated from good works, and yet faith alone apprehends the merit of Christ, and we are justified by means of faith alone.[17]

These snippets from the history of Lutheranism reveal that for post-Reformation Lutheranism, the distinction between law and gospel is reinforced by an instrumental conception of faith. Faith saves, not because of any inherent quality that it possesses, but rather because it connects the sinner to the

---

[15] *The Formula of Concord* 3.7, in Paul Timothy McCain (ed), *Concordia: The Lutheran Confessions*, 2nd ed. (St. Louis: Concordia, 2005), p. 481.

[16] *The Formula of Concord* 3, denials 8-9 [3.20-21], (ed. McCain), p. 482.

[17] J.A. Quenstedt, quoted in Robert D. Preus, 'The Justification of a Sinner before God', p. 46.

righteousness of Jesus Christ.[18] In this way, the gospel—which demands faith as opposed to works—may be more sharply distinguished from the law, for whereas the law commands performance, the gospel commands the passive activity of reception.

Reformed statements such as *The Westminster Confession* tie this bicovenantal soteriology to the historical covenants of works and of grace:

> The first covenant made with man was a covenant of works, wherein life was promised to Adam, and in him to his posterity, upon condition of perfect and personal obedience.
>
>   Man by his fall having made himself incapable of life by that covenant, the Lord was pleased to make a second, commonly called the covenant of grace, wherein he freely offereth unto sinners life and salvation by Jesus Christ, requiring of them faith in him that they may be saved, and promising to give unto all those that are ordained unto life his Holy Spirit, to make them willing and able to believe.[19]

Taken together with the *Confession*'s explicit affirmation of Christ's perfect obedience to the law, these statements indicate that the covenant of works has an ongoing validity and functions as the legal basis upon which righteousness is counted to those who trust in Christ.[20] The great divide between justification by faith and justification by works (as opposed to the Roman doctrine of justification by both faith and works) stems from the absolute necessity of pursuing righteousness either by means of the covenant of works or by means of the covenant of grace, but never by means of both at the same time.

Turretin aptly expresses the dichotomy between the two covenants:

> This double covenant is proposed to us in Scripture: of nature and of grace; of works and of faith; legal and evangelical. The foundation of this distinction rests both on the different relation of God contracting (who can be considered now as Creator and Lord, then as Redeemer and Father) and on the diverse condition of man (who may be viewed either as a perfect or as a fallen creature); also on the diverse mode of obtaining life and happiness (either by proper obedience or by another's imputed); finally on the diverse duties prescribed to man (to wit, works

---

[18] 'Faith is the unique means and instrument through which we lay hold on the righteousness of Christ, receive it, and apply it to ourselves.' Chemnitz, *Justification*, p. 86; 'If man has offered unto him the justification, then he accepts of it by faith, which is, as it were, the spiritual hand, by which the grace of God, the merits of Christ, the forgiveness of sins, righteousness, life, and salvation are laid hold of.' Nikolaus Hunnius, *Epitome Credendorum* 500, in Eric Lund (ed), *Documents from the History of Lutheranism 1517-1750* (Minneapolis: Fortress, 2002), p. 243.
[19] *The Westminster Confession of Faith* 7.2-3, (ed. Pelikan and Hotchkiss), p. 615.
[20] See *The Westminster Confession of Faith* 8.4-5.

or faith). For in the former, God as Creator demands perfect obedience from innocent man with the promise of life and eternal happiness; but in the latter, God as Father promises salvation in Christ to fallen man under the condition of faith. The former rests upon the work of man; the latter upon the grace of God alone. The former upon a just Creator; the latter upon a merciful Redeemer. The former was made with innocent man without a mediator; the latter was made with fallen man by the intervention of a mediator.[21]

Expressed in these terms, it becomes apparent how the Reformed doctrine of justification impacts the whole of theology. The conflation of the covenant of works with the covenant of grace (the Roman doctrine) confuses the God-human relationship by downplaying the extent of human depravity, lowering the divine standard of righteousness, and lessening the redemptive accomplishment of the cross.

John Owen's 1677 treatise *The Doctrine of Justification by Faith* includes an argument very similar to that of Turretin. Owen compares the covenant of works to the covenant of grace, arguing that the blessing of the former depends on personal obedience, that it is an unmediated covenant, and that only perfect, sinless obedience could be rewarded with life. Once the covenant of works had been established (as it was in the Garden of Eden), it was impossible that God could have established a different covenant, *unless that covenant differed in its essential form*. And because the covenant of works offers a reward on the basis of personal obedience, the covenant of grace can in no way depend on such, for if it did it would not be essentially different from the covenant of works and, therefore, could not in principle constitute a distinct covenant. In essence, Owen argues that the newness of the covenant of grace excludes any possibility of justification by personal obedience.[22]

The dichotomy between the covenant of works and the covenant of grace does not entail that the two covenants have absolutely no similarities. As Johannes Wollebius (1589-1629) argues, both covenants 'exhibit a mirror of perfect obedience'. Yet while the covenant of works teaches perfect obedience, the covenant of grace shows where it may be found: in Jesus Christ.[23] The law stands as a signpost pointing to the gospel. The danger of monocovenantalism (even grace-based monocovenantalism) is that it allows the sign to obscure the reality.

Covenant theology, by tying the principles of works and faith to the historical unfolding of the two major covenants, develops and nuances the law-

---

[21] Turretin, *Institutes* 8.3.4 (ed. Dennison), p. 575.
[22] John Owen, *The Doctrine of Justification by Faith through the Imputation of the Righteousness of Christ; Explained, Confirmed, and Vindicated*, in William H. Goold (ed), *The Works of John Owen* (Carlisle, PA: Banner of Truth, 1965), 5, pp. 275-77.
[23] Johannes Wollebius, *Compendium Theologiae Christianae* 1.15.3, in John W. Beardslee III (ed), *Reformed Dogmatics* (Grand Rapids: Baker, 1965), p. 85.

gospel distinction in some ways not present in the Reformers. Yet even among those theologians who do not pursue this line of thinking, the bicovenantal law-gospel distinction remains entrenched in post-Reformation theology.

Alien Righteousness

If God demands perfect obedience, and Adamic humanity is incapable of offering perfect obedience to God; if Christ the mediator between God and man has obeyed the law perfectly and has made satisfaction for sinners, it follows that only the righteousness of Jesus Christ can suffice before God for the sake of his people. If perfect obedience and bicovenantalism constitute the theological background of the Reformation and post-Reformation doctrine of justification, the doctrine of the imputation of Christ's righteousness to the believer takes center-stage. With no hope of justification by means of personal obedience (because personal obedience is always imperfect), sinners must abandon all hope of right standing with God on the basis of works, even if those good works are produced by the grace of God working in them.

For Chemnitz, the doctrine of imputation entails that justified sinners stand before God as if they have fulfilled every obligation of the law:

> Thus we can now draw three conclusions from these true fundamental points pertaining to the word 'imputation' in this article. 1. The 'basis' by reason of which and in respect to which righteousness is imputed unto blessedness does not lie in the believers themselves, not even in Abraham after he was adorned by the Holy Spirit with outstanding gifts of spiritual renewal. 2. A contrary 'basis' is found if God should wish to enter into judgment. This must be covered so that sin is not imputed to us. 3. This imputation is also a 'relationship' of the Divine mind and will, which out of free mercy for the sake of Christ does not impute their sins to the believers but imputes to them righteousness, that is, they are considered before God at the tribunal of His judgment as if they had perfect righteousness dwelling in them, and therefore salvation and eternal life are given to them as righteous people.[24]

Chemnitz's argument is, essentially, that inherent righteousness (even in a man such as Abraham who has been granted the Holy Spirit) cannot suffice for justification. If God chose to judge us on the basis of what is within us, then we would only face his wrath. Yet for the sake of Christ God imputes righteousness to us, and because of him we are reckoned perfect law-keepers.

In the wake of the Osiandrist controversy, *The Formula of Concord* carefully seeks to avoid any possible affirmation that justification results from the indwelling of Christ's divine nature. The confession likewise avoids the opposite conclusion, namely, that the righteousness of sinners is grounded only

---

[24] Chemnitz, *Justification*, p. 150.

in Christ's human nature. Instead, it affirms the unified person of Christ and the imputation of his righteousness to those who believe:

> Against both the errors just mentioned, we unanimously believe, teach, and confess that Christ is our Righteousness neither according to His divine nature alone nor according to His human nature alone. But it is the entire Christ who is our Righteousness according to both natures. In His obedience alone, which as God and man He offered to the Father even to His death, He merited for us the forgiveness of sins and eternal life. For it is written, 'For as by the one man's disobedience the many were made sinners, so by the one man's obedience the man will be made righteous' (Romans 5:19).
>
> We believe, teach, and confess [t]hat our righteousness before God is this: God forgives our sins out of pure grace, without any work, merit, or worthiness of ours preceding, present, or following. He presents and credits to us the righteousness of Christ's obedience. Because of this righteousness, we are received into grace by God and regarded as righteous.[25]

Even though in the Osiandrist view justifying righteousness is given by grace and is properly Christ's own divine righteousness, nevertheless the *Formula* regards it as a false teaching because it obscures the distinction between law and gospel by basing the justifying decree on a righteousness that inheres in the sinner. What is needed is a righteousness that is *extra nos* and is, therefore, left uncontaminated by our sin. This righteousness may be found, not in a divine or human nature, but in the single divine-human person of Christ.

In his 1625 work *Epitome Credendorum*, Lutheran theologian Nikolaus Hunnius (1585-1643) defines the verdict of justification as a twofold act of imputation, the reckoning of righteousness and the forgiveness of sins:

> In the act of our justification two different things are accomplished; namely, in the first place, the righteousness of Christ and his fulfilling the law are imputed unto man, as if he had done these things himself, and second, the sins that he had committed are not imputed to him, as if he had never committed the same. By the first act he is delivered from a debt, which he never possibly could have paid; whilst by the second he is freed from the burden of sin, which he never could have atoned for, and the punishment for which he could never have sustained. By these two acts he is delivered from the judgment of God in such a manner that henceforward he has not any more to fear either guilt or transgression, nor the evils that are the consequence of them.[26]

Other than the fact that he lists these two components in a different order, Hunnius's definition of justification is virtually identical to that of Calvin,

---

[25] *The Formula of Concord* 3.1-2 [3.3-4], (ed. McCain), p. 480.
[26] Nikolaus Hunnius, *Epitome Credendorum* 485, (ed. McCain), p. 242.

displaying the absolute necessity of an alien righteousness.

The most significant development in the Reformed tradition with regard to the doctrine of alien righteousness pertains to the distinction between Christ's active and passive obedience. The doctrine of imputation does not require such a distinction, which is not evident in, for example, Luther's writings, though the concept of imputation certainly is. Nevertheless, the distinction itself represents a further refining of the doctrine of imputation that falls in line with the bicovenantal theology of post-Reformation theology, particularly in the stream of covenant theology. The doctrine of the covenant of works places Adam in a prelapsarian state, not in possession of the fullness of divine blessing, but in a position to merit eternal life by his obedience. The law that governs the divine-human relationship offers the reward of eternal life on that condition. But because Adam sinned, he plunged humanity under the curse of the law. For covenant theologians, this means Christ's atoning work involves more than simply the removal of the guilt of sin. Mere forgiveness of sins, without a corresponding fulfillment of the law's positive demands, does not meet the condition of the covenant of works. For this reason, an active obedience is necessary for true fulfillment of the law, which by the terms of the covenant of works, merits eternal life. Thus the righteousness of Christ is conceived, in covenant theology, as addressing both the negative sanctions of the law and its positive demands. Believers receive an alien righteousness when, joined to Christ by faith, his righteousness—in both of its dimensions—is counted to them.[27]

Several Reformed confessions from this period stop short of an open affirmation of a distinction between Christ's active and passive obedience, but nevertheless the theological concepts involved in this distinction do seem to be present in them. For example, the *Second Helvetic Confession* distinguishes between the forgiveness of sins and the imputation of righteousness that makes sinners worthy of eternal life.[28] By doing so the *Confession* appears to affirm

---

[27] A popular misunderstanding of the distinction between active and passive obedience seeks to distinguish between two distinct periods of distinct types of obedience in the work of Christ: his active obedience during his life and his passive obedience at the time of his death. However, the proper conception of active and passive obedience is that the whole of Christ's obedience consists of both aspects, and that these pertain, respectively, not to distinct periods of time or distinct events, but rather to his entire obedience as fulfillment of the positive demands of righteousness and in its penal aspect. See John Murray, *Redemption Accomplished and Applied* (Grand Rapids: Eerdmans, 1955), pp. 21-22.

[28] 'For Christ took upon Himself and bare the sins of the world, and did satisfy the justice of God. God, therefore, is merciful unto our sins for Christ alone, that suffered and rose again, and does not impute them unto us. But he imputes the justice of Christ unto us for our own; so that we are not only cleansed from sin, and purged, and holy, but also endued with the righteousness of Christ; yea, and acquitted from sin, death, and condemnation (2 Cor. 5:19-21); finally, we are righteous, and heirs of eternal life. To

that mere forgiveness of sins is not enough for eternal life and that positive righteousness is an additional requirement. Merely forgiven sinners are no better off than Adam in his prelapsarian state, not yet in possession of eternal life. However, forgiven sinners who are clothed in the righteousness of Christ receive the reward of eternal life because they are reckoned as having fulfilled the positive demands of the law, which Christ has fulfilled for them. The same theological presupposition seems to underlie the statement of the *Irish Articles*: 'He [Christ], for them [believers], paid their ransom by his death. He, for them, fulfilled the law in his life; that now, in him, and by him, every true Christian man may be called a fulfiller of the law.'[29] The ransom paid by Christ's death and the fulfillment of the law by his life seem to indicate distinct but inseparable aspects of Christ's obedience, which results in a righteousness that is imputed to believers, who are counted as having satisfied the divine demand for perfect obedience.

While the Westminster divines make no explicit reference to Christ's active and passive obedience, they do speak of 'his perfect obedience, and sacrifice of himself' as though to distinguish two aspects of his redemptive accomplishment.[30] Furthermore, Christ's obedience and satisfaction are clearly regarded as two aspects of his redemptive work in Article 11 on justification: 'Yet, inasmuch as he was given by the Father for them, and his obedience and satisfaction accepted in their stead, and *both* freely, not for anything in them, their justification is only of free grace, that both the exact justice, and rich grace of God, might be glorified in the justification of sinners' (emphasis added).[31] The word 'both' indicates that 'obedience' and 'satisfaction' are not being used interchangeably. The omission of any explicit mention of Christ's active and passive obedience in the *Westminster Confession* remains something of a mystery. Nevertheless, the distinction the *Confession* draws between 'obedience' and 'satisfaction' indicates that the Westminster divines were working with such categories.[32]

On the other hand, leading Reformed theologians of the post-Reformation period leave no ambiguity whatsoever regarding their commitment to the distinction between active and passive obedience and the imputation of both to believers. Wollebius writes, 'Just as the passion of Christ is necessary for the expiation of sin, so his active obedience and righteousness are necessary for the

---

speak properly, then, it is God alone that justifieth us, and that only for Christ, by not imputing unto us our sins, but imputing Christ's righteousness unto us (Rom. 4:23-25).' *The Second Helvetic Confession* 15.3 (ed. Schaff), pp. 862-63.

[29] *The Irish Articles* 35 (ed. Pelikan and Hotchkiss), p. 558.

[30] *The Westminster Confession of Faith* 8.5 (ed. Pelikan and Hotchkiss), p. 617.

[31] *The Westminster Confession of Faith* 11.3 (ed. Pelikan and Hotchkiss), p. 621.

[32] On this question, see Jeffery K. Jue, 'The Active Obedience of Christ and the Theology of the Westminster Standards: A Historical Investigation', in K. Scott Oliphint (ed), *Justified in Christ: God's Plan for Us in Justification* (Fearn, UK: Mentor, 2007), pp. 99-130.

gaining of eternal life.'[33] He supports this claim with several arguments, among which is the primary argument that the law binds human beings both to punishment and to obedience. In their sinful state, human beings have a twofold misery: guilt for their sins and a lack of righteousness. It is for this reason that a twofold satisfaction of the law is required, a satisfaction offered by Christ's active and passive obedience. The active obedience of Christ, which merits eternal life for those in him, corresponds to the active disobedience of Adam, which merits condemnation for those in him.[34]

Turretin makes the same argument, claiming that it is one thing to be released from prison and quite another to be set upon a throne; it is one thing for a fugitive slave's punishment to be remitted but quite another for the slave to be named a son.[35] In the same way, the innocent Adam was not in possession of eternal life, which awaited his obedience to attain. By the same token, it should not be automatically assumed that God should reward eternal life to those whose sins have been forgiven. If mere forgiveness of sins is all that is granted, then God could place such forgiven sinners under an obligation similar to Adam's to earn the reward of eternal life by their works.[36] But because Christ's atoning work is sufficient not merely for the remission of punishment but also for the securing of eternal life, his obedience includes both passive and active dimensions.[37] Thus, his imputed righteousness is sufficient for justification.

Owen bases his argument for the imputation of Christ's active and passive

---

[33] Wollebius, *Compendium* 1.18.2.1 (ed. Beardslee), p. 106.

[34] Wollebius, *Compendium* 1.18.2.1 (ed. Beardslee), pp. 106-07.

[35] 'It is one thing to redeem from punishment; another to assign a reward also. It is one thing to deliver from death; another to bestow life and happiness. It is one thing to bring out of prison; another to seat upon a throne. The former takes away evil, but the latter superadds good also; as if a fugitive slave should not only be acquitted of the punishment due, but also raised to the dignity and right of a son.' Turretin, *Institutes* 16.4.8 (ed. Dennison), 2, p. 658.

[36] 'For although these two things are connected together indissolubly from the covenant of grace, still from the nature of the thing they could be separated; as Adam, although innocent from the beginning of his creation and worthy of no punishment, still was not at once worthy of a reward until he had perfected the round of obedience, so it was not absolutely necessary that he whose sins have been remitted and who is delivered from the guilt of death, should straightway be gifted with a crown of immortality (since, if it pleased God, he might have afterwards directed man to work by which he should obtain the reward.' Turretin, *Institutes* 16.4.8 (ed. Dennison), 2, p. 658.

[37] 'Third, we remark that the obedience of Christ has a twofold efficacy, satisfactory and meritorious; the former by which we are freed from the punishments incurred by sin; the latter by which (through the remission of sin) a right to eternal life and salvation is acquired for us. For as sin has brought upon us two evils—the loss of life and exposure to death—so redemption must procure the two opposite benefits—deliverance from death and a right to life, escape from hell and an entrance into heaven.' Turretin, *Institutes* 14.13.10 (ed. Dennison), 2, p. 447.

obedience to the believer on the glory and honor of God.[38] His argument proceeds in two steps. First, he argues that the only reason Christ underwent the penalty of the law for sinners was so that God's righteousness might not be violated through the infringement of the law in the relaxation of its penal demands. Second, he asks why, if God will not allow the penal sanctions of the law to be infringed, he should allow the positive demands of the law to go unfulfilled. To treat forgiven sinners who have not fulfilled the law as though they have fulfilled it would constitute an infringement of the law, unless Christ has fulfilled the positive requirements of the law for them. Thus the imputation of Christ's active obedience to the believer hinges on God's commitment to defend his glory and honor by defending the holy standards of his law.[39]

Owen proceeds to defend this doctrine against two objections. First, in answer to the objection of Socinus that Christ's active obedience cannot be vicarious because he, as a man, owed obedience to God for himself, Owen responds by an appeal to the hypostatic union. While the human nature of Christ was 'made under the law' (Gal. 4:4), and Christ's obedience was performed through his human nature, nevertheless it was the obedience of the single theanthropic person. While his obedience has special reference to his human nature, nevertheless it cannot be sundered from the divine person, the Son of God, who owed no obedience to the law for himself and indeed stands above the law as God. In other words, apart from the incarnation, there is no sense in which the Son of God could be under the law, and the specific purpose for which he freely took to himself a human nature and came under the law was so that he could fulfill the law for us. As an illustration of his point, Owen refers to the argument of Hebrews 7 that Levi, in the loins of Abraham, paid tithes to Melchizedek and thus demonstrated the latter's superiority. Why, Owen asks, would the author not suppose that Christ likewise paid tithes to

---

[38] A good discussion of Owen's doctrine of justification is provided by Carl R. Trueman, 'John Owen on Justification', in K. Scott Oliphint (ed), *Justified in Christ: God's Plan for Us in Justification*, (Fearn, UK: Mentor, 2007), pp. 81-98. Trueman draws attention to the fact that Owen's commitment to the doctrine of Christ's active and passive obedience can be seen by his role in the development of the *Savoy Declaration* of 1658, a revision of the *Westminster Confession*, which makes active and passive obedience explicit articles of faith.

[39] 'For why was it necessary, or why would God have it so, that the Lord Christ, as the surety of the covenant, should undergo the curse and penalty of the law, which we had incurred the guilt of by sin, that we may be justified in his sight? Was it not that the glory and honour of his righteousness, as the author of the law, and the supreme governor of all mankind thereby, might not be violated in the absolute impunity of the infringers of it? And if it were requisite unto the glory of God that the penalty of the law should be undergone for us, or suffered by our surety in our stead, because we had sinned, wherefore is it not as requisite unto the glory of God that the *preceptive part* of the law be complied withal for us, inasmuch as obedience thereunto is required of us?' Owen, *Justification by Faith*, p. 251 (emphasis original).

Melchizedek, since he too was in the loins of Abraham (at least in regard to his human nature)? The answer is that Christ, as the eternal Son of God, 'without father, without mother, without genealogy, without beginning of days or end of life' (and so typified by Melchizedek), was not in the loins of Abraham in the same sense that Levi was. For the personhood of Christ is the personhood of the eternal Son of God, who exists independent of Abraham. And so there is a sense, unique to his human nature, in which Christ was present in Abraham, and yet one cannot cast aside his divine nature or theanthropic personhood and relegate him to the same status as Levi. In the same way, Christ's status as one under the law is not the same as that of all others who are under the law, for as the theanthropic person he has come under the law freely not for himself, but to fulfill it on behalf of his elect.[40]

The second objection that Owen addresses is that the imputation of Christ's active obedience is unnecessary due to the fact that justification consists of the forgiveness of sins. What more is necessary once one's sins have been forgiven? In response, Owen argues that one who is pardoned of sins may have his punishment remitted, but he is not thereby counted as having done everything required of him. His argument merits a substantive quotation:

> The like may be said of what is in like manner supposed,—namely, that not to be unrighteous, which a man is on the pardon of sin, is the same with being righteous. For if not to be unrighteous be taken *privatively*, it is the same with being just or righteous: for it supposeth that he who is so hath done all the duty that is required of him that he may be righteous. But not to be unrighteous *negatively*, as the expression is here used, it doth not do so: for, at best, it supposeth no more but that a man as yet hath done nothing actually against the rule of righteousness. Now this may be when yet he hath performed none of the duties that are required of him to constitute him righteous, because the times and occasions of them are not yet. And so it was with Adam in the state of innocency; which is the height of what can be attained by the complete pardon of sin.[41]

Pardon alone does not constitute justification. In order to be declared righteous, one must be reckoned as having done everything the law demands. For this reason, Christ's active obedience must be imputed to the believer. Without it, there is no hope for a satisfaction of God's demand for perfect obedience.

The doctrine of alien righteousness, whether unfolded with the nuances of active and passive obedience or not, remains the defining mark of the Protestant doctrine of justification throughout the post-Reformation period. Given the theological structure of post-Reformation theology, with its demand for perfect obedience and its corresponding law-gospel distinction, there could be no other

---

[40] Owen, *Justification by Faith*, pp. 252-62.
[41] Owen, *Justification by Faith*, p. 264.

basis for the justification of sinners than the righteousness of Christ imputed to believers.

Conclusion

Developments within post-Reformation theology with regard to the doctrine of justification do not essentially alter the basic dividing line that had previously been drawn between the Reformers and Rome. On the contrary, these developments follow the trajectory of the Reformers and, in many cases, give further theological nuance to their formulations. Perfect obedience remains an immutable divine standard, tying the doctrine of justification to the immutable holiness of God. Because perfect obedience is unattainable for sinners, obedience to the law can have no place in the doctrine of justification, either in a Pelagian scheme of justification by works or in a Roman doctrine of final justification on the basis of grace-empowered merit. Abandoning any hope for justification by means of the law, post-Reformation theologians continuously point to the imputed righteousness of Christ, granted to believers through the instrument of faith, as the only hope for justification.

Within the Reformed tradition, covenant theology adds new dimensions to these three aspects of justification. Covenant theologians link perfect obedience to a prelapsarian covenant of works that the first Adam transgressed but the last Adam fulfilled on behalf of his elect. With regard to the bicovenantal framework of justification, covenant theology asserts that the principles of the covenant of works and of the covenant of grace are mutually exclusive of one another and that works must be excluded entirely (as a legal basis of justification) for sinners seeking right standing with God under the covenant of grace. Covenant theologians also typically affirm that what is necessary for justification is not mere pardon of sins but also the imputation of Christ's active obedience in fulfillment of the positive demands of the law, and in this way they add further nuance to the doctrine of alien righteousness.

The words of Turretin indicate how these three aspects of Reformed theology—perfect obedience, bicovenantalism, and alien righteousness—coalesce into a coherent doctrine of justification:

> However, we must premise here that God, the just Judge, cannot pronounce anyone just and give him a right to life except on the ground of some perfect righteousness which has a necessary connection with life; but that righteousness is not of one kind. For as there are two covenants which God willed to make with men—the one legal and the other of grace—so also there is a twofold righteousness—legal and evangelical. Accordingly there is also a double justification or a double method of standing before God in judgment—legal and evangelical. The former consists in one's own obedience or a perfect conformity with the law, which is in him who is to be justified; the latter in another's obedience or a perfect observance of the law, which is rendered by a surety in

the place of him who is to be justified—the former in us, the latter in Christ. . . . Hence a twofold justification flows: one in the legal covenant by one's own righteousness according to the clause, 'Do this and live'; the other in the covenant of grace, by another's righteousness (Christ's) imputed to us and apprehended by faith according to the clause, 'Believe and thou shalt be saved.' Each demands a perfect righteousness. The former requires it in the man to be justified, but the latter admits the vicarious righteousness of a surety. The former could have a place in a state of innocence, if Adam had remained in innocence. But because after sin it became impossible to man, we must fly to the other (i.e., the gospel), which is founded upon the righteousness of Christ.[42]

Thus the dividing line between Rome and the post-Reformation tradition hinges not on justification by grace versus justification by works, but rather on the clear distinction between law and gospel.

As was noted in the previous chapter, it is in these categories that the 'old perspective' on Paul developed, not in a simple dichotomy between grace and works based on a proto-Weberian misreading of Judaism. The hermeneutical presupposition that drives the new perspective's revised readings of Paul does not accurately represent the Reformation doctrine of justification as it developed in history. Given what has been demonstrated here about the nature of the Reformation doctrine of justification, the argument of Sanders' *Paul and Palestinian Judaism*, as historically enlightening as it may or may not be, cannot sustain the radical conclusion that an entirely new approach to Paul's doctrine of justification is warranted.

---

[42] Turretin, *Institutes* 16.2.2 (ed. Dennison), 2, p. 637.

CHAPTER 5

Conclusion

The hermeneutical presupposition of the new perspective on Paul, which has been generated in the wake of E.P. Sanders' *Paul and Palestinian Judaism*, was formulated in chapter 1 of this study as follows: *covenantal nomism could not have served as Paul's foil in the promotion of a doctrine of justification that resembles that of the Reformation.* The grace-based character of covenantal nomism, so it might seem, would apparently rule out such a possibility. New perspective proponents instead interpret the grace/works antithesis in Paul as a sociological and ecclesiological, rather than an anthropological and soteriological, reality. The foregoing survey of the development of the Protestant doctrine of justification during the Reformation period and beyond has demonstrated that such a presupposition is unwarranted. The aim of this final chapter is to tie together the various threads that have been traced throughout this study in order to demonstrate the expendability of the new perspective's hermeneutical presupposition. Finally, some concluding exegetical observations on the bicovenantal structure of Paul's doctrine of justification will be offered in order to demonstrate that the Reformation doctrine, formulated as a bicovenantal response to the monocovenantal soteriology of Rome, has roots in the text of Scripture.

Summary of Observations

The emerging Roman Catholicism of the late medieval and Reformation periods, like Sanders' Judaism, was itself a grace-based religion. As demonstrated in both the pre-Reformation scholastic tradition and in the definitive decree of the Council of Trent, late medieval Catholic theology steadfastly proclaimed a doctrine of justification by grace.

A survey of Peter Lombard's *Sentences*, Thomas Aquinas's *Summa Theologica*, and Bonaventure's *Breviloquium* has shown a common soteriological pattern. The divine initiative is primary in salvation. Justification occurs through the infusion of habitual grace through the sacrament of baptism, which heals the soul and enables the performance of works of merit, empowered by cooperative grace, for the purpose of attaining eternal life. Knowing the weakness of humanity, God has instituted the sacrament of penance as a way of restoring habitual grace once it has been lost, so that justification may be repeated after the commission of a mortal sin. Justification is distinct from the final judgment. It represents a movement from a state of sin to a state of grace, but it represents only the beginning of a journey toward the final judgment. In Sanders' terminology, after one 'gets in' by grace, one must 'stay in' by a combination of grace and works until one reaches the beatific vision. There are certainly differences among these three theologians. For example, Thomas develops a more robust doctrine of predestination, and Bonaventure places greater emphasis on free will. Nevertheless, there is a common pattern that is best described as grace-based and monocovenantal. There is no clear distinction between law and gospel, for the purpose of the gospel is to transform the pilgrim believer (*viator*) and make him capable of fulfilling, in an imperfect but nevertheless adequate way, God's righteous demands.

The *via moderna* conforms this soteriological pattern to its own voluntarist theology. For theologians of this school of thought, God has taken the initiative in the salvation of humanity by entering into a covenant (*pactum*) in which works that are intrinsically nothing before him are accepted as worthy of reward. It is within this gracious framework that the slogan 'To those who do what is in them God does not deny grace' (*Facientibus quod in se est Deus non denegat gratiam*) must be understood. The statement cannot be taken as an endorsement of Pelagianism. It seems, rather, to be a species of semi-Pelagianism, for it speaks of human initiative in the personal reception of grace, but it does so within the context of a gracious covenant established by the divine initiative. Furthermore, it denies the intrinsic worthiness of human works and affirms the necessity of a reception of internal grace for final salvation once the individual has taken the initiative to do what is in him. The *via moderna* likewise exhibits a pattern of religion that is grace-based and monocovenantal, though with a greater emphasis on the human initiative in the initial reception of grace.

The decree of the Council of Trent on justification represents Rome's official response to the bicovenantal doctrine of justification proclaimed by the Reformers. Trent denies both Pelagianism and semi-Pelagianism, affirming that divine grace is necessary to prepare the soul to receive grace. However, at the same time Trent carefully spells out a doctrine of free will in which the sinner has the capacity to submit to or resist the grace of God that is offered. Justification, which is the infusion of habitual grace, occurs through the sacrament of baptism. God grants the gift of perseverance in grace to those who will receive it, but he has also provided penance as a second means of justification after habitual grace is lost through mortal sin. By transferring the *viator* from a state of sin to a state of grace, justification makes possible the acquisition of merit that will result in eternal life. Trent stands squarely within the tradition of medieval scholasticism, but it moves beyond its predecessors by anathematizing specific Protestant doctrines: the bound will, *sola fide*, the imputation of Christ's righteousness, and assurance of salvation. Trent therefore represents a clear reaffirmation of a grace-based monocovenantal soteriology in the face of the bicovenantal theology of the Reformation.

The works of three prominent Reformers—Martin Luther, Philip Melanchthon, and John Calvin—have been surveyed in an attempt to understand the rise of the Protestant doctrine of justification in the context of late medieval theology. It has been argued that what distinguishes the Reformers from Rome is not that the former argue for justification by grace and the latter argue for justification by works. Rather, the dividing line is the doctrine of alien righteousness, which depends in turn on a clear law-gospel distinction within the context of a divine demand for perfect obedience.

Martin Luther espouses a doctrine of unconditional justification. God justifies the ungodly by creating faith within them through the gospel. Christ himself is present in faith, and so by the unconditional decree of justification God so unites the believer and Christ that, like a bride united to her bridegroom, everything that Christ has—including his righteousness—is counted to the sinner. Justification is the central organizing principle for the theology of the mature Luther, and the law-gospel distinction is the driving force behind his hermeneutic. Luther does not clearly distinguish between the legal and transformative aspects of salvation, but his doctrine, in contrast to that of Rome, does propose a justification of the ungodly through the unconditional, creative work of the gospel. God's justifying verdict, which creates faith in the elect, represents a present anticipation of the final judgment, so that one's standing with God is based solely on God's mercy in Christ and not on anything inherent in the sinner. Nevertheless, since Christ is present in faith, good works flow from faith just like good fruit comes from a healthy tree.

Philip Melanchthon stands in significant continuity with Luther, affirming clearly a law-gospel distinction that is based on the divine demand for perfect obedience. Likewise, he argues that justification is by faith alone, based on the imputed righteousness of Christ. Nevertheless, the mature Melanchthon does show some signs of independence from Luther. He departs from Luther's doctrine of the bondage of the will, arguing that the will retains some limited freedom in external, civil matters, as well as the freedom to receive or reject grace. He argues that faith itself is not righteousness but is merely instrumental toward the attainment of righteousness in Christ. He promotes a third use of the law for believers. In spite of these differences, Luther and Melanchthon share the same bicovenantal structure that marks their division with Rome.

John Calvin argues that there are two ways of righteousness: the way of faith and the way of works. Because righteousness by works is unattainable for Adamic humanity, those who seek righteousness before God must seek it by faith in Christ. Justification is defined as the remission of sins and the imputation of Christ's righteousness to the believer. Calvin's doctrine of alien righteousness fits squarely within the context of his monergistic soteriology, for both doctrines—justification by the imputation of an alien righteousness and monergistic regeneration—magnify the grace of God by showing that all hope for salvation lies outside the sinner. These three Reformers do not sing in complete unison on the doctrine of justification, but they do share the same basic soteriological framework: a bicovenantal structure rooted in a divine demand for perfect obedience, issuing in a doctrine of alien righteousness as the basis of justification.

The post-Reformation period extends and develops the theology of the Reformation on the doctrine of justification in both the Lutheran and Reformed streams of Protestantism. The necessity for perfect obedience remains a fixture in post-Reformation thought, binding the doctrine of justification to the nature of God's holiness. The law-gospel distinction remains firmly in place in light of the impossibility of meeting the standard of perfection. Post-Reformation theologians stand with their predecessors by arguing for the necessity of the alien righteousness of Christ imputed to the believer as the legal basis of right standing with God.

Covenant theology develops all three of these aspects of justification. Post-Reformation Reformed theologians explicate the demand for perfect obedience in terms of the covenant of works, first given to Adam in the Garden of Eden and then subsequently republished in the law of Moses. The law-gospel distinction is then spelled out as a distinction between the covenant of works and the covenant of grace, which differ from one another in form and thereby reveal two different, mutually exclusive ways of attaining eternal life. The unmediated covenant of works offers life on the condition of perfect obedience, but the covenant of grace, mediated through Christ, gives life to the elect on the condition of faith alone. Life is granted to the elect because of the righteousness of Jesus Christ, which in covenant theology is often explicated in terms of his passive obedience, which satisfies the penal sanctions of the law, and his active obedience, which fulfills the law's positive requirements. Because the covenant of works promises life on the condition of obedience and not mere innocence, the forgiveness of sins is not enough for believers; they also need the imputation of Christ's active obedience in order to surpass Adam's prelapsarian state in Christ and thereby receive eternal life.

The Expendability of the New Perspective's Hermeneutical Presupposition

E.P. Sanders' *Paul and Palestinian Judaism* is a seminal work on Second Temple Judaism. While his conclusions continue to be debated, few would argue that he has not made a significant contribution to that field of study. However, Sanders' resulting portrayal of Paul has been received with less enthusiasm. Yet Sanders remains a figure of great importance in Pauline studies because he has given a number of other scholars a platform on which to construct a new perspective on Paul, even though this new Paul often looks very different from the Paul of Sanders himself.[1] Taking for granted that Sanders has overturned the Reformation paradigm for reading Paul, new perspective proponents have sought to explain the nature of Paul's faith/works antithesis in different ways. The hermeneutical presupposition at work in such explanations is that covenantal nomism could not have served as Paul's foil in the development of a doctrine of justification that resembles that of the Reformation.

The foregoing survey has demonstrated that such a presupposition is a *non sequitur*. Accepting Sanders' thesis for the sake of argument, the fact that first-century Jews might be better described as 'covenantal nomists' rather than 'legalists' has no bearing on the categories that gave shape to the historic Protestant doctrine of justification. Strict legalism was not an error the Reformers or their heirs ever encountered. Pelagianism was universally condemned as a heresy among Protestant and Catholic alike. In fact, even semi-Pelagianism was widely regarded as an errant teaching. The Reformation doctrine of justification arose specifically in response to the monocovenantal doctrine of Rome, a doctrine of justification in which law and gospel are not clearly distinguished, and right standing with God is attained by grace-empowered merit. The Roman Catholic doctrine is not a mirror image of Sanders' portrayal of first-century Judaism, but the similarities between the two are quite striking. Both affirm that 'getting in' is by grace and that 'staying in' results from a blend of grace and works. Both provide ongoing means of atonement for sin: the sacrificial system in Judaism and the sacrament of penance in Roman Catholicism. Both locate salvation at the end of a process of divine-human cooperation. Neither draws a sharp distinction between the principle of demand in the law and the principle of reception in the gospel; Second Temple Judaism really has no gospel to speak of, and Roman Catholicism views the gospel primarily through the lens of moral reformation, thereby finding its chief value in its capacity to aid sinners in obeying the law. Neither Judaism nor Roman Catholicism upholds a divine demand for perfect obedience, and so neither requires a doctrine of perfect vicarious obedience as the only hope for sinners.

If the Reformation doctrine of justification arose in response to the grace-based, monocovenantal foil of late medieval Catholicism, there is absolutely no reason to suppose that Paul's doctrine of justification could not follow a similar line of thought in response to the foil of a grace-based, monocovenantal Second Temple Judaism. It is yet to be explained why Paul could not have argued for a doctrine of faith that receives the imputed righteousness of Christ in response to the law-based piety of covenantal nomism. New perspective scholars have misread the implications of Sanders' argument. Nothing that Sanders has argued necessarily implies that the Reformation reading of Paul cannot be sustained. The new perspective on Paul has provided greater sensitivity to

---

[1] See chapter 1 for a survey of the work of several new perspective scholars.

Paul's first-century Jewish context, thereby providing numerous exegetical insights that had been lacking in centuries past. But while this historical sensitivity may yield some nuances to the interpretation of Paul's letters, it does not lead to the kind of radical revisions proposed by new perspective advocates. Helpful nuances should be warmly welcomed, but what is not needed is a completely new perspective.

Concluding Exegetical Observations

It is one thing to argue that the Reformers and their heirs upheld a demand for perfect obedience, together with a doctrine of alien righteousness, incorporated into a bicovenantal scheme, as the primary soteriological dividing line with Rome. To say that Paul's doctrine of justification follows a similar pattern is another claim entirely. The purpose of this work has not been to establish the latter claim but only the former in an attempt to expose fallacious reasoning in new perspective exegesis. Nevertheless, because the greatest significance of this debate lies in its impact on the church's reading of Scripture, it is important to note, at the conclusion of this study, that the historical-theological observations offered here do have the potential to illumine the interpretation of Paul's letters. That is not to say that Reformation theology should exercise a rigid control over biblical interpretation. It is, rather, to argue that understanding with precision the claims made by theologians of the past yields an exegetical richness that results when interpreters of today transcend the concerns of their own generation and learn from the past some ways that they might pose questions of the text. In light of the foregoing study, two questions worth posting are these: (1) Do Paul's letters indicate that a divine demand for perfect obedience necessitates a bicovenantal structure for the doctrine of justification, as opposed to a monocovenantal blurring of law and gospel upheld by his opponents? (2) If so, does this bicovenantal structure cohere with Paul's statements about the role of works at the final judgment and James's doctrine of justification by works? The following observations are offered, not as full-fledged exegetical treatments, but rather as preliminary answers to these questions and suggestions for further study.

BICOVENANTALISM IN PAUL

Paul unpacks his doctrine of justification most fully in his letters to the Galatians, to the Romans, and in the third chapter of his letter to the Philippians. Evidence from all three letters indicates that Paul held to a bicovenantal structure that forms the framework of his doctrine of justification, one that presupposes a divine demand for perfect obedience. This framework sets his doctrine of justification against any monocovenantal scheme, whether it be a strict form of legalism, a grace-based covenantal nomism, or anything in between.

Galatians 3:10-14

An initial glance at Paul's argument in Galatians 3:10 reveals an apparent incongruity between the claim he makes and the proof-text he employs to back it up. Having argued that the blessing of Abraham—justification—comes to those who are of faith (Gal. 3:1-9), Paul then proceeds to argue that only curse—the opposite of blessing—comes to those who are of the law: 'For all who rely on works of the law are under a curse' (v. 10).[2] Paul quotes Deuteronomy 27:26 to establish this claim, a verse that pronounces a curse on all who do not abide by all things written in the law. It would seem that the verse establishes the opposite of what Paul argues, namely, that in order to avoid the curse, one must strive diligently to abide by all things written in the law. At first glance it appears that Paul has gift-wrapped a winning argument for the Judaizers. More attention to Paul's argument, however, reveals that this is not the case.

Traditionally, interpreters have understood Paul's argument to contain an unstated premise, namely, that no one is capable of keeping the law, and thus all who seek justification by that route are doomed to inherit the curse of Deuteronomy 27:26.[3] This interpretation has been called into question in recent years by new perspective proponents. James Dunn, Joel Green, and Mark Baker espouse what might be termed the 'ecclesiological' reading of Galatians 3:10-14.[4] According to these scholars, the nature of the curse is not that the law cannot be fulfilled. It is, rather, that Israel has misused the law, turning it into a boundary marker that stokes the flames of nationalistic pride and excludes Gentiles from fellowship. Those who 'rely on works of the law' (v. 10), therefore, are 'those who have understood the scope of God's covenant people

---

[2] Unless otherwise indicated, Scripture quotations are taken from the English Standard Version.

[3] Martin Luther, *Commentary on Galatians*, Modern English Edition (Grand Rapids: Fleming H. Revell, 1988), pp. 159-89; Steve Jeffery, Mike Ovey, and Andrew Sach, *Pierced for Our Transgressions: Rediscovering the Glory of Penal Substitution* (Nottingham, UK: IVP, 2007), pp. 89-95; Leon Morris, *The Apostolic Preaching of the Cross*, 3rd ed. (Grand Rapids: Eerdmans, 1965), pp. 56-59; Moisés Silva, *Interpreting Galatians: Explorations in Exegetical Method*, 2nd ed. (Grand Rapids: Baker Academic, 2001), pp. 217-35; Thomas R. Schreiner, *The Law and Its Fulfillment: A Pauline Theology of Law* (Grand Rapids: Baker, 1993), pp. 44-63. F.F. Bruce (*The Epistle to the Galatians: A Commentary on the Greek Text*, NIGTC [Grand Rapids: Eerdmans, 1982], pp. 157-67) generally follows the traditional reading, but his argument that at this time in redemptive history eternal life could not be gained by perfect obedience (if it were possible) departs from the traditional reading somewhat.

[4] James D.G. Dunn, 'Works of the Law and the Curse of the Law (Galatians 3.10-14)', in *The New Perspective on Paul: Collected Essays* (Tübingen: Mohr Siebeck, 2005), pp. 111-30; Joel B. Green and Mark D. Baker, *Recovering the Scandal of the Cross: Atonement in New Testament and Contemporary Contexts* (Downers Grove, IL: InterVarsity, 2000), pp. 60-62.

as Israel *per se*, as that people who are defined by the law and marked out by its distinctive requirements.'[5] This exclusionary attitude mistakenly elevates matters of secondary importance and thereby falls short of what the law actually requires. Having misused the law, therefore, Israel finds herself under its curse, and the Gentiles likewise experience the curse because they have been excluded: 'It was a curse which fell primarily on the Jew (3:10; 4:5), but Gentiles were affected by it so long as that misunderstanding of the covenant and the law remained dominant'.[6] Christ's work on the cross addresses this problem. By putting himself under the curse and outside the scope of the blessing of the covenant people, he essentially put himself in the place of the Gentile. God's vindication of him through the resurrection indicates that God is for the Gentiles, thereby undercutting the notion that the law serves as a boundary between Jews and Gentiles. Jews who recognize this truth find redemption from the curse when they give up their exclusive attitude, and that in turn creates a new situation where Gentiles are welcomed as Gentiles into the international people of God.[7]

This construal of Paul's argument must be deemed implausible for several reasons. First, it rests on a highly unlikely view of the curse of the law. In Deuteronomy 28:15ff., the curse is threatened against disobedience to the law in general, not against exclusive nationalism. Paul's quotation from Deuteronomy 27:26 (v. 10) says nothing about Jewish nationalism but threatens those who do not obey 'all things written in the Book of the Law'.[8] Second, this reading involves a fair amount of equivocation.[9] Dunn speaks inconsistently about the nature of the curse of the law and how it applies to both Jews and

---

[5] Dunn, 'Works of the Law', p. 124. Green and Baker (*Recovering the Scandal*, p. 61) argue similarly, '[T]hose who use the law to drive a wedge between Jews and Gentiles have abused the law and, therefore, fall under the same curse as that assumed to accrue to Gentiles on account of their lawlessness.'

[6] Dunn, 'Works of the Law', p. 127.

[7] Dunn, 'Works of the Law', pp. 128-29; Green and Baker, *Recovering the Scandal*, p. 61.

[8] Stephen Westerholm (*Perspectives Old and New on Paul: The "Lutheran" Paul and His Critics* [Grand Rapids: Eerdmans, 2004], p. 318), asks a number of probing questions that expose the inadequacy of this reading: 'According to Paul, Jews before Christ lived "under sin" no less than did the Gentiles (Gal. 3:22); they lived in the 'flesh'—a flesh for whose typical expressions Paul has a handy list (5:19-21), none of whose items is readily rendered "ethnocentrism". How is it, then, that their failure to "abide by all the things written in the book of the law" can be limited to the claims of racial privileges? Did the Sinaitic covenant itself provide atonement for all transgression *except* this one? For that matter, were *all* Jews guilty of racism—or were the select few who escaped *this* sin in no need of Christ's death? Was the death of Christ the only way Jews could be disabused of their misunderstanding? Had it no broader function?'

[9] Seyoon Kim, *Paul and the New Perspective: Second Thoughts on the Origin of Paul's Gospel* (Grand Rapids: Eerdmans, 2002), pp. 132-34.

Gentiles.[10] On the one hand, Dunn writes of the curse of the law being directed against Israel on the basis of nationalism.[11] This implies that, by excluding the Gentiles, Israel has broken the law and fallen under the wrath of God. However, he writes later that Christ's redemptive work has accomplished 'the deliverance of the heirs of the covenant promise from *the ill effects of the too narrow understanding* of covenant and law held by most of Paul's Jewish contemporaries'.[12] As Kim points out, 'It is no longer the curse [pronounced by the law] *for* a wrong understanding of the law, but the curse *of* a wrong understanding.'[13] Furthermore, how do Gentiles come under this curse? They cannot be implicated in Israel's nationalism. Instead, Dunn sees the Gentiles being affected by the curse because Jewish misunderstanding leaves them outside the covenant people.[14] What remains unclear is whether the curse has anything to do with the wrath of God directed against law-breakers or if it is merely the natural consequence of Israel's nationalism exhibited in racial segregation. On the one hand, this reading almost reduces the curse of the law to a horizontal reality, which extracts it completely from its biblical context. In Deuteronomy 27-29, the curse is God's response to the sin of the people, not the tragic sociological situation created by an exclusive attitude. On the other hand, Dunn's reading makes no sense of the context of Galatians itself, a letter written to combat Judaizers who sought to *include* Gentiles in the covenant people by bringing them under the law. One can imagine the Judaizers responding to Dunn's Paul by appealing to their great love for the Gentiles exemplified in their desire to extend Torah-observance beyond the borders of Israel.

Third, the ecclesiological reading truncates the biblical theme of redemption. According to Dunn, Christ redeemed Jews and Gentiles by, in effect, becoming a Gentile in order to reveal that God is for the Gentiles. Jews who understand this will give up their exclusive attitude and welcome the Gentiles as Gentiles into the covenant people, thereby removing from themselves the curse of misunderstanding and removing from the Gentiles the exclusionary effects of the curse. As Westerholm points out, 'So limited a view of the atonement would have astonished even the most dogmatic TULIP theologian.'[15] The biblical concept of redemption involves much more than a revelation that results in a changed attitude. The verbs ἀγοράζω and ἐξαγοράζω (the latter appears in Gal. 3:13) connote the ideas of purchase and ownership (Matt.

---

[10] These comments are directed at Dunn's exegesis because his discussion of the text is much more detailed than that of Green and Baker, who basically offer a condensed version of his argument.

[11] Dunn, 'Works of the Law', p. 125.

[12] Dunn, 'Works of the Law', p. 127, emphasis added.

[13] Kim, *Paul and the New Perspective*, p. 133.

[14] Dunn, 'Works of the Law', p. 127.

[15] Westerholm, *Perspectives Old and New*, pp. 317-18.

13:44, 46; Mark 6:36, 37; John 6:5; 13:29; 1 Cor. 6:20; 7:23, 30; 2 Pet. 2:1; Rev. 3:18)[16] pointing toward an objective accomplishment on the cross, not a visible demonstration of an existing reality (God's favor for Gentiles). In Paul's writings redemption is linked to forgiveness of sins (Eph. 1:7; Col. 1:14), justification (Rom. 3:24), and adoption into God's family (Gal. 4:5; Rom. 8:23). This indicates that his concept of redemption involves a change in one's standing before God, not merely a subjective change of heart toward outsiders. The ecclesiological reading, as N.T. Wright notes, is simply 'tortuous and improbable' and must, therefore, be deemed inadequate.[17]

Wright has offered another alternative to the traditional reading, and in this he has been joined by Richard B. Hays and Hans Boersma.[18] The interpretive proposal put forth by these scholars might best be deemed the 'national-historical' reading of Galatians 3:10-14. They argue that the traditional reading misunderstands Paul's view of the law. Paul did not assume that no individual Jew could ever fulfill the law. He did not uphold a standard of perfection, for the law itself allowed for human failure by providing various means of atonement. Looking back on his preconversion life, Paul indicates that he had indeed kept the law sufficiently (Phil. 3:6).[19] Hays adds the thought that the traditional reading involves 'a ridiculous caricature of Judaism'.[20] How, then, could Paul argue that all who rely on works of the law fall under the curse of the law? The answer lies in the narrative of Israel's history. Israel as a nation had failed to keep the law and was, therefore, experiencing the curse of the exile. Whoever takes on Israel's identity markers ('works of the law'), therefore, joins Israel under the curse.[21] However, in Christ a shift in redemptive history has occurred. In verse 13, Paul declares, 'Christ redeemed us [i.e., believing Jews] from the curse of the law by becoming a curse for us'.

---

[16] Morris, *Apostolic Preaching*, pp. 53-60. The use of ἐξαγοράζω in Eph. 5:16 and Col. 4:5 does not constitute an exception, for there Paul exhorts his readers to 'buy up' the time, which means to 'redeem' it or make the most of it.

[17] N.T. Wright, *The Climax of the Covenant: Christ and the Law in Pauline Theology* (Minneapolis: Fortress, 1992), p. 153.

[18] Wright, *Climax*, pp. 137-56; idem, *Paul: In Fresh Perspective* (Minneapolis: Fortress, 2005), pp. 139-40; idem, *Paul for Everyone: Galatians and Thessalonians* (London: SPCK, 2002), pp. 31-35; Richard B. Hays, *The Letter to the Galatians*, in vol. 11 of Leander E. Keck (ed), *The New Interpreter's Bible* (Nashville: Abingdon, 2000), pp. 256-62; idem, *The Faith of Jesus Christ: The Narrative Substructure of Galatians 3:1-4:11*, 2nd ed. (Grand Rapids: Eerdmans, 2002), pp. 177-83; Hans Boersma, *Violence, Hospitality, and the Cross: Reappropriating the Atonement Tradition* (Grand Rapids: Baker Academic, 2004), pp. 170-77.

[19] Wright, *Climax*, p. 145; Hays, *The Letter to the Galatians*, p. 257; Boersma, *Violence*, p. 174.

[20] Hays, *The Letter to the Galatians*, 257.

[21] Wright, *Climax*, pp. 146-49; Hays, *The Letter to the Galatians*, pp. 257-59; Boersma, *Violence*, pp. 174-76.

That is, Christ took upon himself Israel's exile (the curse threatened in Deuteronomy 28) and exhausted it. He suffered as Israel's representative, thereby removing the curse from Israel and putting back on course God's redemptive purpose for the world, which had been blocked by Israel's failure. This is why Paul concludes by saying that the blessing of Abraham has come to the Gentiles (v. 14).[22]

The national-historical reading of Galatians 3:10-14 is not without merit. Its proponents rightly discern the importance of the redemptive-historical shift that has occurred with the atoning work of Christ. Israel's exile does indeed represent a vivid, climactic expression of the curse of the law from which believers in the new covenant age have been delivered. Wright, Hays, and Boersma do well to trace elements of Scripture's storyline in Paul's argument, for the sequence of events in the Old Testament forms a major role in his argument in Galatians 3-4.[23] Nevertheless, the national-historical reading does not offer the most plausible interpretation of the passage in question. It must be noted that while Wright, Hays, and Boersma reject the unstated premise of the traditional reading (universal human inability), they nevertheless posit their own unstated premise (the historical reality of Israel's failure and exile).[24] At the very least, then, it is evident that the traditional reading is not the only one forced to infer a major step in the argument that Paul did not make explicit. Which inference, therefore, makes the most sense within the context of Paul's argument? Several considerations indicate that the premise of universal human inability better explains the totality of the evidence than does the premise of Israel's continuing exile.

First, the national-historical reading illegitimately limits both the nature and scope of the curse. On this reading, the curse is reduced to the historical event of the exile and is, therefore, limited in scope to Israel. However, Deuteronomy itself speaks of multiple curses for disobedience: 'But if you will not obey the voice of the LORD your God or be careful to do all his commandments and his statutes that I command you today, then *all these curses* shall come upon you and overtake you' (Deut. 28:15, emphasis added). The list of curses that follows (vv. 16-68) climaxes with exile, but the concept of curse cannot simply be reduced to exile. In fact, Deuteronomy 21:23 (which Paul quotes in v. 13 in reference to Christ's crucifixion) has nothing to do with exile but rather pronounces a curse on all who are hanged on a tree. The five kings executed by

---

[22] Wright, *Climax*, pp. 151-56; Hays, *The Letter to the Galatians*, pp. 260-63; Boersma, *Violence*, pp. 176-77. Hays and Wright differ in their understanding of the scope of 'we' in v. 14. Wright takes it to refer to believing Jews, and Hays takes it as a reference to Jews and Gentiles together.

[23] Most notable is Paul's argument that the Mosaic Covenant—characterized by law—is subordinate to the Abrahamic Covenant—characterized by promise—because of the latter's historical precedence (Gal. 3:15-18).

[24] Wright, *Climax*, pp. 146-48.

Joshua fall under this curse (Josh. 10:26-27), indicating that the scope of divine curse extends beyond Israel. The curse on the ground of Genesis 3:17-19 indicates that all humanity has come under God's wrath, not just Israel. Wright and company mistakenly subsume the idea of curse under exile, when it should actually be the other way around. The exile represents one particular historical demonstration of God's wrath, but God's wrath is directed against all humanity under sin (Rom. 3:9-20; 5:12).

Second, apart from the question of whether or not the continuing exile theme can be sustained as a genuine Pauline category transferred from Second Temple Judaism,[25] the fact remains that positing the continuing exile as the missing step in Paul's argument enables the Judaizers to put him in checkmate with only one move. Agreeing with Paul that Jesus the Messiah had exhausted the exile in himself, thereby bringing it to an end, the Judaizers would have claimed a golden opportunity to recommit themselves (and those under their teaching) to the law. They would have been able to reply to Paul's argument in Galatians 3:10-14 by saying, 'We went into exile for disobedience to the law in the first place. Now that the exile is over, we must reaffirm our commitment to the law so as to avoid going into exile again.'[26] It is difficult to see how Paul's argument on this reading leads to the conclusion that to remain under the law after the coming of Christ puts one back under the curse. Wright and company want to say that because the law led to exile, Gentile believers must not identify themselves with the law. But this only works as an argument if the law always leads to exile, which in turn only follows if human beings are unable to keep the law. Thus, the only way the national-historical reading can make sense is when it smuggles in the unstated premise of the traditional reading: human inability. The redemptive-historical shift away from the law that has occurred in Christ only makes sense if the law was unable to provide salvation because of the universality of sin. If Paul did not presuppose universal human inability, then he would have no answer to the argument that, now that the Messiah has brought the exile to an end, the people of God should go back to the law and get it right this time.

Third, the wording of Paul's quotation of Deuteronomy 27:26 indicates that

---

[25] N.T. Wright (*Justification: God's Plan and Paul's Vision* [Downers Grove, IL: IVP Academic, 2009], pp. 57-63) rightly notes that Daniel 9 paints the future of Israel as one in which the seventy-year exile has been extended. However, it is one thing to take note of a legitimate biblical-theological category and quite another to demonstrate that this particular category forms a major hinge of Paul's theological argumentation. Wright's continuing exile thesis has been critiqued by Mark A. Seifrid, 'Blind Alleys in the Controversy over the Paul of History', *TynBul* 45 (1994), pp. 89-91; Douglas J. Moo, 'Israel and the Law in Romans 5-11: Interaction with the New Perspective', in D.A. Carson, Peter T. O'Brien, and Mark A. Seifrid (eds), *Justification and Variegated Nomism*, vol. 2, *The Paradoxes of Paul* (Grand Rapids: Baker Academic, 2005), pp. 200-05.

[26] Kim, *Paul and the New Perspective*, pp. 138-40.

the law pronounces a curse on anyone who falls short of perfect obedience.[27] The Hebrew text simply pronounces a curse on 'anyone who does not confirm the words of this law by doing them', lacking the adjective 'all' to specify the extent of obedience required. By contrast, the LXX translation pronounces a curse on 'every man who does not abide by all the words of this law to do them'.[28] Significantly, Paul's quotation stands closer to the LXX than to the Hebrew by including the word 'all', yet his wording differs at several points.[29] Whatever thought process lies behind the wording of Paul's quotation (whether a loose adherence to the LXX or his own personal translation of the Hebrew), it appears that Paul made a deliberate choice to include the word 'all' when he could have omitted it. That Paul deliberately chose to specify the extent of obedience required by the law as a total obedience speaks strongly in favor of the traditional reading. The unstated premise of human inability falls right into place once the quotation from Deuteronomy 27:26 establishes a divine standard of perfection, to which no one can attain.

Fourth, the contrast between law and faith that Paul establishes in verses 11-12 speaks not merely of redemptive-historical realities but of underlying principles, namely, the principles of 'doing' and 'receiving'. In verse 11 Paul appeals to Habakkuk 2:4 to establish the principle that eschatological life is received by faith, not law.[30] Even more significant is Paul's direct assertion, 'the law is not of faith' (v. 12). This statement establishes a general principle; it is not a mere observation of a historical contingency. Paul's proof-text for this

---

[27] For a discussion of perfect obedience in Paul, see Thomas R. Schreiner, 'Is Perfect Obedience to the Law Possible? A Re-Examination of Galatians 3:10', *JETS* 27, no. 2 (1984), pp. 151-60; idem, 'Paul and Perfect Obedience to the Law: An Evaluation of the View of E.P. Sanders', *WTJ* 47 (1985), pp. 245-78.

[28] My translation.

[29] אָרוּר אֲשֶׁר לֹא־יָקִים אֶת־דִּבְרֵי הַתּוֹרָה־הַזֹּאת לַעֲשׂוֹת אוֹתָם (MT)

ἐπικατάρατος πᾶς ἄνθρωπος ὃς οὐκ ἐμμενεῖ ἐν πᾶσιν τοῖς λόγοις τοῦ νόμου τούτου τοῦ ποιῆσαι αὐτούς (LXX)

ἐπικατάρατος πᾶς ὃς οὐκ ἐμμενεῖ πᾶσιν τοῖς γεγραμμένοις ἐν τῷ βιβλίῳ τοῦ νόμου τοῦ ποιῆσαι αὐτά (Paul)

[30] Paul's use of Habakkuk 2:4 here and in Romans 1:17 is full of exegetical landmines, and it is beyond the scope of this work to investigate them here. The best interpretation of both Habakkuk and Paul is provided by Mark A. Seifrid, *Christ, Our Righteousness: Paul's Theology of Justification* (Downers Grove: InterVarsity, 2000), pp. 37-38. For a lengthy exegetical and theological treatment that follows the main contours of Seifrid's proposal, see Alexander Stewart, 'The Hermeneutical Validity of Paul's Use of Habakkuk 2:4 in Romans 1:17' (paper presented at the southeastern regional meeting of the Evangelical Theological Society, Chattanooga, TN, 4 April 2009). However, the argument for opposing principles of 'doing' and 'receiving' that forms the hinge of the law-faith antithesis in these verses is not dependent on any one particular interpretation of Paul's use of Habakkuk 2:4. For example, Bruce (*Galatians*, pp. 161-62) takes an approach that differs from Seifrid but nevertheless reaches a similar theological conclusion.

assertion is Leviticus 18:5: 'The one who does them [the requirements of the law] shall live by them.' Paul quotes this verse to establish the point that eschatological life is promised to the one who 'does' the law, but this way of attaining life is not the way of faith, for it operates by a different principle.[31] Thus, the law is not of faith. Paul has drawn a clear distinction between law and gospel, a distinction that exists *in principle* and therefore also in redemptive history. The exile of Israel-under-Torah may indeed lie in the background of Paul's thought here, but when an exegete allows the background to swallow up the foreground, the result is reductionism. The national-historical reading fails to grasp that Paul's argument reaches back through the failure of Israel to an underlying Adamic condition common to all nations.

Fifth, the wider context of Paul's argument confirms the unstated premise of the traditional reading. The 'climax and capstone' of Paul's argument in Galatians 3-4 appears in 4:21-5:1, where Paul connects Hagar and Sarah to Mount Sinai/the present Jerusalem and the heavenly Jerusalem, respectively.[32] The primary difference between the two women is that Hagar the slave gave birth to a son 'born according to the flesh', whereas Sarah the free woman gave birth to a son 'born through promise' (Gal. 4:23). Ishmael was born when Abram and Sarai took it upon themselves to act independently of God in an attempt to attain his blessing. His birth was the result of mere human effort. By contrast, the unlikely birth of Isaac was the fulfillment of a divine promise. As Fesko rightly notes, 'the contrast is between sinful human effort, or works-righteousness, and grace'.[33] This is the same contrast evident in the traditional reading of Galatians 3:10-14. The point of the Hagar/Sarah contrast is not to establish that Israel has, in fact, failed to keep the law and now lies under the punishment of an ongoing exile. The point, rather, is that the law itself represents a way of relating to God that is incompatible with receiving the promise. Paul links Hagar and Ishmael to the law in order to demonstrate that no autonomous effort on the part of sinful humanity can bring the promise of God to fulfillment. The law is not of faith.

Following right on the heels of Paul's capstone argument in Galatians 4:21-

---

[31] It may be true that Leviticus 18:5, in its original context, speaks of a faithful Israelite living a blessed life in the promised land without specific reference to eschatological life. However, it appears that Paul uses the promise in a typological manner to encompass eschatological life, which is promised to those who obey the law perfectly. The reason for this assertion is the parallel use of the verb ζήσεται from both Habakkuk 2:4 and Leviticus 18:5 (vv. 11, 12). The former clearly refers to eschatological life because it is tied conceptually to justification. By implication, then, the latter also refers to eschatological life.

[32] J.V. Fesko, *Justification: Understanding the Classic Reformed Doctrine* (Phillipsburg, NJ: P & R, 2008), 175. It is beyond the scope of this work to investigate the nature of Paul's interpretive method here, whether it stands closer to what modern scholars refer to as 'typology' or 'allegory'.

[33] Fesko, *Justification*, p. 175.

5:1 is his warning in 5:2-6 that acceptance of circumcision entails a nullification of the benefits of Christ, a falling away from grace. Why does Paul make such a radical claim? It is because 'every man who accepts circumcision …is obligated to keep the whole law [ὅλον τὸν νόμον]' (v. 3). The man who binds himself to the law through circumcision puts himself under the obligation of perfect obedience, which is impossible for sinners to attain.[34] Therefore, to accept circumcision is to accept the inevitable consequence of failing to keep the law, and that is the curse of the law. Significantly, Paul's argument here focuses not on the plight of national Israel but on the demands placed upon the individual. Paul does not say that acceptance of circumcision identifies one with Israel-in-exile. Nowhere does he paint the threat of Judaizing with that particular brush. Rather, the threat represented in Galatians 5:2-6 is specifically the threat of an individual taking on an impossible obligation and thereby incurring the consequence of failing to fulfill it. In other words, Paul's warning is not based on the reality that Israel *has* failed to keep the law (true though that may be); rather, it is based on the reality that no one *can* fulfill the law, ever. Therefore, as a means of right standing with God, acceptance of the gospel entails leaving the law behind. Insofar as they pertain to the legal basis of justification, the way of the law and the way of faith are antithetical in principle.

These five considerations indicate that, with regard to Galatians 3:10-14, the unstated premise of the traditional reading makes better sense in context than does the unstated premise of the national-historical reading. If, therefore, Paul presupposes in Galatians 3:10 that no one is capable of fulfilling the law, the bicovenantal structure of his doctrine of justification becomes evident. Because no one can live up to the demand for perfect obedience (Deut. 27:26), which is the condition by which the law promises eternal life (Lev. 18:5), the only pathway to justification for a sinful race is faith (Hab. 2:4) directed to the crucified Christ, who has taken the curse of the law upon himself (Deut. 21:23). Strict legalism is not a necessary foil to this argument. Any blurring of the distinction between law and gospel could have summoned this response from Paul.

Romans 9:30-10:13

In a passage situated within a larger argument concerning Israel's unbelief and the divine purpose behind it (Romans 9-11), Paul explores the failure of Israel by drawing a contrast between two kinds of righteousness. This contrast is stated three times in Romans 9:30-10:13:

---

[34] Galatians 6:13 further confirms this point by indicating that the Judaizers themselves were not really law-keepers, in spite of appearances to the contrary. No doubt the Judaizers would have disagreed with Paul's assessment, showing that Paul, who viewed the law through the lens of the gospel, understood the law's demand as much higher than any sinful human being could attain.

(1) 'the righteousness based on faith' versus 'the law of righteousness'
     (9:30-31);
(2) 'the righteousness of God' versus 'their own righteousness' (10:3);
(3) 'the righteousness based on the law' versus 'the righteousness
     based on faith' (10:5-6).[35]

These two different kinds of righteousness represent, respectively, the righteous
status promised by the law for perfect obedience, which is unattainable for
fallen human beings, and the righteousness that is freely given by God through
the gospel and is received by faith. This reading makes the best sense of the
flow of Paul's argument.

In 9:30-32, Paul contrasts the Gentiles as those who have attained
righteousness, even though they did not pursue it, with Israel, who pursued 'a
law that would lead to righteousness'[36] but did not attain it. 'Righteousness'
here must refer to a forensic reality, that of right standing in God's courtroom,
not a moral condition, for certainly Paul was well aware that many pagans
pursued virtue with great energy.[37] Paul goes on to explain that Israel 'did not
succeed in reaching that law' because 'they did not pursue it by faith, but as if it
were based on works'. The primary question that surrounds this passage is this:
what is the nature of Paul's contrast between these two kinds of righteousness?
Is it a contrast between law and gospel, or does Paul place law and gospel on
one side over against Israel's *misuse* of the law on the other?

Scholars who favor the latter view include C.E.B. Cranfield, Daniel P.
Fuller, James D.G. Dunn, and N.T. Wright.[38] Cranfield and Fuller identify
Israel's misuse of the law as a form of legalism by which they sought to place
God in their debt, while Dunn and Wright identify Israel's misuse of the law as
a form of nationalism by which they took pride in their status as those marked

---

[35] Douglas J. Moo, *The Epistle to the Romans*, NICNT (Grand Rapids: Eerdmans, 1996),
p. 619.
[36] The ESV rendering of νόμον δικαιοσύνης is clearly interpretive, but it makes the best
sense in context. Paul's statement that Israel 'did not succeed in reaching that law' is
antithetical to the statement that the Gentiles have attained righteousness. The
conceptual parallel between the 'righteousness' that the Gentiles have attained and the
'law' that Israel has not attained implies that Paul is thinking of the law as a means to
righteousness.
[37] Moo, *Romans*, p. 621.
[38] C.E.B. Cranfield, *The Epistle to the Romans*, vol. 2, ICC (Edinburgh: T & T Clark,
1979), pp. 508-10; Daniel P. Fuller, *Gospel and Law: Contrast or Continuum? The
Hermeneutics of Dispensationalism and Covenant Theology* (Grand Rapids: Eerdmans,
1980), pp. 71-79; idem, *The Unity of the Bible: Unfolding God's Plan for Humanity*
(Grand Rapids: Zondervan, 1992), pp. 465-67; James D.G. Dunn, *Romans 9-16*, WBC,
vol. 38B (Dallas: Word, 1988), p. 593; Wright, *Climax*, p. 240.

out by Torah over against Gentile outsiders. The view that Israel's misuse of the law, as opposed to the law itself, stands in contrast with 'the righteousness based on faith' is an attractive option specifically because of Paul's statement that Israel did not attain the law of righteousness '[b]ecause they did not pursue it by faith [ἐκ πίστεως], but as if it were based on works [ὡς ἐξ ἔργων]' (v. 32). With some measure of plausibility, the scholars who favor this view have argued that all along Israel should have pursued the law by faith. According to Cranfield, this kind of pursuit of the law would have entailed

> accepting, without evasion or resentment, the law's criticism of one's life, recognizing that one can never so adequately fulfil its righteous requirements as to put God in one's debt, accepting God's proffered mercy and forgiveness and in return giving oneself to Him in love and gratitude and so beginning to be released from one's self-centredness and turned in the direction of a humble obedience that is free from self-righteousness.[39]

Dunn agrees that Israel should have pursued the law by faith, but he differs in his explanation of what this would have entailed:

> But the obedience God looked for was the obedience of faith, obedience from the heart (6:17), that is, from a commitment and lifestyle which penetrated far below matters of race and of ritual and which could be sustained and maintained independently of either. This was the lesson Israel ought to have learned from its own scriptural record of God's choice of Isaac and Jacob (9:6-13) but evidently had failed to do so.[40]

That Israel has misused the law is plain from Paul's argument.[41] However, it does not necessarily follow that Israel's misuse of the law implies that the law itself must be regarded 'as an offer of grace which is to be fulfilled "in faith"'.[42] A recognition of the misuse of the law on Israel's part does not entail a denial of the law-gospel antithesis. In spite of the apparent merits of the view represented by Cranfield, Dunn, and others, this construal of Paul's argument must ultimately be rejected, for the following reasons.[43]

First, within the immediate context there is clear evidence of a contrast

---

[39] Cranfield, *Romans*, p. 510.
[40] Dunn, *Romans 9-16*, p. 593.
[41] Israel's failure to recognize Christ as the τέλος of the law (Rom 10:4) is the primary exemplification of this failure.
[42] Seifrid, *Christ, Our Righteousness*, p. 120. Seifrid here does not represent his own position but describes what has become a popular view of the law.
[43] Scholars who stand on the other side of this question, locating the antithesis between law and gospel instead of between Israel's misuse of the law on the one hand and law-gospel on the other, include Moo, *Romans*, pp. 620-30; Seifrid, *Christ, Our Righteousness*, pp. 120-23; Westerholm, *Perspectives Old and New*, pp. 325-30.

between law and gospel. Romans 10:5-6 contrasts 'the righteousness that is based on the law' with 'the righteousness based on faith'. Here 'law' and 'faith' stand over against one another. Paul again quotes Leviticus 18:5 in Romans 10:5 in order to demonstrate that the principle of 'doing' is at work in the law according to the law's own testimony, as opposed to faith. Second, there is clear evidence elsewhere in Paul of a law-gospel contrast, most notably in Galatians 3:12, which explicitly affirms that the law is not of faith. Philippians 3:9 likewise distinguishes between the righteousness of the law and the righteousness of faith.[44] In light of these clear statements, it strains credulity to imagine that Paul would have set law and gospel on a continuum in Romans 9:30-32.

Third, and perhaps most significant, the law-gospel contrast can be maintained in Romans 9:30-32 even while acknowledging Israel's misuse of the law as a major component of Paul's argument. Paul's argument becomes clear once it is recognized that the particular failure on Israel's part that Paul has in mind is neither a legalistic distortion of the law (as Cranfield argues) nor a nationalistic distortion of it (as Dunn argues), even though both claims might be true to some degree. Rather, what Paul specifically affirms about Israel is that they 'have stumbled over the stumbling stone' (v. 32), and this constitutes their failure to pursue the 'law that would lead to righteousness' by faith.[45] In other words, Israel has failed with respect to the law by failing to heed the law's own testimony to Christ and, consequently, to the law's own limitations. The main problem with respect to the law is, at root, neither legalistic nor nationalistic, but Christological in character. Israel has distorted the law by absolutizing it, when the law itself always looked forward to the day when its guardian role would be brought to end by the advent of faith (Gal. 3:23-25). Thus, Paul does argue that Israel has misused the law, but this misuse is tied specifically to a failure to recognize that law must give way to gospel. Israel pursued by works the law that would lead to righteousness, but was ultimately unable to offer the obedience required by the law. Instead, Israel should have

---

[44] Westerholm, *Perspectives Old and New*, pp. 327-28

[45] Seifrid (*Christ, Our Righteousness*, 120-21) rightly argues, 'This "pursuit of the law by faith" does not constitute some special form of accomplishment of the demands of the law. We can hardly set aside the message which Paul has presented thus far in Romans when we arrive at this passage. He surely has not forgotten his declaration that "apart from the law . . . the righteousness of God has been manifest" (3:21), or his assertion that "the law works wrath" (4:15). This same understanding of the law is implicit in Paul's citation of Leviticus 18:5 in 10:5 ("the one who does these things shall live by them"). Furthermore, "faith" for Paul cannot be regarded as the special means by which one may obey the law properly, since it is not a mere disposition of the human being. Faith is defined by its content: Israel stumbled against the stone which God placed in Zion and did not submit to Christ, the righteousness of God (9:33; 10:3; cf. 2 Cor. 1:20). To "pursue the law from faith", as Israel might have done, would have been to look for and expect "Christ", who, Paul says, "is the goal (*telos*) of the law" (10:4)'.

recognized the law as a sign pointing away from itself and to Christ.[46] In short, to pursue the 'law that would lead to righteousness' by works means to strive to obey the demands of the law, which are impossible for fallen human beings to fulfill, as a means of right standing with God. On the other hand, to pursue the 'law that would lead to righteousness' by faith means to recognize from the law itself its own inherent limitations and believe in Christ, to whom it points and gives way. In this latter sense, the law does in fact lead to righteousness, but only by pointing beyond itself. In Romans 9:30-32, Paul's thought with regard to the law moves in the same orbit as his statement in Galatians 2:19: 'For *through the law* I died to the law, so that I might live to God' (emphasis added).[47]

The second contrast between two kinds of righteousness in this passage is that between Israel's own righteousness and the righteousness of God (10:3). Israel, Paul says, did not submit to God's righteousness because they are ignorant of it and are, consequently, bent on establishing their own righteousness.[48] Some have argued that the nature of this contrast pertains to Israel's nationalism. According to this view, Israel has jealously sought to guard its own privileged status through the boundary markers of the law, thereby establishing 'their own' righteousness, a righteousness that does not extend to the Gentiles. But this narrow view of God's saving purpose demonstrates their ignorance of the fact that God's plan has always been to establish an international people. In this way, Israel has failed to submit to the

---

[46] In light of his precise definition of 'law of righteousness' (*Romans*, 622-26), Moo would likely argue that this interpretation equivocates on the meaning of 'law', switching back and forth between law as 'demand' and law as 'revelation', the former referring more narrowly to the commands of the law and the latter referring more broadly to the Torah as canonical Scripture. In response, I would argue that Paul himself uses the term 'law' in this kind of flexible manner in other places. He can oppose faith to 'works of the law' in Romans 3:28 and then immediately claim, 'we uphold the law' in 3:31, followed by a reference to Abraham's justification, an event announced by the law itself (4:1-5). He can argue that 'the righteousness of God has been manifested apart from the law', and then immediately say that 'the Law and the Prophets bear witness to it' (Rom 3:21). Moo's argument on this latter verse appears overly pedantic.

[47] A similar reading of Romans 9:30-32 is presented by John Piper, *The Future of Justification: A Response to N.T. Wright* (Wheaton: Crossway, 2007), pp. 191-95. Piper distinguishes between the 'overall, long-term aim of the law', which is to point to Christ and so give testimony to faith, and the 'short-term aim of the law', which is rightly described as 'not of faith' (Gal. 3:12). According to its short-term aim, the law demands perfect obedience. But according to its overall, long-term aim, the law points to the gospel.

[48] Moo, *Romans*, p. 636, rightly argues that both participles ἀγνοοῦντες and ζητοῦντες are causal.

righteousness of God.[49] As Wright cleverly remarks, 'It is as though the postman were to imagine that all the letters in his bag were intended for him.'[50] This view sees no inherent contrast between law and gospel, but rather, as in 9:30-32, a contrast between Israel's (nationalistic) misuse of the law and the saving purpose of God expressed through both the law and the gospel. This interpretation views Israel's own righteousness as a corporate reality dependent on her elect status as opposed to a possession of individual Israelites dependent on obedience to the law.

Moo rightly argues, however, that 'their own' is better interpreted in a distributive sense here, referring to a righteousness sought by each individual Israelite on the basis of law-keeping.[51] He offers three convincing reasons for this interpretation. First, Paul's reference to 'their own righteousness' has Old Testament antecedents, the most notable of which is the reference in Deuteronomy 9:4-6:

> Do not say in your heart, after the LORD your God has thrust them out before you, 'It is because of my righteousness that the LORD has brought me in to possess this land', whereas it is because of the wickedness of these nations that the LORD is driving them out before you. Not because of your righteousness or the uprightness of your heart are you going in to possess their land, but because of the wickedness of these nations the LORD your God is driving them out from before you, and that he may confirm the word that the LORD swore to your fathers, to Abraham, to Isaac, and to Jacob.

Significantly, this passage defines Israel's own (non-existent) righteousness in opposition to the wickedness of the nations, indicating that righteousness refers to doing what is right. Here Moses forbids Israel, not from jealously guarding her covenant membership and thereby excluding the nations from blessing, but rather from thinking that she has done anything to deserve the Lord's favor. Furthermore, in the Hebrew this passage contains all singular pronouns, adding a personalized dimension to the command. To be sure, this command is directed to Israel as a whole, but it is given in terms that would be applicable to every Israelite as an individual.[52] This is an illuminating Old Testament background for Paul's statement in Romans 10:3, and that Paul had it in mind is

---

[49] Dunn, *Romans 9-16*, pp. 595-96; N.T. Wright, *What Saint Paul Really Said: Was Paul of Tarsus the Real Founder of Christianity?* (Grand Rapids: Eerdmans, 1997), p. 108.
[50] Wright, *What Saint Paul Really Said*, p. 108.
[51] Moo, *Romans*, pp. 634-35. Although Moo does not say so, it would be incorrect to exclude the corporate dimension from this text. Individual Israelites pursued righteousness, but they did so as part of the covenant people. Both realities are true at the same time, and it is reductionistic to use one to exclude the other.
[52] The *shema* of Deuteronomy 6:4-9 follows the same individual/corporate dynamic. It is addressed to the nation ('Hear, O Israel!'), and yet the pronouns are all singular.

evident from his quotation of the phrase 'Do not say in your heart' in Romans 10:6.

Second, within the immediate context Israel's attempt to establish their own righteousness parallels their pursuit of the law of righteousness by works instead of by faith (9:32) and, most convincingly, 'the righteousness that is based on the law' of 10:5, which Paul specifically defines according to the demand of Leviticus 18:5. In other words, the nature of the contrast that runs through this passage is between doing and receiving, just as in Galatians 3:10-14.

Third, the closest parallel to this passage is Philippians 3:9, where Paul contrasts 'a righteousness of my own that comes from the law' with 'that which comes through faith in Christ', which he further defines as 'the righteousness from God that depends on faith'. Although this too is a disputed passage that will be discussed below, two observations are noteworthy here: (1) Paul speaks of his own personal righteousness as a faithful Jew, which demonstrates that corporate righteousness is not the only category in his thinking; (2) this righteousness is specifically said to be 'from the law' (ἐκ νόμου), which, in light of Paul's use of Leviticus 18:5 in other contexts, implies that righteousness, and thus eternal life, is a reward for obedience. In light of these considerations, it is best to conclude that Israel's attempt to establish their own righteousness constitutes an attempt to pursue righteousness by obedience to the law, in spite of the law's own testimony to its limitations. Paul says of Israel, 'they did not submit to God's righteousness' (Rom 10:3), which is conceptually parallel to his previous statement, 'They have stumbled over the stumbling stone' (Rom 9:32). In short, Israel has failed to believe in Christ, and so they go on pursuing the law in the time of its obsolescence. The hinge of the entire section appears in 10:4, where Paul declares, 'For Christ is the end of the law for righteousness to everyone who believes.'[53] So far, Paul's argument in Romans 9:30-10:4 is primarily redemptive-historical, drawing a distinction between the Law of Moses and the gospel of Christ because of their respective places in history.

However, beginning in 10:5, the argument turns toward a matter of inherent principle, and here appears the contrast between 'the righteousness that is based on the law' (τὴν δικαιοσύνην τὴν ἐκ νόμου) and 'the righteousness based on faith' (ἡ ἐκ πίστεως δικαιοσύνη). As in Galatians 3:12, Paul appeals to Leviticus 18:5 in reference to the righteousness offered by the law and then contrasts the principle of having eschatological life by means of obedience with the principle of grace operative in the gospel. Interestingly, Paul sets Leviticus 18:5 in contrast with Deuteronomy 30:12-14. The nature of the contrast is apparent: 'the person who does the commandments' (Rom. 10:5/Lev. 18:5) is the person who could claim to have performed a magnificent feat, such as

---

[53] Moo, *Romans*, pp. 638-43, rightly argues that τέλος carries both the sense of termination and goal, and thus he prefers the term 'culmination'.

ascending into heaven or descending into the abyss (Rom. 10:6/Deut. 30:12-13). But because the righteousness of faith stands opposed to the righteousness of the law, there is no need to perform such an impossible feat. Christ does not need to be retrieved either from heaven or from the abyss by the strength of human effort. The righteousness of faith declares, instead, 'The word is near you, in your mouth and in your heart', which Paul goes on to define as the word of faith proclaimed in the gospel (Rom. 10:8-10). Divine grace has brought Christ near through the gospel, where he is to be received in faith, not attained by effort. Paul operates with a works/grace contrast here, which corresponds to that between law and faith. The argument follows these lines of thought, but it is difficult to see how Paul could quote one Old Testament passage that, in context, refers to the accessibility of the law (Deut. 30:12-14) in order to express a gospel principle in opposition to another Old Testament passage that refers to the demands of the law (Lev. 18:5). In other words, how can Paul use a passage about the law to refer to the gospel, specifically as the gospel stands in contrast to the law?

Dunn argues that Deuteronomy 30:12-14 emphasizes both inward and outward obedience, whereas Leviticus 18:5 emphasizes only 'doing', which slides easily into a mere externalism, and so herein lies the contrast between the two.[54] This view, by arguing that only Israel's misuse of the law is in view and not the law itself, does not adequately grasp the law-faith contrast that runs throughout this passage. The promise of life as a reward for 'doing' contained in Leviticus 18:5 is presented as a genuine promise, though admittedly no fallen human being could ever attain it. As such, it establishes a law-principle that is inherently different from the gospel. In contrast to Dunn, Schreiner locates the contrast between these two Old Testament passages in the new covenant idea of Deuteronomy 30:1-10, which promises circumcision of the heart on the other side of exile, so that Paul is actually speaking of different epochs in redemptive history.[55] This view rightly maintains the law-faith antithesis, but it suffers from one major weakness: it fails to note the shift that takes place within Deuteronomy 30. Certainly, verses 1-10 speak of new covenant realities, but verse 11 refocuses attention on the Israel of Moses' day, exhorting them to obey the law by removing from them any claim that they did not know what God had commanded. Since the verses Paul quotes stand outside the section dealing with new covenant realities, it seems unlikely that Paul would set up the contrast in precisely the way that Schreiner argues. The best view of Paul's contrast is that offered by Moo, who finds in the quotation from Deuteronomy 30:12-14 a principle of grace evident in Israel's history and now even more evident in the proclamation of Christ crucified.[56] In other words, Paul focuses

---

[54] Dunn, *Romans 9-16*, pp. 613-14.

[55] Thomas R. Schreiner, *Romans*, BECNT (Grand Rapids: Baker, 1998), pp. 557-58.

[56] Moo, *Romans*, p. 653. He writes, 'The grace of God that underlies the Mosaic covenant is operative now in the New Covenant; and, just as Israel could not plead the

on the law as demand when he quotes Leviticus 18:5, but he focuses on the law as a gracious act of divine revelation when he quotes Deuteronomy 30:12-14. The former stands in opposition to faith, whereas the latter stands in continuity with it.

Thus, there is evident in Romans 9:30-10:13 the same kind of law-gospel distinction that was seen in Galatians 3:10-14. The righteousness of faith (9:30; 10:6), which is another way of referring to the righteousness of God (10:3), stands opposed to the righteousness of the law (10:5), and it is the latter that Israel aimed for in their pursuit of 'a law that would lead to righteousness' (9:31), which is another way of saying that they tried establish 'their own' righteousness (10:3). Israel has failed to see the law's testimony to its own obsolescence, and so they go on pursuing the law for what they cannot attain through it. Only the gospel gives what the law cannot provide. This bicovenantal distinction stands opposed to any attempt to achieve right standing with God by means of the law, whether it be a strict legalism, as in Weber's portrayal of Judaism, or in the softer legalism of Sanders' covenantal nomism.

Philippians 3:2-11

For the purpose of this study, only two questions about Paul's argument concerning justification in Philippians 3 demand attention. First, what does Paul mean when he refers to his former observance of the law as 'blameless' (v. 6)? Second, what is the nature of the contrast between 'a righteousness of my own that comes from the law' and 'the righteousness from God that depends on faith' (v. 9)? Each question will be pursued in turn.

The question of Paul's blamelessness with respect to the law impacts the thesis of this section, for if one understands Paul to mean that he had obeyed the law sufficiently to meet its demands, then it follows that he did not regard the law as demanding perfect obedience.[57] Sanders argues that Paul saw no inherent deficiency in his former obedience: 'Paul had no trouble fulfilling the law satisfactorily. It is most important that Paul's argument concerning the law does not in fact rest on man's inability to fulfil it.'[58] The nature of the contrast between the righteousness of faith and the righteousness of the law, according to Sanders, is not that the latter is deficient and the former is not. It is, rather,

---

excuse that she did not know God's will, so now, Paul says, neither Jew nor Gentile can plead ignorance of God's revelation in Jesus Christ.' See also the helpful discussion in Seifrid, *Christ, Our Righteousness*, pp. 122-23.

[57] Krister Stendahl appealed to Philippians 3:6 in order to argue against the idea that the pre-Christian Paul had a troubled conscience in his groundbreaking article, 'The Apostle Paul and the Introspective Conscience of the West', *Harvard Theological Review* 56 (1963), pp. 199-215. This article was reprinted in Krister Stendahl, *Paul among Jews and Gentiles* (Philadelphia: Fortress, 1976), pp. 78-96.

[58] E.P. Sanders, *Paul and Palestinian Judaism: A Comparison of Patterns of Religion* (Minneapolis: Fortress, 1977), p. 443; idem, *Paul, the Law, and the Jewish People* (Philadelphia: Fortress, 1983), pp. 44-45.

that the righteousness of faith supersedes the righteousness of the law in such a way that by comparison the latter becomes nothing.

It is better, however, to understand Paul's claim to blamelessness as one that proceeds from a Pharisaic perspective. Insofar as he adhered to the law's demands, viewed through the lens of his former Pharisaic piety, Paul really was blameless (ἄμεμπτος). In other words, his public reputation was without blemish; no one could charge him with wrongdoing with respect to the standards of the law as interpreted within his community.[59] A similar concept is present in the demand of the Pastoral Epistles that overseers/elders should be 'above reproach' (1 Tim. 3:2; Tit. 1:6), that is, without any overt character deficiencies.[60] The blamelessness in view in Philippians 3:6 (as well as in the Pastorals) pertains to one's standing before men, and it does not conflict with Paul's clear teaching elsewhere that the law has no power to justify sinful human beings before God (Rom. 3:20).

Furthermore, there are positive indications in the context of Philippians 3 that Paul the Christian does not share the evaluation of Paul the Pharisee regarding the praiseworthiness of his former obedience to the law. In other words, where Paul the Pharisee could claim to be blameless by Pharisaic standards, Paul the Christian understands that his former life was full of sin. The most obvious clue from the immediate context is the fact that Paul cites his persecution of the church as a demonstration of his zeal for the law (v. 6).[61] It is beyond question that Paul the Christian regards as sinful what Paul the Pharisee once regarded as honoring to God (1 Cor. 15:9; 1 Tim. 1:12-16). In addition, Paul begins his argument in this section by warning, 'Look out for the dogs, look out for the evildoers, look out for those who mutilate the flesh' (v. 2). He then proceeds to list his own former credentials as one who used to belong to that group.[62] It is obvious, then, that Paul's blamelessness in verse 6 is relative to the standards of his community as a Pharisee. From the perspective of the gospel, his ritual purity is like the uncleanness of a dog; his works are those of an evildoer; his circumcision is mutilation of the flesh. And so he counts it all as loss and dung (vv. 7-8). This language is not merely a hyperbolic expression

---

[59] Peter T. O'Brien, *The Epistle to the Philippians*, NIGTC (Grand Rapids: Eerdmans, 1991), pp. 379-81; Gordon D. Fee, *Paul's Letter to the Philippians*, NICNT (Grand Rapids: Eerdmans, 1995), pp. 309-10; Schreiner, 'Paul and Perfect Obedience', p. 260-62.

[60] The word ἄμεμπτος is not used in either 1 Timothy 3:2 or Titus 1:6, but the terms ἀνεπίλημπτον and ἀνέγκλητος communicate a similar idea.

[61] O'Brien, *Philippians*, pp. 375-76 rightly argues that while Paul does not specifically mention the law in connection with his zeal, the law is implied as the focus of his zeal.

[62] Of course, Paul is warning about the threat of Judaizers, a group to which he never belonged. But as a Pharisee who persecuted the church, Paul's zeal for the law and opposition to the truth of the gospel parallels that of the Judaizers who troubled his churches. And that is why he is able to capitalize on his former experience as a Pharisee in his argument against them.

showing how much Christ surpasses everything else by comparison. It is a true statement of what sinful opposition to the truth of the gospel is, opposition represented by Paul's former persecution of the church as well as the Judaizing threat to some of the churches he planted. It is no wonder, then, that Paul attributes every former credential to the flesh (v. 4), which he says elsewhere is incapable of pleasing God (Rom. 8:7-8; 7:14, 18). Westerholm aptly makes the case for this understanding of Paul's 'blamelessness':

> The point Paul is making is that he knows the righteousness of the law as well as any and surpassed others in its performance, so that the Philippians may safely trust his judgment, follow his example, and reject the advocates of the law: that is his *point*. From what he says one may also *infer* that he did not suffer from poor self-esteem, nor was his conscience of an introspective, troubled sort. On the other hand, it would be wrong to conclude from what Paul says here that he saw nothing unsatisfactory in the righteousness of the law and only opted for faith in Christ because it somehow seemed even better. Though 'blameless' from his former perspective, his persecution of the church (3:6) could only have appeared to him, from the moment he encountered the risen Christ, as a bad thing to have done (cf. 1 Cor. 15:9). And all his merits under the law he characterizes as belonging to the realm of the flesh (Phil. 3:3-4). For Paul that means they could not please God (cf. Gal. 3:3; Rom. 8:7-8); true service is carried out by the *Spirit* of God (Phil. 3:3).[63]

In no way does Paul's claim to a certain kind of blamelessness in his former piety amount to a denial of the divine demand for perfect obedience. Paul the Christian fully understands that the blamelessness of Paul the Pharisee, originating from the flesh, amounts to nothing before God.

Having addressed the first question, we can now proceed to the second: what is the nature of the contrast between 'a righteousness of my own that comes from the law' and 'the righteousness from God that depends on faith'? According to Wright, Paul does not refer here to 'a moralistic or self-help righteousness, but the status of orthodox Jewish covenant membership'.[64] In keeping with the new perspective's hermeneutical presupposition, Wright apparently wishes to deny that any form of merit theology lies in the background of Paul's statement regarding his own righteousness. By framing an antithesis between 'self-help righteousness' and 'orthodox Jewish covenant membership', Wright implies that Paul's 'own' righteousness consists exclusively in his Jewish identity *as opposed* to his personal piety. But these two things cannot be divided, as is evident from Paul's list of Pharisaic credentials in verses 4-6. He lists four items that pertain to his birth and

---

[63] Westerholm, *Perspectives Old and New*, p. 403, emphasis original.
[64] Wright, *What Saint Paul Really Said*, p. 124; idem, *Justification*, pp. 141-43.

heritage and then three that pertain to his works.[65] Paul's boast in his Jewish heritage moves seamlessly into a boast in his personal devotion to the law.[66] Jewish heritage and personal achievement with respect to the law cannot be divorced from one another, as is further evident in Paul's statement in Galatians 1:14 that he, a Jewish man who shared the same national heritage as his Jewish contemporaries, nevertheless surpassed many of them by his zeal for the law.

When Paul speaks of 'a righteousness of my own that comes from the law', he means a righteous status that is based on doing as opposed to receiving, a righteousness that arises from personal obedience to what the law demands.[67] This righteousness is set in opposition to the righteousness of faith, that which comes from God as a gift through Jesus Christ. Again, Paul sets forth an antithesis between doing and receiving, between law and gospel. Two primary considerations confirm this reading of the passage. First, the strong note of personal achievement with respect to the law has already been noted in Philippians 3:4-6. The mix of Jewish identity and piety unfolded in these verses is specifically what Paul counts as loss in verses 7-8, which in turn may be identified as the basis for the righteousness that Paul rejects in verse 9. To deny any element of obedience to the law as a basis for right standing with God in this passage is to tear Paul's argument asunder. Second, the contrasting righteousness to that which comes from the law is 'the righteousness from God' (τὴν ἐκ θεοῦ δικαιοϛύνην). The preposition ἐκ indicates that the righteousness in view comes from God as a gift and is received by faith (cf. Rom. 5:17). Thus, Paul opposes the gospel to the law in principle once again, showing that to adhere to one for righteousness means to abandon completely the other.

These observations are by no means exhaustive, either in terms of the exegetical detail offered or the range of passages selected. Nevertheless, these three passages provide an adequate sample of the theological reality behind Paul's doctrine of justification: a divine demand for perfect obedience that requires in turn an antithesis between law and gospel. Because the law, which by its very nature demands its hearers to do certain things, cannot be fulfilled by sinful human beings, it must give way to the gift of righteousness that can only be received by faith in Christ. Strict legalism of the Pelagian variety is not

---

[65] In v. 5 Paul lists items of his Jewish heritage: 'circumcised on the eighth day, of the people of Israel, of the tribe of Benjamin, a Hebrew of Hebrews'. Then in vv. 5-6 he lists his own pious works: 'as to the law, a Pharisee; as to zeal, a persecutor of the church; as to righteousness under the law, blameless'.

[66] Paul's Pharisaic devotion to the law cannot be reduced to a mere devotion to the law's external boundary markers. Certainly, devotion to the law would include devotion to its ceremonial aspects, but Paul mentions specifically his standing as a Pharisee, his persecution of the church, and his blamelessness with respect to the law, none of which can be reduced to mere badges of Jewish identity. Thomas R. Schreiner (*The Law and Its Fulfillment: A Pauline Theology of Law* [Grand Rapids: Baker, 1993], pp. 112-14) provides a helpful discussion of the legalistic elements of this passage.

[67] Westerholm, *Perspectives Old and New*, p. 311; O'Brien, *Philippians*, pp. 391-96.

the only teaching that functions as a foil to this Pauline doctrine. Covenantal nomism would also fall under Paul's rebuke. The Reformers, who themselves never encountered a strict legalism in their theological opponents, did not read the law-gospel distinction into Paul. They correctly read it out of him.

JUSTIFICATION AND WORKS

One more exegetical question merits attention here, though it may be answered much more briefly. That question is whether or not Paul's statements regarding judgment according to works (Rom. 2:1-16; 1 Cor. 3:10-15; 2 Cor. 5:10) and James's argument for justification by works (Jas. 2:14-26) necessarily stand at odds with the bicovenantal framework advocated here. Does Paul smuggle the law into the equation of justification through the backdoor by linking the final judgment to works? Does James openly contradict a bicovenantal theology by arguing that justification is by works and not by faith alone? Both questions may be answered in the negative.

Leaving aside the book of James for the time being, it is important to note three theological concepts that Protestant interpreters typically employ when addressing Pauline statements about judgment according to works. All three concepts preserve the law-gospel distinction and the bicovenantal theology that defines the Reformation tradition. The first concept is the standard of judgment under the divine law.[68] Several interpreters have argued that Paul's statement that it is 'the doers of the law who will be justified' (Rom. 2:13) refers to the criterion of judgment according to the law.[69] So far as the law is concerned, the standard of judgment is doing, not merely hearing, and thus the law only justifies those who fulfill it. The fact that no fallen human being will actually fulfill the law in such a way (Rom. 3:20) does not rule out the genuine condition of justification by means of the law on the basis of perfect obedience. The second theological concept employed by Protestant interpreters when approaching passages about judgment according to works is that of rewards that do not belong to the essence of justification. First Corinthians 3:10-15 is a case in point. Paul specifically states that the one whose work does not endure the fire of judgment will nevertheless be saved in the end, 'but only as through fire', that is, with a loss of reward. This passage does not address justification but rather rewards that will be given to those charged with the task of building God's church.[70] Finally, the third theological concept that enables a bicovenantal theology to cohere with the Pauline statements about works is that

---

[68] The divine law in view here is that which is revealed in the Mosaic legislation and in the innate sense of divine demand present in every human heart (Rom. 2:14-16).

[69] Moo, *Romans*, pp. 139-41; 166-68; Westerholm, *Perspectives Old and New*, pp. 267-72; John Murray, *The Epistle to the Romans* (Grand Rapids: Eerdmans, 1968), pp. 71-72; Fesko, *Justification*, pp. 312-13.

[70] See Gordon D. Fee, *The First Epistle to the Corinthians*, NICNT (Grand Rapids: Eerdmans, 1987), pp. 128-45, for a helpful discussion of this passage.

of works as the fruit or manifestation of faith. Although they may differ in their manner of explanation, some interpreters argue that the works of believers will form the evidential basis of their standing with God on the last day. Justification is by faith alone, but faith is necessarily manifested by good works, and thus if the latter are missing, so must the former necessarily be missing as well. Only in this sense, then, will works function as a criterion of judgment on the last day.[71]

Among Protestants there is no widespread agreement about whether all three concepts should be employed at all, or which passages might express which concept. For example, Fesko argues that at the general resurrection, which itself constitutes the final judgment, the works of believers will not be evaluated as manifestations of saving faith. Works only have significance for believers at the final judgment insofar as they result in rewards that are not essentially related to justification.[72] This represents, in effect, a denial of the third concept described above. On the other hand, Schreiner, Seifrid, and Bird deny that the first concept outlined above is present in Romans 2, arguing that justification of the doers of the law refers to the justification of believers, whose works represent manifestations of faith.[73] The exegetical issues involved in adjudicating between these conflicting interpretations would take this study too far away from its purpose at this point, which is merely to affirm the presence of a bicovenantal structure in Paul. Thus, the important point to note here is that wherever one might settle in regard to these in-house debates among Protestants, there is no necessary contradiction between the bicovenantal theology of the Reformation and the Pauline statements regarding judgment according to works.

But what about James's bald assertion, 'You see that a person is justified by works and not by faith alone' (Jas. 2:24)? Does this statement represent a scriptural affirmation that works do have a necessary role to play in the attainment of right legal standing before God?[74] In fact, James does not

---

[71] It is important to note that N.T. Wright's doctrine of justification in relation to the final judgment presents a different strategy altogether. For Wright, justification by faith is only the present anticipation of a final justification on the basis of Spirit-wrought works, that is, 'on the basis of the entire life' (Wright, *What Saint Paul Really Said*, p. 129). Wright's proposal actually entails a twofold justification that blends together law and gospel and is thus incompatible with a bicovenantal theology.

[72] Fesko, *Justification*, pp. 299-331.

[73] Thomas R. Schreiner, *The Law and Its Fulfillment: A Pauline Theology of Law* (Grand Rapids: Baker, 1993), pp. 179-204; idem, *Romans*, pp. 104-45; Seifrid, *Christ, Our Righteousness*, pp. 147-50; Michael Bird, *The Saving Righteousness of God: Studies on Paul, Justification, and the New Perspective* (Eugene, OR: Wipf and Stock, 2007), pp. 155-78.

[74] The apparent tension between Paul and James on this question does not matter if one's concern is only to investigate Paul's understanding of justification. However, the evangelical principle of the unity of Scripture, based on the unity of its divine origin,

contradict the bicovenantal structure or the affirmation of *sola fide* present in Paul. James's concern is different from Paul's, as is his use of important terminology.

It is crucial to recognize the question that James treats throughout 2:14-26. This question is introduced in verse 14: 'What good is it, my brothers, if someone says he has faith but does not have works? Can that faith save him?'[75] This is not the question of justification in the Pauline sense. In fact, James' question already presupposes the Pauline teaching that salvation is by faith.[76] Rather, the question relates to the nature of true, saving faith. Can a faith that does not issue forth in works truly save the one who possesses it? James offers an illustration in verses 15-16 to make his point: well-wishers who see a brother or sister in need and offer nothing more than empty words accomplish nothing. James' conclusion, then, is that faith without works is dead, which means that it is useless and incapable of effecting salvation (v. 17). This statement, the primary argument of the entire section, will be repeated in substance two more times (vv. 20, 26). To this point James has not mentioned justification; his focus is on what constitutes genuine, saving faith.

Verse 18a introduces an objection that faith and works could be viewed as separate spiritual virtues. One believer may exhibit faith, and another may exhibit works, but, according to the objection, there is no reason to suppose the two must always go together. James responds in 18b-19 by affirming that faith can only be demonstrated by deeds. The proof of this assertion lies in the fact that even the demons, who have an intellectual apprehension of central theological truths, possess a kind of faith that is clearly not a saving faith because it is not manifested by works that exhibit trust in God's promise in the gospel. No professing believer would want to possess a kind of faith on par with that of demons. Verse 20 then restates (in a question form) James' primary contention that faith without works is useless, and this question leads into the two illustrations of Abraham and Rahab (vv. 21-25), a section that contains James' most controversial statements. It is important to recognize that the question of verse 20, which concerns the uselessness of faith without works, drives the argument of verses 21-25, demonstrating that James' concern remains, not to discuss justification in its Pauline sense, but to explicate the true

---

demands an explanation of the tension, especially with regard to such an important question for theology.

[75] This discussion follows the outline of the passage provided by Douglas J. Moo, *The Letter of James*, Pillar New Testament Commentary (Grand Rapids: Eerdmans, 2000), p. 119.

[76] J.A. Motyer (*The Message of James*, The Bible Speaks Today [Downers Grove, IL: IVP, 1985], p. 109) writes, 'It is important to ask what James is assuming about his readers. Unless they are accustomed to say "Salvation is by faith" there is no point in James approaching them in this way. But he approaches them with this challenge question, not because he would propose a different way of salvation, but because he would have them understand what "by faith alone" really means.'

nature of saving faith.

In verse 21 he appeals to Genesis 22 in order to prove his point that Abraham was justified by works when he offered up Isaac on the altar. What does James mean when he uses the verb 'justify' (δικαιόω) in this context? Moo argues that the verb most likely means 'vindicate in the judgment'.[77] Tying the present section to James' primary contention about the kind of religion that avails before God (Jas. 1:27), Moo argues that James' point is to affirm that Abraham (and, consequently, all believers) are vindicated in the final judgment before God by works, and this is the sense in which justification is by works. However, this doctrine does not contradict Paul's affirmation of justification by faith, Moo argues, because Paul's doctrine pertains to the initiatory aspect of justification, whereby God puts the ungodly in right standing with himself, and James' doctrine pertains to the final judgment, where those who are believers are vindicated by their works.[78] Moo affirms that this distinction between initial and final justification represents a kind of covenantal nomism, but he seeks to set this teaching apart from Second Temple Judaism by arguing that a monergistic doctrine of salvation (as affirmed by both Paul and James) sets the Christian view apart from the Jewish view.[79] Thus, James can affirm 'that a person is justified by works and not by faith alone' (v. 24) without contradicting Paul because James has the final judgment in view, not the initiatory aspect of salvation.

Moo's helpful exegetical arguments require some minor tweaking, and his theological synthesis between Paul and James requires some major revision. It is doubtful that Paul's doctrine of justification can be limited to an initiatory aspect. For Paul, the final judgment has already been anticipated in the present justification of the ungodly (Rom. 8:1, 33-34). One who relegates Paul's teaching to the beginning aspects of salvation and James' teaching to the final judgment runs the risk of creating two distinct acts of justification, the initial act that is by faith and a subsequent act that is based on works.[80] Is there a better way to fit Paul and James together? Indeed there is. One can adopt Moo's understanding of James' use of δικαιόω as 'vindicate in the judgment' without tying this meaning exclusively to the final judgment. In fact, James' two examples of Abraham and Rahab lead in precisely this direction, for neither example pertains to the final judgment, but both pertain to vindication of their faith during times of testing. When James argues that Abraham was justified by works when he offered his son Isaac on the altar (v. 21), he likely has the divine pronouncement of Genesis 22:12 in mind: 'for now I know that you fear God,

---

[77]Moo, *James*, pp. 133-35.

[78] Moo, *James*, p. 141.

[79] Moo, *James*, pp. 37-43.

[80] Theologically, this is the same kind of distinction between initial and final justification that is present in Roman Catholic theology and in N.T. Wright.

seeing you have not withheld your son, your only son, from me'.[81] James argues that this event constitutes a fulfillment of Abraham's prior justification by faith in Genesis 15:6. Significantly, James agrees with Paul by tracing Abraham's justification to his faith (Rom. 4:3; Gal. 3:6). However, he sees this faith being 'fulfilled'[82] when Abraham demonstrates his belief in God's promise of a multitude of descendants by his willingness to sacrifice his only son in obedience to the divine command, trusting that God will fulfill his promise in some wondrous way in spite of Isaac's death. The implication is that if Abraham had refused to heed the divine command, then his faith would have been revealed as a sham, and the declaration of Genesis 15:6 would have been left empty. The same principle applies to Rahab (v. 25), whose declaration of faith in God's promise to give Israel the land (Josh. 2:9-11) would have been revealed as fraudulent if she had been unwilling to align herself with Israel by protecting the Israelite spies from danger.

What James is saying, then, is that both Abraham and Rahab were vindicated in judgment before God, who was testing them through particular circumstances to reveal the true character of their faith. In this sense, both were justified by works. Significantly, however, in both cases Abraham and Rahab were *vindicated by their works as those who trusted in the promise of God.*[83] In other words, the particular kind of justification in view is not a declaration that one has kept the law and so has attained eternal life by obedience. Rather, the question before the divine court in each instance is whether one is or is not truly believing God's promise, which in turn is the basis upon which eternal life is granted. Justification by works pertains only to this secondary aspect of vindication in judgment. Thus, what James espouses is not a form of covenantal nomism, for the works in view are not driven by the law but by the promise. The obedience of believers is a gospel obedience. Works that are performed in faith are, in a sense, nothing more than faith in its public aspect (Gal. 5:6).

There is no reason to tie James' view primarily to the final judgment and thereby bifurcate the doctrine of justification into two distinct divine acts.[84] It is

---

[81] Motyer, *James*, pp. 106-15, rightly argues that God's statement (which implies that he has learned new information) is anthropomorphic in nature.

[82] Moo, *James*, p. 138, rightly argues that 'fulfill' in this context means 'fill up' or 'give ultimate significance'.

[83] Other commentators who do not understand 'justify' in this context to mean 'vindicate in the judgment' nevertheless come very close to this idea. See Peter H. Davids, *The Epistle of James*, NIGTC (Grand Rapids: Eerdmans, 1982), p. 127; Fesko, *Justification*, pp. 292-94; Ralph P. Martin, *James*, WBC, vol. 48 (Waco, TX: Word, 1988), p. 91; Motyer, *James*, pp. 105-16.

[84] Moo, *James*, p. 135, argues that the overall thrust of this section of James focuses on 'true religion' that will survive the judgment of God (1:21-27; 2:12-13). While his observation is correct, there is no reason to assume that James' doctrine of justification by works pertains exclusively to the final judgment. In fact, there are at least two reasons to suppose that it pertains to any incident in which the faith of a believer is

better to understand the Pauline reality of justification by faith as the final judgment brought forward into time, thereby giving rise to the strangeness of existence in the overlap of the ages. Because faith itself is an invisible reality, those who have already been declared right with God and thus belong to the new age must nevertheless undergo testing while the present evil age remains in order to prove that their faith in the promise is real, in contrast to those who profess faith and yet remain captive to the present age because their faith is akin to that of demons.[85] Living out their faith with concrete acts of obedience, true believers are justified by works in the sense that God vindicates them as true believers when they obey through times of testing.

This theological synthesis of Paul and James implies that there remains a future vindication for believers at the final judgment, but this vindication is only the final in a series of vindications that occur as believers progress through periods of testing. In a sense, one might say that the justifying verdict pronounced at the moment of faith is ratified again and again and again as the believer demonstrates faith through times of testing in acts of obedience that show trust in the divine promise. James' doctrine of justification by works does not contradict the bicovenantal theology of Paul.

Conclusion

The new perspective on Paul rests largely on an unfounded hermeneutical presupposition. The illegitimacy of that presupposition has been exposed by an investigation of the development of the Reformation doctrine of justification in response to the grace-based monocovenantal theology of late medieval Roman Catholicism. Furthermore, the preceding exegetical section has offered an interpretation of Paul that includes a strong bicovenantal element, showing that, even if Sanders' pattern of covenantal nomism holds true for Second Temple Judaism, Paul still could have used such a monocovenantal pattern as a foil in the explication of his doctrine of justification on the basis of the imputed righteousness of Christ. The primary burden of this study has been to expose the fallacy in the new perspective's hermeneutic, but a secondary aim in this final chapter has been to give at least some positive evidence for the presence of Reformation categories in Paul as a suggestion for more fruitful study to be

---

tested, including but not limited to the final judgment. The first reason has already been discussed: James cites the examples of Abraham and Rahab, both of whom were justified by works at a point prior to the final judgment. The second reason is that James' purpose is to cause his readers to consider whether or not their faith is real by observing the works they have done during times of testing. They do not have to wait until the final judgment to make this evaluation. In fact, it is imperative that they do not.
[85] Further vindication of this interpretation comes from the opening of James' letter, which focuses on the testing of believers' faith (Jas. 1:2-3). I am grateful to Lee Tankersley for drawing this observation to my attention.

taken up by others.

New insights into Paul will continue to be offered by scholars of all perspectives. But it is always a wise course of action to listen closely and carefully to the voices who have come before us. In the recent paradigm shift that has occurred in Pauline studies, it does not appear that the Reformers and their heirs have been extended this courtesy, and this study is offered in hope of helping to remedy that defect. After all, if the old perspective is not broken, then there is no need to fix it.

Bibliography

Pauline and Related Studies

Avemarie, Friedrich. *Tora und Leben: Untersuchungen zur Heilsbedeutung der Tora in der frühen rabbinischen Literatur*. Tübingen: Mohr Siebeck, 1996.

Baugh, S.M. 'The New Perspective, Mediation, and Justification'. In R. Scott Clark (ed), *Covenant, Justification, and Pastoral Ministry*, pp. 137-63. Phillipsburg, NJ: P & R, 2007.

Bird, Michael. *The Saving Righteousness of God: Studies on Paul, Justification, and the New Perspective*. Eugene, OR: Wipf and Stock, 2007.

Boersma, Hans. *Violence, Hospitality, and the Cross: Reappropriating the Atonement Tradition*. Grand Rapids: Baker Academic, 2004.

Boyarin, Daniel. *A Radical Jew: Paul and the Politics of Identity*. Berkeley: University of California Press, 1994.

Bruce, F. F. *The Epistle to the Galatians: A Commentary on the Greek Text*. New International Greek Testament Commentary. Grand Rapids: Eerdmans, 1982.

Bultmann, Rudolf. *Theology of the New Testament*. 2 vols. Edited and translated by Kendrick Grobel. New York: Charles Scribner's Sons, 1951.

Carson, D.A., Peter T. O'Brien, and Mark A. Seifrid (eds). *Justification and Variegated Nomism*. 2 vols. Grand Rapids: Baker Academic, 2001-2004.

Chester, Tim. 'Justification, Ecclesiology, and the New Perspective'. *The Northern Training Institute Papers* 12 (March 2008): 1-14.

Clark, R. Scott (ed). *Covenant, Justification, and Pastoral Ministry: Essays by the Faculty of Westminster Seminary California*. Phillipsburg, NJ: P & R, 2007.

Cranfield, C.E.B. *The Epistle to the Romans*. 2 vols. International Critical Commentary. Edinburgh: T & T Clark, 1979.

Das, A. Andrew. *Paul, the Law, and the Covenant*. Peabody, MA: Hendrickson, 2001.

Davids, Peter H. *The Epistle of James*. New International Greek Testament Commentary. Grand Rapids: Eerdmans, 1982.

Donaldson, Terence L. *Paul and the Gentiles: Remapping the Apostle's Convictional World*. Minneapolis: Fortress, 1997.

Dunn, James D.G. *The Epistle to the Galatians*. Black's New Testament Commentaries. London: A & C Black, 1993.

_____. *Jesus, Paul, and the Law: Studies in Mark and Galatians*. Louisville: Westminster John Knox, 1990.

_____. 'The Justice of God: A Renewed Perspective on Justification by Faith'. In *The New Perspective on Paul: Collected Essays*, pp. 187-205. Tübingen: Mohr Siebeck, 2005.

_____. 'The New Perspective on Paul'. In *The New Perspective on Paul: Collected Essays*, pp. 89-110. Tübingen: Mohr Siebeck, 2005.

_____. 'The New Perspective: Whence, What, and Wither?' In *The New Perspective on Paul: Collected Essays*, pp. 1-88. Tübingen: Mohr Siebeck, 2005.

_____. 'New Perspective View'. In James K. Beilby and Paul Rhodes Eddy (eds), *Justification: Five Views*, pp. 176-201. Downers Grove, IL: IVP Academic, 2011.

_____. 'Paul and Justification by Faith'. In *The New Perspective on Paul: Collected Essays*, pp. 361-74. Tübingen: Mohr Siebeck, 2005.

_____. 'Philippians 3.2-14 and the New Perspective on Paul'. In *The New Perspective on Paul: Collected Essays*, pp. 463-84. Tübingen: Mohr Siebeck, 2005.

_____. *Romans*. 2 vols. Word Biblical Commentary, vols. 38a-38b. Dallas: Word, 1988.

_____. *The Theology of Paul the Apostle*. Grand Rapids: Eerdmans, 1998.

_____. 'Whatever Happened to "Works of the Law"?' In *The New Perspective on Paul: Collected Essays*, pp. 375-88. Tübingen: Mohr Siebeck, 2005.

_____. 'Works of the Law and the Curse of the Law (Galatians 3.10-14)'. In *The New Perspective on Paul: Collected Essays*, pp. 111-30. Tübingen: Mohr Siebeck, 2005.

Dunn, James D.G., and Alan M. Suggate. *The Justice of God: A Fresh Look at the Old Doctrine of Justification by Faith*. Grand Rapids: Eerdmans, 1993.

Elliot, Neil. *The Rhetoric of Romans: Argumentative Constraint and Strategy in Paul's Dialogue with Judaism*. Sheffield, UK: Sheffield Academic, 1990.

Eriksson, Bart Anders. 'Luther, Paul and the New Perspective'. Th.M. thesis, Wycliffe College, University of Toronto, 2004.

Estelle, Bryan D., J.V. Fesko, and David VanDrunen, eds. *The Law Is Not of Faith: Essays on Works and Grace in the Mosaic Covenant*. Phillipsburg, NJ: P & R, 2009.

Fee, Gordon D. *The First Epistle to the Corinthians*. New International Commentary on the New Testament. Grand Rapids: Eerdmans, 1987.

_____. *Paul's Letter to the Philippians*. New International Commentary on the New Testament. Grand Rapids: Eerdmans, 1995.

Fesko, J.V. *Justification: Understanding the Classic Reformed Doctrine*. Phillipsburg, NJ: P & R, 2008.

Fuller, Daniel P. *Gospel and Law: Contrast or Continuum? The Hermeneutics of Dispensationalism and Covenant Theology*. Grand Rapids: Eerdmans, 1980.

_____. *The Unity of the Bible: Unfolding God's Plan for Humanity*. Grand Rapids: Zondervan, 1992.

Gaffin, Richard B. 'Review Essay: Paul the Theologian'. *Westminster Theological Journal* 62 (2000), pp. 121-41.

Gathercole, Simon J. 'The Doctrine of Justification in Paul and Beyond: Some Proposals'. In Bruce L. McCormack (ed), *Justification in Perspective: Historical Developments and Contemporary Challenges*, pp. 219-41. Grand Rapids: Baker, 2006.

_____. *Where Is Boasting? Early Jewish Soteriology and Paul's Response in Romans 1-5*. Grand Rapids: Eerdmans, 2002.

Green, Joel B. and Mark D. Baker. *Recovering the Scandal of the Cross: Atonement in New Testament and Contemporary Contexts*. Downers Grove, IL: InterVarsity, 2000.

Hays, Richard B. *The Faith of Jesus Christ: The Narrative Substructure of Galatians 3:1-4:11*, 2nd ed. Grand Rapids: Eerdmans, 2002.

_____. 'Justification'. In David Noel Freedman (ed), *The Anchor Bible Dictionary*. New York: Doubleday, 1992.

_____. *The Letter to the Galatians*. In Leander E. Keck (ed), *The New Interpreter's Bible*, vol. 11, pp. 181-348. Nashville: Abingdon, 2000.

Horton, Michael S. *Covenant and Salvation: Union with Christ*. Louisville: Westminster John Knox, 2007.

_____. 'Traditional Reformed Response [to the New Perspective View]'. In James K. Beilby and Paul Rhodes Eddy (eds), *Justification: Five Views*, pp. 202-07. Downers Grove, IL: IVP Academic, 2011.

_____. 'Which Covenant Theology?' In R. Scott Clark (ed), *Covenant, Justification, and Pastoral Ministry: Essays by the Faculty of Westminster Seminary California*, pp. 197-228. Phillipsburg, NJ: P & R, 2007.

Jeffery, Steve, Mike Ovey, and Andrew Sach. *Pierced for Our Transgressions: Rediscovering the Glory of Penal Substitution*. Nottingham, UK: IVP, 2007.

Kim, Seyoon. *Paul and the New Perspective: Second Thoughts on the Origin of Paul's Gospel*. Grand Rapids: Eerdmans, 2002.

Longenecker, Bruce W. *The Triumph of Abraham's God: The Transformation of Identity in Galatians*. Nashville: Abingdon, 1998.

Martin, Ralph P. *James*. Word Biblical Commentary, vol. 48. Waco, TX: Word, 1988.

Moo, Douglas J. *The Epistle to the Romans*. New International Commentary on the New Testament. Grand Rapids: Eerdmans, 1996.

_____. 'Israel and the Law in Romans 5-11: Interaction with the New Perspective'. In D.A. Carson, Peter T. O'Brien, and Mark A. Seifrid (eds), *Justification and Variegated Nomism*, vol. 2, *The Paradoxes of Paul*, pp. 185-216. Grand Rapids: Baker Academic, 2005.

_____. *The Letter of James*. Pillar New Testament Commentary. Grand Rapids: Eerdmans, 2000.

Morris, Leon. *The Apostolic Preaching of the Cross*. 3rd ed. Grand Rapids: Eerdmans, 1965.

Motyer, J. A. *The Message of James*. The Bible Speaks Today. Downers Grove, IL: IVP, 1985.

Murray, John. *The Epistle to the Romans*. Grand Rapids: Eerdmans, 1968.

O'Brien, Peter T. *The Epistle to the Philippians*. New International Greek Testament Commentary. Grand Rapids: Eerdmans, 1991.

Piper, John. *The Future of Justification: A Response to N.T. Wright*. Wheaton, IL: Crossway, 2007.

Sanders, E.P. *Paul*. Past Masters. New York: Oxford University Press, 1991.

_____. *Paul, the Law, and the Jewish People*. Philadelphia: Fortress, 1983.

_____. *Paul and Palestinian Judaism: A Comparison of Patterns of Religion*. Minneapolis: Fortress, 1977.

Schreiner, Thomas R. 'Is Perfect Obedience to the Law Possible? A Re-Examination of Galatians 3:10'. *Journal of the Evangelical Theological Society* 27, no. 2 (1984), pp. 151-60.

_____. *The Law and Its Fulfillment: A Pauline Theology of Law*. Grand Rapids: Baker, 1993.

_____. 'Paul and Perfect Obedience to the Law: An Evaluation of the View of E.P. Sanders'. *Westminster Theological Journal* 47 (1985), pp. 245-78.

_____. *Romans*. Baker Exegetical Commentary on the New Testament. Grand Rapids: Baker, 1998.

Seifrid, Mark A. 'Blind Alleys in the Controversy over the Paul of History'. *Tyndale Bulletin* 45 (1994), pp. 73-95.

_____. *Christ, Our Righteousness: Paul's Theology of Justification*. Downers Grove, IL: InterVarsity, 2000.

Silva, Moisés. *Interpreting Galatians: Explorations in Exegetical Method*, 2nd ed. Grand Rapids: Baker Academic, 2001.

Stendahl, Krister. 'The Apostle Paul and the Introspective Conscience of the West'. *Harvard Theological Review* 56 (1963), pp. 1-14.

_____. *Paul among Jews and Gentiles*. Philadelphia: Fortress, 1976.

Stewart, Alexander. 'The Hermeneutical Validity of Paul's Use of Habakkuk 2:4 in Romans 1:17'. Paper presented at the southeastern regional meeting of the Evangelical Theological Society, Chattanooga, TN, 4 April 2009.

Stuhlmacher, Peter. *Revisiting Paul's Doctrine of Justification: A Challenge to the New Perspective*. Downers Grove, IL: InterVarsity, 2001.

Vickers, Brian. *Jesus' Blood and Righteousness: Paul's Theology of Imputation*. Wheaton, IL: Crossway, 2006.

Waters, Guy Prentiss. *Justification and the New Perspectives on Paul: A Review and Response*. Phillipsburg, NJ: P & R, 2004.

Watson, Francis. *Paul, Judaism, and the Gentiles*. New York: Cambridge University Press, 1986.

_____. *Paul, Judaism, and the Gentiles: Beyond the New Perspective*. Grand Rapids: Eerdmans, 2007.

Westerholm, Stephen. 'Justification by Faith Is the Answer: What Is the Question?' *Concordia Theological Quarterly* 70 (2006), pp. 197-217.

_____. 'The "New Perspective" at Twenty-Five'. In D.A. Carson, Peter T. O'Brien, and Mark A. Seifrid (eds), *Justification and Variegated Nomism*, vol. 2, *The Paradoxes of Paul*, pp. 1-38. Grand Rapids: Baker Academic, 2004.

_____. *Perspectives Old and New on Paul: The "Lutheran" Paul and His Critics*. Grand Rapids: Eerdmans, 2004.

Wright, N.T. *The Climax of the Covenant: Christ and the Law in Pauline Theology*. Minneapolis: Fortress, 1991.

_____. *The Epistles of Paul to the Colossians and to Philemon: An Introduction and Commentary*. Tyndale New Testament Commentaries. Grand Rapids: Eerdmans, 1986.

_____. *Justification: God's Plan and Paul's Vision*. Downers Grove, IL: IVP Academic, 2009.

_____. *The Letter to the Romans*. In Leander A. Keck (ed), *The New Interpreter's Bible*, vol. 10, pp. 393-770. Nashville: Abingdon, 2002.

_____. 'New Perspectives on Paul'. In Bruce L. McCormack (ed), *Justification in Perspective: Historical Developments and Contemporary Challenges*, pp. 243-64. Grand Rapids: Baker Academic, 2006.

_____. 'On Becoming the Righteousness of God: 2 Corinthians 5:21'. In David M. Hay (ed), *Pauline Theology*, vol. 2, *1 & 2 Corinthians*, pp. 200-08. Minneapolis: Fortress, 1993.

_____. *Paul for Everyone: Galatians and Thessalonians*. London: SPCK, 2002.

_____. *Paul: In Fresh Perspective*. Minneapolis: Fortress, 2005.

_____. 'The Paul of History and the Apostle of Faith'. *Tyndale Bulletin* 29 (1978), pp. 61-88.

_____. 'Romans and the Theology of Paul'. In David M. Hay and E. Elizabeth Johnson (eds), *Pauline Theology*, vol. 3, *Romans*, pp. 30-67. Atlanta: Society of Biblical Literature, 2002.

_____. *What Saint Paul Really Said: Was Paul of Tarsus the Real Founder of Christianity?* Grand Rapids: Eerdmans, 1997.

Catholic Theology in the Late Medieval and Reformation Periods

PRIMARY SOURCES

Biel, Gabriel. *Collectorium circa Quattour Libros Sententiarum*. 5 vols. Edited by Wilfrid Werbeck and Udo Hofmann. Tübingen: Mohr Siebeck, 1973-1992.

_____. 'The Circumcision of the Lord'. In Heiko A. Oberman (ed), *Forerunners of the Reformation: The Shape of Late Medieval Thought Illustrated by Key Documents*, pp. 165-74. New York: Holt, Rinehart, & Winston, 1966.

Bonaventure. *Breviloquium.* In *Doctoris Seraphici S. Bonaventurae S. R. E. Episcopi Cardinalis Opera Omnia*, vol. 5, pp. 199-291. Quaracchi: Ex Typographia Collegii S. Bonaventurae, 1891.

_____. *Breviloquium.* In José de Vinck (ed), *The Works of Bonaventure*, Paterson, NJ: St. Anthony Guild, 1963.

Council of Trent. *The Canons and Decrees of the Sacred and Oecumenical Council of Trent.* Translated by J. Waterworth. London: Dolman, 1848.

_____. *Council of Trent—1545-1563.* In Norman P. Tanner (ed), *Decrees of the Ecumenical Councils*, vol. 2, *Trent—Vatican II*, pp. 655-799. Washington, DC: Georgetown University Press, 1990.

Peter Lombard. *Libri IV Sententiarum.* 2 vols. Quaracchi: Ex Typographia Collegii St. Bonaventurae, 1916.

Thomas Aquinas. *Summa Theologiae.* Vol. 5. Edited by Thomas Gilby. New York: McGraw-Hill, 1967.

_____. *Summa Theologiae.* Vol. 30. Edited by Cornelius Ernst. New York: McGraw-Hill, 1972.

_____. *Summa Theologiae.* Vol. 34. Edited by R. J. Batten. New York: McGraw-Hill, 1974.

_____. *Summa Theologiae.* Vol. 56. Edited by David Bourke. New York: McGraw-Hill, 1974.

_____. *Summa Theologiae.* Vol. 57. Edited by James J. Cunningham. New York: McGraw-Hill, 1974.

_____. *Summa Theologiae.* Vol. 60. Edited by Reginald Masterson and T.C. O'Brien. New York: McGraw-Hill, 1965.

_____. *The "Summa Theologica" of St. Thomas Aquinas.* Part 1. Volume 1. Translated by the Fathers of the English Dominican Province. London: R & T Washbourne, 1911.

_____. *The "Summa Theologica" of St. Thomas Aquinas.* Part 2 (First Part). Volume 3. Translated by the Fathers of the English Dominican Province. London: R & T Washbourne, 1915.

_____. *The "Summa Theologica" of St. Thomas Aquinas.* Part 3. Volume 3. Translated by the Friars of the English Dominican Province. London: R & T Washbourne, 1914.

_____. *Compendium of Theology.* Translated by Cyril Vollert. St. Louis: Herder, 1947.

_____. *Summa Contra Gentiles.* Edited and translated by Charles J. O'Neil. 4 vols. Notre Dame: University of Notre Dame Press, 1957.

William of Ockham. *Questiones in Librum Tertium Sententiarum (Reportatio).* Edited by Francis E. Kelley and Girard I. Etzkom. Vol. 6 of *Guillelmi de Ockham Opera Philosophica et Theologica ad Fidem Codicum Manuscriptorum Edita.* New York: St. Bonaventure, 1982.

SECONDARY SOURCES

Anderson, Marvin W. 'Trent and Justification (1546): A Protestant Reflection'. *Scottish Journal of Theology* 21, no. 4 (1968), pp. 385-406.

Armitage, J. Mark. 'A Certain Rectitude of Order: Jesus and Justification According to Aquinas'. *The Thomist* 72/1 (2008), pp. 45-66.

Colish, Marcia L. *Peter Lombard*. 2 vols. New York: Brill, 1994.

_____. 'Peter Lombard'. In G.R. Evans (ed), *The Medieval Theologians: An Introduction to Theology in the Medieval Period*, pp. 168-83. Malden, MA: Blackwell, 2001.

Cullen, Christopher M. *Bonaventure*. New York: Oxford University Press, 2006.

Evans, G.R. '*Vis Verborum*: Scholastic Method and Finding Words in the Debates on Justification of the Council of Trent'. *Downside Review* 106 (1988), pp. 264-75.

_____, ed. *The Medieval Theologians*. Malden, MA: Blackwell, 2001.

Froehlich, Karlfried. 'Justification Language and Grace: The Charge of Pelagianism in the Middle Ages'. In Elsie Anne McKee and Brian G. Armstrong (eds), *Probing the Reformed Tradition: Historical Studies in Honor of Edward A. Dowey, Jr.*, pp. 21-47. Louisville: Westminster John Knox, 1989.

_____. 'Justification Language in the Middle Ages'. In George Anderson, T. Austin Murphy, and Joseph A. Burgess (eds), *Justification by Faith: Lutherans and Catholics in Dialogue VII*, pp. 143-61. Minneapolis: Augsburg, 1985.

Garrigou-Lagrange, Reginald. *Grace: Commentary on the* Summa Theologica *of St. Thomas Ia IIae, q. 109-114*. Translated by the Dominican Nuns. St. Louis: Herder, 1952.

Gilson, Etienne. *The Philosophy of St. Bonaventure*. Translated by Dom Illtyd Trethowan and Frank J. Sheed. Paterson, NJ: St. Anthony Guild, 1965.

Jedin, Hubert. *A History of the Council of Trent*. 2 vols. Translated by Dom Ernest Graf. St. Louis: B. Herder, 1961.

Laporte, Jean-Marc. 'Dynamics of Grace in Aquinas: A Structural Approach'. *Theological Studies* 34, no. 2 (1973), pp. 203-26.

Levering, Matthew. *Christ's Fulfillment of Torah and Temple: Salvation According to Thomas Aquinas*. South Bend, IN: University of Notre Dame Press, 2002.

Lonergan, Bernard. *Grace and Freedom: Operative Grace in the Thought of Saint Thomas Aquinas*. Toronto: University of Toronto Press, 2000.

McGinn, Bernard. 'The Development of the Thought of Thomas Aquinas on the Reconciliation of Divine Providence and Contingent Action'. *The Thomist* 39 (1975), pp. 741-52.

McGrath, Alister E. 'The Anti-Pelagian Structure of "Nominalist" Doctrines of Justification'. *Epheremerides Theologicae Lovanienses* 57, no. 1 (1981), pp. 107-19.

_____. *Iustitia Dei: A History of the Christian Doctrine of Justification.* 3rd ed. New York: Cambridge University Press, 2005.

McSorley, Harry J. 'Was Gabriel Biel a Semipelagian?' In Leo Scheffczyk, Wemer Detloff, and Richard Heinzmann (eds), *Warheit und Verkündigung: Michael Schmaus zum 70. Geburtstag,* vol. 2, pp. 1109-20. München: Ferdinand Schöningh, 1967.

Oberman, Heiko A. *The Harvest of Medieval Theology: Gabriel Biel and Late Medieval Nominalism.* Grand Rapids: Baker Academic, 2000.

_____. 'The Tridentine Decree on Justification in the Light of Late Medieval Theology'. *Journal for Theology and the Church* 3 (1967), pp. 28-54.

O'Meara, Thomas Franklin. *Thomas Aquinas Theologian.* Notre Dame, IN: University of Notre Dame Press, 1997.

Payne, Gordon R. 'Augustinianism in Calvin and Bonaventure'. *Westminster Theological Journal* 44, no. 1 (1982), pp. 1-31.

Peter, Carl J. 'The Decree on Justification in the Council of Trent'. In George Anderson, T. Austin Murphy, and Joseph A. Burgess (eds), *Justification by Faith: Lutherans and Catholics in Dialogue VII,* pp. 218-29. Minneapolis: Augsburg, 1985.

Ritschl, Albrecht. *A Critical History of the Christian Doctrine of Justification and Reconciliation.* Translated by John S. Black. Edinburgh: Edmonston and Douglas, 1872.

Rosemann, Philipp W. *Peter Lombard.* New York: Oxford University Press, 2004.

_____. *The Story of a Great Medieval Book: Peter's Lombard's Sentences.* Orchard Park, NY: Broadview, 2007.

Rydstrøm-Poulsen, Aage. *The Gracious God: Gratia in Augustine and the Twelfth Century.* Copenhagen: Akademisk Forlag, 2002.

Van Nieuwenhove, Rik, and Joseph Wawrykow, eds. *The Theology of Thomas Aquinas.* South Bend, IN: University of Notre Dame Press, 2005.

Wawrykow, Joseph. *God's Grace and Human Action: "Merit" in the Theology of Thomas Aquinas.* Notre Dame, IN: University of Notre Dame Press, 1996.

_____. 'Grace'. In Rik Van Nieuwenhove and Joseph Wawrykow (eds), *The Theology of Thomas Aquinas.* Notre Dame, IN: University of Notre Dame Press, 2005.

Justification and the Reformers

PRIMARY SOURCES

Calvin, John. *Acta Synodi Tridentinae cum Antidoto*. In G. Baum, E. Cunitz, and E. Reuss (eds), *Ioannis Calvini Opera quae supersunt omnia*, vol. 7, pp. 365-506. Corpus Reformatorum, vol. 35. Brunswick, NJ: C. A. Schwetschke and Son, 1868; reprint, Johnston Reprint Corp., 1964.

_____. 'Ad Sadoleti Epistolam'. In P. Barth (ed), *Joannis Calvini Opera Selecta*, vol. 1., pp. 457-89 Munich: Chr. Kaiser, 1926.

_____. *Christianae Religionis Institutio 1536*. In P. Barth (ed), vol. 1 of *Joannis Calvini Opera Selecta*, vol. 1, pp. 11-283. Munich: Chr. Kaiser, 1926.

_____. *Institutio Christianae Religionis 1559*. Vols. 3-5 of *Joannis Calvini Opera Selecta*. Edited by P. Barth and G. Niesel. Munich: Chr. Kaiser, 1957-62.

_____. *Acts of the Council of Trent, with the Antidote*. Translated by Henry Beveridge. In Thomas F. Torrance (ed), *Tracts and Treatises on the Reformation of the Church*, pp. 17-188. Grand Rapids: Eerdmans, 1958.

_____. *Articles Agreed Upon by the Faculty of Sacred Theology of Paris in Reference to Matters of Faith at Present Controverted; With the Antidote*. Translated by Henry Beveridge. In Thomas F. Torrance (ed), *Tracts and Treatises on the Reformation of the Church*, vol. 1, pp. 69-120. Grand Rapids: Eerdmans, 1958.

_____. *The Epistles of Paul the Apostle to the Galatians, Ephesians, Philippians and Colossians*. Translated by T. H. L. Parker. *Calvin's Commentaries*, ed. David W. Torrance and Thomas F. Torrance. Grand Rapids: Eerdmans, 1965.

_____. *The Epistles of Paul the Apostle to the Romans and to the Thessalonians*. Translated by Ross MacKenzie. *Calvin's Commentaries*, ed. David W. Torrance and Thomas F. Torrance. Grand Rapids: Eerdmans, 1961.

_____. *Institutes of the Christian Religion* [1536]. Translated by Ford Lewis Battles. Grand Rapids: Eerdmans, 1975.

_____. *Institutes of the Christian Religion* [1559]. Edited by John T. McNeill. Translated by Ford Lewis Battles. Library of Christian Classics, vols. 20-21. Philadelphia: Westminster, 1960.

_____. 'Reply to Sadoleto'. Translated by Henry Beveridge. In John C. Olin (ed), *A Reformation Debate*, pp. 49-94. Grand Rapids: Baker, 2002.

_____. *The Second Epistle of Paul the Apostle to the Corinthians and the Epistles to Timothy, Titus, and Philemon*. Translated by T. A. Smail. *Calvin's Commentaries*, ed. David W. Torrance and Thomas F. Torrance. Grand Rapids: Eerdmans, 1964.

_____. *Sermons on Galatians*. Translated by Arthur Golding. Edited by W. Robert Godfrey. Audobon, NJ: Old Paths, 1995.

_____. *Sermons on the Epistle to the Ephesians*. Translated by Arthur Golding. Revised by Leslie Rawlinson and S. M. Houghton. Carlisle, PN: Banner of Truth, 1987.

Erasmus, Desiderius. *De Libero Arbitrio*. In *Desiderii Erasmi Opera Omnia*, vol. 9, pp. 1215-47. New York: Georg Olms Verlag, 2001.

_____. *The Free Will*. In Ernst F. Winter (ed), *Discourse on Free Will*, pp. 1-94. New York: Ungar, 1961.

Luther, Martin. *Acta Augustana*. In *D. Martin Luthers Werke: Kritische Gesamtausgabe*, vol. 2, pp. 1-26. Weimar: Hermann Böhlaus Nachfolger, 1884.

_____. 'Borrede zum ersten Bande der Gesamtausgaben seiner lateinischen Schriften'. In *D. Martin Luthers Werke: Kritische Gesamtausgabe*, vol. 54, pp. 176-87. Weimar: Hermann Böhlaus Nachfolger, 1928.

_____. *De libertate Christiana*. In *D. Martin Luthers Werke: Krtische Gesamtausgabe*, vol. 7, pp. 49-73. Weimar: Hermann Böhlaus Nachfolger, 1897.

_____. *De servo arbitrio*. In *D. Martin Luthers Werke: Kritische Gesamtausgabe*, vol. 18, pp. 600-787. Weimar: Hermann Böhlaus Nachfolger, 1908.

_____. *Dictata super Psalterium: Ps. I-LXXXIII*. Vol. 3 of *D. Martin Luthers Werke: Kritische Gesamtausgabe*. Weimar: Hermann Böhlaus Nachfolger, 1886.

_____. *Dictata super Psalterium: Ps LXXXIV-CL*. In *D. Martin Luthers Werke: Kritische Gesamtausgabe*, vol. 4, pp. 1-462. Weimar: Hermann Böhlaus Nachfolger, 1885.

_____. *Divi Pauli apostoli ad Romanos Epistola*. Vol. 56 of *D. Martin Luthers Werke: Kritische Gesamtausgabe*. Weimar: Hermann Böhlaus Nachfolger, 1938.

_____. *In epistolam Pauli ad Galatas commentarius (1519)*. In *D. Martin Luthers Werke: Kritische Gesamtausgabe*, 2:436-618. Weimar: Hermann Böhlaus Nachfolger, 1884.

_____. *In epistolam Pauli ad Galatas Commentarius (1535)*. Vol. 40/1 of *D. Martin Luthers Werke: Kritische Gesamtausgabe*. Weimar: Hermann Böhlaus Nachfolger, 1911.

_____. *The Bondage of the Will*. Translated by Philip S. Watson and Benjamin Drewery. Vol. 33 of *Luther's Works*, ed. Philip S. Watson and Helmut T. Lehmann. St. Louis: Concordia, 1972.

_____. *First Lectures on the Psalms I: Psalms 1-75*. Edited by Hilton C. Oswald. Translated by Herbert J. A. Bouman. Vol. 10 of *Luther's Works*, ed. Hilton C. Oswald. St. Louis: Concordia, 1974.

_____. *First Lectures on the Psalms II: Psalms 76-126*. Edited by Hilton C. Oswald. Translated by Herbert J. A. Bouman. Vol. 11 of *Luther's Works*, ed. Hilton C. Oswald. St. Louis: Concordia, 1976.

_____. *The Freedom of a Christian*. Translated by W. A. Lambert and Harold J. Grimm. In Harold J. Grimm and Helmut T. Lehmann (eds), *Luther's Works*, vol. 31, pp. 327-77. St. Louis: Concordia, 1957.

_____. *Lectures on Galatians (1519)*. Translated by Richard Jungkuntz. In Walter A. Hansen (ed), *Luther's Works*, vol. 27, pp. 151-410. St. Louis: Concordia, 1964.

_____. *Lectures on Galatians (1535): Chapters 1-4*. Translated by Jaroslav Pelikan. Vol. 26 of *Luther's Works*, ed. Walter A. Hansen. St. Louis: Concordia, 1963.

_____. *Lectures on Romans: Glosses and Scholia*. Edited by Hilton C. Oswald. Translated by Walter G. Tillmanns (Chaps. 1-2) and Jacob A. O. Preus (Chaps. 3-16). Vol. 25 of *Luther's Works*, ed. Hilton C. Oswald. St. Louis: Concordia, 1972.

_____. 'Preface to the Epistles of St. James and St. Jude'. Translated by Charles M. Jacobs. In Theodore Bachmann (ed), *Luther's Works*, ed. Theodore, vol. 35, pp. 395-98. St. Louis: Concordia, 1960.

_____. 'Preface to the New Testament'. Translated by Charles M. Jacobs. In Theodore Bachmann (ed), *Luther's Works*, vol. 35, pp. 357-62. St. Louis: Concordia, 1960.

_____. *The Small Catechism*. In Timothy F. Lull (ed), *Martin Luther's Basic Theological Writings*, 2nd ed., pp. 317-36. Minneapolis: Fortress, 2005.

_____. *Table Talk*. Edited and Translated by Theodore G. Tappert. Vol. 54 of *Luther's Works*, ed. Jaroslav Pelikan. St. Louis: Concordia, 1967.

_____. 'Two Kinds of Righteousness'. Translated by Lowell J. Satre. In Harold J. Grimm (ed), *Luther's Works*, vol. 31, pp. 293-306. St. Louis: Concordia, 1957.

Melanchthon, Philip. *Apologia Confessionis Augustana* (1531). In Henry Ernest Bindseil (ed), *Philippi Melanthonis Opera quae supersunt omnia*, vol. 27, pp. 419-646. Corpus Reformatorum, vol. 27. Brunswick, NJ: C.A. Schwetschke and Son, 1859; reprint, Johnston Reprint Corp., 1964.

_____. *Commentarii in Epistolam Pauli ad Romanos*. In Carolus Gottlieb Bretschneider (ed), *Philippi Melanthonis Opera quae supersunt omnia*, vol. 15, pp. 493-795. Corpus Reformatorum, vol. 15. Brunswick, NJ: C.A. Schwetschke and Son, 1848; reprint, Johnston Reprint Corp., 1964.

_____. *Prima Aetas Locorum Theologicorum ab Ipso Melanthone Editorum*. In Henry Ernest Bindseil (ed), *Philippi Melanthonis Opera quae supersunt omnia*, vol. 21, pp. 59-228. Corpus Reformatorum, vol. 21. Brunswick, NJ: C.A. Schwetschke and Son, 1854; reprint, Johnston Reprint Corp., 1964.

_____. *Secunda Aetas Locorum Theologicorum ab Ipso Melanthone Editorum*. In Henry Ernest Bindseil (ed), *Philippi Melanthonis Opera quae supersunt omnia*, vol. 21, pp. 230-559. Corpus Reformatorum, vol. 21. Brunswick, NJ: C.A. Schwetschke and Son, 1854; reprint, Johnston Reprint Corp., 1964.

_____. *Tertia Aetas Locorum Theologicorum ab Ipso Melanthone Editorum*. In Henry Ernest Bindseil (ed), *Philippi Melanthonis Opera quae supersunt omnia*, vol. 21, pp. 560-1106. Corpus Reformatorum, vol. 21. Brunswick, NJ: C.A. Schwetschke and Son, 1854; reprint, Johnston Reprint Corp., 1964.

_____. *Commentary on Romans*. Translated by Fred Kramer. St. Louis: Concordia, 1992.

_____. *Loci Communes 1543*. Translated by J.A.O. Preus. St. Louis: Concordia, 1992.

_____. *Loci communes theologici*. Translated by Lowell J. Sartre. Revised by Wilhelm Pauck. In vol. 19 of the Library of Christian Classics, 18-152. Philadelphia: Westminster, 1969.

_____. *Paul's Letter to the Colossians*. Translated by D.C. Parker. Sheffield, UK: Almond, 1989.

Sadoleto, Jacopo. 'Epistola ad Senatum Poplumque Genevensem'. In P. Barth (ed), *Joannis Calvini Opera Selecta*, ed. P. Barth, vol. 1, pp. 441-56. Munich: Chr. Kaiser, 1926.

_____. 'Letter to the Genevans'. Translated by Henry Beveridge. In John C. Olin (ed), *A Reformation Debate*, pp. 29-48. Grand Rapids: Baker, 2002.

SECONDARY SOURCES

Althaus, Paul. *The Theology of Martin Luther*. Translated by Robert C. Schultz. Philadelphia: Fortress, 1966.

Barth, Karl. *The Theology of John Calvin*. Translated by Geoffrey W. Bromiley. Grand Rapids: Eerdmans, 1995.

Bayer, Oswald. *Martin Luther's Theology: A Contemporary Interpretation*. Translated by Thomas H. Trapp. Grand Rapids: Eerdmans, 2008.

Braaten, Carl E., and Robert W. Jenson, eds. *Union with Christ: The New Finnish Interpretation of Luther*. Grand Rapids: Eerdmans, 1998.

Bray, Gerald. 'The Reformers and Recent New Testament Scholarship'. *The Churchman* 109 (1995), pp. 102-26.

Carpenter, Craig B. 'A Question of Union with Christ? Calvin and Trent on Justification'. *Westminster Journal of Theology* 64 (2002), pp. 363-86.

Casteel, Theodore W. 'Calvin and Trent: Calvin's Reaction to the Council of Trent in the Context of His Conciliar Thought'. *Harvard Theological Review* 63 (1970), pp. 91-117.

Cavanaugh, William T. 'A Joint Declaration? Justification as Theosis in Aquinas and Luther'. *The Heythrop Journal* 41, no. 3 (2000), pp. 265-80.

Clark, R. Scott. '*Iustitia Imputata Christi*: Alien or Proper to Luther's Doctrine of Justification?' *Concordia Theological Quarterly* 70 (2007), pp. 269-310.

Coates, Thomas. 'Calvin's Doctrine of Justification'. *Concordia Theological Monthly* 34 (1963), pp. 325-34.

Ebeling, Gerhard. *Luther: An Introduction to His Thought*. Translated by R. A. Wilson. Philadelphia: Fortress, 1970.

Edwards, Mark U. 'Luther's Polemical Controversies'. In Donald K. McKim (ed), *The Cambridge Companion to Martin Luther*, pp. 192-205. New York: Cambridge University Press, 2003.

Forde, Gerhard O. *The Captivation of the Will: Luther vs. Erasmus on Freedom and Bondage*. Edited by Steven Paulson. Lutheran Quarterly Books. Grand Rapids: Eerdmans, 2005.

George, Timothy. 'Martin Luther'. In Jeffrey P. Greenman and Timothy Larsen (ed), *Reading Romans through the Centuries: From the Early Church to Karl Barth*, pp. 101-19. Grand Rapids: Brazos, 2005.

Grane, Leif. *Contra Gabrielem: Luthers Auseinandersetzung mit Gabriel Biel in der Disputatio contra scholasticam theologiam 1517*. Copenhagen: Gyldendal, 1962.

Green, Lowell C. 'Faith, Righteousness, and Justification: New Light on Their Development Under Luther and Melanchthon'. *Sixteenth Century Journal* 4, no. 1 (1973), pp. 65-86.

Hamm, Berndt. 'What Was the Reformation Doctrine of Justification?' In C. Scott Dixon (ed), *The German Reformation: The Essential Readings*, pp. 53-90. Malden, MA: Blackwell, 1999.

Hart, Trevor. 'Humankind in Christ and Christ in Humankind: Salvation as Participation in Our Substitute in the Theology of John Calvin'. *Scottish Journal of Theology* 42 (1989), pp. 67-84.

Johnson, Marcus. 'New or Nuanced Perspective on Calvin? A Reply to Thomas Wenger'. *Journal of the Evangelical Theological Society* 51, no. 3 (2008), pp. 543-58.

Lillback, Peter A. 'Calvin's Development of the Doctrine of Forensic Justification: Calvin and the Early Lutherans on the Relationship of Justification and Renewal'. In K. Scott Oliphint (ed), *Justified in Christ: God's Plan for Us in Justification*, pp. 51-80. Fearn, UK: Mentor, 2007.

Mannermaa, Tuomo. *Christ Present in Faith: Luther's View of Justification*. Edited by Kirsi Stjerna. Minneapolis: Fortress, 2005.

_____. 'Justification and *Theosis* in Lutheran-Orthodox Perspective'. In Carl E. Braaten and Robert W. Jenson (eds), *Union with Christ: The New Finnish Interpretation of Luther*, pp. 25-41. Grand Rapids: Eerdmans, 1998.

Marcel, Pierre. 'The Relation Between Justification and Sanctification in Calvin's Thought'. *The Evangelical Quarterly* 27 (1955), pp. 132-45.

McCormack, Bruce. 'What's at Stake in the Current Debates over Justification? The Crisis of Protestantism in the West'. In Mark Husbands and Daniel J. Treier (eds), *Justification: What's at Stake in the Current Debates*, pp. 81-117. Downers Grove, IL: IVP, 2004.

McGrath, Alister E. *Luther's Theology of the Cross: Martin Luther's Theological Breakthrough*. Grand Rapids: Baker, 1990.

Metzger, Paul Louis. 'Luther and the Finnish School. Mystical Union with Christ: An Alternative to Blood Transfusions and Legal Fictions'. *Westminster Theological Journal* 65 (2003), pp. 201-13.

Muller, Richard A. *The Unaccommodated Calvin: Studies in the Foundation of a Theological Tradition*. Oxford Studies in Historical Theology. New York: Oxford University Press, 2000.

Niesel, Wilhelm. *The Theology of Calvin*. Translated by Harold Knight. Philadelphia: Westminster, 1956.

Oberman, Heiko A. *The Two Reformations: The Journey from the Last Days to the New World*. New Haven, CT: Yale University Press, 2003.

Oden, Thomas C. *The Justifiation Reader*. Grand Rapids: Eerdmans, 2002.

O'Kelley, Aaron T. 'Luthern and Melanchthon on Justification: Continuity or Discontinuity?' In Michael Parsons (ed), *Since We Are Justified by Faith: Justification in the Theologies of the Reformation*, pp. 30-43. Milton Keynes, UK: Paternoster, 2012.

Parker, T.H.L. 'Calvin's Doctrine of Justification'. *The Evangelical Quarterly* 24 (1952), pp. 101-07.

Pelikan, Jaroslav. *Reformation of Church and Dogma*. Vol. 4 of *The Christian Tradition: A History of the Development of Doctrine*. Chicago: University of Chicago Press, 1984.

_____, ed. *Interpreters of Luther: Essays in Honor of Wilhelm Pauck*. Philadelphia: Fortress, 1968.

Rainbow, Jonathan. 'Double Grace: John Calvin's View of the Relationship of Justification and Sanctification'. *Ex Auditu* 5 (1989), pp. 99-105.

Reid, W. Stanford. 'Justification by Faith According to John Calvin'. *Westminster Theological Journal* 42 (1980), pp. 290-307.

Root, Michael. 'Aquinas, Merit, and Reformation Theology after the Joint Declaration on the Doctrine of Justification', *Modern Theology* 20, no. 1 (2004), pp. 5-22.

Santmire, H. Paul. 'Justification in Calvin's 1540 Romans Commentary'. *Church History* 33 (1964), pp. 294-313.

Scheible, Heinz. 'Philip Melanchthon (1497-1560)'. In Carter Lindberg (ed), *The Reformation Theologians*, pp. 67-82. Malden, MA: Blackwell, 2002.

Seifrid, Mark A. 'Luther, Melanchthon and Paul on the Question of Imputation: Recommendations on a Current Debate'. In Mark Husbands and Daniel J. Treier (eds), *Justification: What's at Stake in the Current Debate*, pp. 137-52. Downers Grove, IL: InterVarsity, 2004.

Strehle, Stephen. *The Catholic Roots of the Protestant Gospel: Encounter between the Middle Ages and the Reformation*. Studies in the History of Christian Thought. New York: Brill, 1995.

Trueman, Carl R. 'Is the Finnish Line a New Beginning? A Critical Assessment of the Reading of Luther Offered by the Helsinki Circle'. *Westminster Theological Journal* 65/2 (2003), pp. 231-44.

Waldron, Samuel E. 'Faith, Obedience, and Justification: Current Evangelical Departures from *Sola Fide*'. Ph.D. diss., The Southern Baptist Theological Seminary, 2005.

Wendel, François. *Calvin: Origins and Development of His Religious Thought.* Translated by Philip Mairet. Durham, NC: Labyrinth, 1987.

Wenger, Thomas. 'The New Perspective on Calvin: Responding to Recent Calvin Interpretations'. *Journal of the Evangelical Theological Society* 50 (2007), pp. 311-28.

_____. 'Theological Spectacles and a Paradigm of Centrality: A Reply to Marcus Johnson'. *Journal of the Evangelical Theological Society* 51, no. 3 (2008), pp. 559-72.

Wengert, Timothy J. *Law and Gospel: Philip Melanchthon's Debate with John Agricola of Eisleben over* Poenitentia. Grand Rapids: Baker, 1997.

_____. Review of Carl E. Braaten and Robert W. Jenson (eds), *Union with Christ: The New Finnish Interpretation of Luther. Theology Today* 56 (1999), pp. 432-34.

Wriedt, Markus. 'Luther's Theology'. Translated by Katharina Gustavs. In Donald K. McKim (ed), *The Cambridge Companion to Martin Luther*, pp. 86-119. New York: Cambridge University Press, 2003.

Justification in the Post-Reformation Period

PRIMARY SOURCES

The Belgic Confession. In Jaroslav Pelikan and Valerie Hotchkiss (eds), *Creeds and Confessions of Faith in the Christian Tradition*, vol. 2, pp. 405-26 New Haven, CT: Yale University Press, 2003.

Chemnitz, Martin. *Examination of the Council of Trent: Part I*. Translated by Fred Kramer. St. Louis: Concordia, 1971.

_____. *Justification: The Chief Article of Christian Doctrine as Expounded in* Loci Theologici. Translated by J.A.O. Preus. Edited by Delpha Holleque Preus. St. Louis: Concordia, 1985.

Confessio Helvetica Posterior. In Philip Schaff (ed), *The Creeds of Christendom*, vol. 3, pp. 233-306. New York: Harper and Brothers, 1877.

Formula Concordiae. In Philip Schaff (ed), *The Creeds of Christendom*, vol. 3, pp. 93-180. New York: Harper and Brothers, 1877.

The Formula of Concord. In Paul Timothy McCain (ed), *Concordia: The Lutheran Confessions*, 2nd ed., pp. 471-619. St. Louis: Concordia, 2005.

The Heidelberg Catechism. In Jaroslav Pelikan and Valerie Hotchkiss (eds), *Creeds and Confessions of Faith in the Christian Tradition*, vol. 2, pp. 427-57. New Haven, CT: Yale University Press, 2003.

Grotius, Hugo. *Defensio Fidei Catholicae de Satisfactione Christi Adversus Faustum Socinum Senensem.* In Edwin Rabbie (ed), *Opera Theologica*, vol. 1, pp. 1-277. Assen, The Netherlands: Van Gorcum, 1990.

Hunnius, Nikolaus. *Epitome Credendorum.* Translated by Paul Edward Gottheil. Nürnberg: Sebald, 1847.

Lund, Eric, ed. *Documents from the History of Lutheranism, 1517-1750.* Minneapolis: Fortress, 2002.

The Irish Articles. In Jaroslav Pelikan and Valerie Hotchkiss (eds), *Creeds and Confessions of Faith in the Christian Tradition*, vol. 2, pp. 551-68. New Haven, CT: Yale University Press, 2003.

Owen, John. *The Doctrine of Justification by Faith through the Imputation of the Righteousness of Christ; Explained, Confirmed, and Vindicated.* In William H. Goold (ed), *The Works of John Owen*, vol. 5, pp. 1-400. Carlisle, PA: Banner of Truth, 1965.

The Second Helvetic Confession. In Jaroslav Pelikan and Valerie Hotchkiss (eds), *Creeds and Confessions of Faith in the Christian Tradition*, vol. 2, pp. 458-525. New Haven, CT: Yale University Press, 2003.

Synod of Dort. *Canones Synodi Dordrechtanae.* In Philip Schaff (ed), *The Creeds of Christendom*, vol. 3, pp. 550-80. New York: Harper and Brothers, 1877.

_____. *The Canons of the Synod of Dort.* In Jaroslav Pelikan and Valerie Hotchkiss (eds), *Creeds and Confessions of Faith in the Christian Tradition*, vol. 2, pp. 571-600. New Haven, CT: Yale University Press, 2003.

Turretin, Francis. *Francisci Turretini Opera.* 4 vols. Edinburgh: J. D. Lowe, 1847-1848.

_____. *Institutes of Elenctic Theology.* 3 vols. Translated by George Musgrave Giger. Edited by James T. Dennison, Jr. Phillipsburg, NJ: P & R, 1992-1997.

Ursinus, Zacharias. *The Commentary of Dr. Zacharias Ursinus on the Heidelberg Catechism.* Translated by G. W. Williard. Grand Rapids: Eerdmans, 1954.

The Westminster Confession of Faith. In Jaroslav Pelikan and Valerie Hotchkiss (eds), *Creeds and Confessions of the Christian Tradition*, vol. 2, pp. 601-49. New Haven, CT: Yale University Press, 2003.

Wollebius, Johannes. *Compendium Theologiae Christianae.* Translated by John W. Beardslee III. In John W. Beardslee III (ed), *Reformed Dogmatics*, pp. 27-262. Grand Rapids: Baker, 1965.

SECONDARY SOURCES

Bavinck, Herman. *Reformed Dogmatics.* Vol. 3, *Sin and Salvation in Christ.* Edited by John Bolt. Translated by John Vriend. Grand Rapids: Baker Academic, 2006.

Beach, J. Mark. *Christ and the Covenant: Francis Turretin's Federal Theology as a Defense of the Doctrine of Grace*. Göttingen: Vandenhoeck & Ruprecht, 2007.

Berkhof, Louis. *Systematic Theology*. Combined ed. Grand Rapids: Eerdmans, 1996.

Berkouwer, G.C. 'Justification by Faith in the Reformed Confessions'. Translated by Lewis B. Smedes. In Donald K. McKim (ed), *Major Themes in the Reformed Tradition*, pp. 132-41. Grand Rapids: Eerdmans, 1992.

Clark, R. Scott. *Caspar Olevian and the Substance of the Covenant: The Double Benefit of Christ*. Edinburgh: Rutherford, 2005.

Jue, Jeffery K. 'The Active Obedience of Christ and the Theology of the Westminster Standards: A Historical Investigation'. In K. Scott Oliphint (ed), *Justified in Christ: God's Plan for Us in Justification*, pp. 99-130. Fearn, UK: Mentor, 2007.

Klempa, William. 'The Concept of the Covenant in Sixteenth- and Seventeenth-Century Continental and British Reformed Theology'. In Donald K. McKim (ed), *Major Themes in the Reformed Tradition*, pp. 94-107. Grand Rapids: Eerdmans, 1992.

Murray, John. *Redemption Accomplished and Applied*. Grand Rapids: Eerdmans, 1955.

Olson, Roger E. *Arminian Theology: Myths and Realities*. Downers Grove, IL: IVP Academic, 2006.

Preus, Robert D. 'The Doctrine of Justification in the Theology of Classical Lutheran Orthodoxy' In Klemet I. Preus (ed), *Doctrine Is Life: The Essays of Robert D. Preus on Justification and the Lutheran Confessions*, pp. 79-96. St. Louis: Concordia, 2006.

_____. 'The Justification of a Sinner Before God as Taught in Later Lutheran Orthodoxy'. In Klemet I. Preus (ed), *Doctrine Is Life: The Essays of Robert D. Preus on Justification and the Lutheran Confessions*, pp. 39-53. St. Louis: Concordia, 2006.

_____. *The Theology of Post-Reformation Lutheranism*. St. Louis: Concordia, 1970.

Trueman, Carl R. 'John Owen on Justification'. In K. Scott Oliphint (ed), *Justified in Christ: God's Plan for Us in Justification*, pp. 81-98. Fearn, UK: Mentor, 2007.

Vainio, Olli Pekka. *Justification and Participation in Christ: The Developments of the Lutheran Doctrine of Justification from Luther to the Formula of Concord (1580)*. Boston: Brill, 2008.

Scripture Index

General Index

active obedience 110-14, 120
alien righteousness 20-21, 43-44, 51, 53-
   55-56, 59-63, 65-67, 69, 71, 73-74, 77-
   78, 80, 81, 83, 87, 92, 94-95, 98-99,
   108-115, 119-20, 122
Althaus, Paul 62-63 fn.32
Anderson, Marvin W. 44 fn.94
antinomianism 47, 79, 86 fn.126, 104
   fn.10
assurance of salvation 47, 118
Augustine 7, 23-24, 25 fn.11, 59, 69, 86,
   90
Augustinian theology 24-25, 44, 47, 50,
   58-59
auxilium divinum 31-32, 37
Avemarie, Friedrich 2 fn.3
Baker, Mark D. 123-24, 125 fn.10
baptism 26-27, 34, 38, 43, 45-46, 51, 57,
   61, 117-18
Barth, Karl 81 fn.108
Battles, Ford Lewis 82 fn.110
Baugh, S.M. 19 fn.59
Bavinck, Herman 101 fn.8
Bayer, Oswald 60 fn.22
Beach, J. Mark 98 fn.2, 103
Belgic Confession 104
Berkhof, Louis 101 fn.8
Berkouwer, G.C. 98 fn.2
bicovenantalism 19 fn.60, 20-21, 43, 51,
   76, 80, 81, 90, 93, 96-97, 98, 104-08,
   104, 106, 108, 110, 115, 117-20, 122,
   131, 139, 143-45, 148
Biel, Gabriel 39-43, 56
Billerbeck, Paul 8, 11, 17
Bird, Michael 3 fn.5, 144
Boersma, Hans 126-27
Bonaventure 36-39, 117-18
Bousset, Wilhelm 8, 11, 17
Boyarin, Daniel 17 fn.55
Braaten, Carl E. 71 fn.69, 72 fn.72
Bruce, F.F. 123 fn.3, 129 fn.30
Bucer, Martin 55 fn.4

Bultmann, Rudolf 8, 10 fn.32, 11, 16
   fn.53, 17
Calvin, John 3, 20, 55, 65, 70, 80-95, 103,
   109, 119-20
Carpenter, Craig B. 81 fn.108, 84 fn.121,
   85 fn.124, 91 fn.145
Carson, D.A. 2 fn.3
Casteel, Theodore W. 91 fn.145
charity 25-27, 33, 35, 38-42, 46, 48, 50
   fn.126, 51, 54, 60, 69
Chemnitz, Martin 100-01, 106 fn.18, 108
Chester, Tim 3 fn.5
Clark, R. Scott 2 fn.3, 19, 56 fn.6, 69
   fn.65, 72 fn.72, 73 fn.78
Coates, Thomas 81 fn.108
Colish, Marcia L. 24 fn.3, 25
condign merit 33, 46 fn.108, 57, 67
congruous merit 33, 46 fn.108, 57-59, 67
cooperative grace 25, 27, 32-34, 117
Council of Trent 20, 22, 26 fn.18, 43-51,
   88, 91-93, 117-19
covenant of grace, the 19 fn.60, 106-07,
   112 fn.36, 115-16, 120
covenant of works, the 19 fn.60, 102-03,
   106-07, 110, 115-16, 120
covenantal nomism 9-10, 16, 18, 51, 26,
   117, 121, 139, 143, 146-48
Cranfield, C.E.B. 132-34
Cullen, Christopher M. 36 fn.64
Das, A. Andrew 2 fn.3
Davids, Peter H. 147 fn.83
De Greef, Wulfert 89 fn.141
Donaldson, Terence L. 17 fn.55
Dunn, James D.G. 4 fn.10, 6-7, 8 fn.24,
   14-16, 123-26, 132-34, 136 fn.49, 138
Ebeling, Gerhard 63 fn.32
election of Israel 8, 51, 136
Elliot, Neil 17 fn.55
Erasmus, Desiderius 66-68, 77
Eriksson, Bart Anders 2 fn.4
Estelle, Bryan D. 102 fn.10
Evans, G.R. 44 fn.94

ND - #0104 - 090625 - C0 - 229/152/10 - PB - 9781842277942 - Gloss Lamination